Transcendent Summits

one climber's route to self-discovery

Gerry Roach

Fulcrum Publishing
Golden, Colorado

Library of Congress Cataloging-in-Publication Data

Roach, Gerry.
Transcendent summits : one climber's route to self-discovery / Gerry Roach.
p. cm.
ISBN 1-55591-471-3 (pbk. : alk. paper) 1. Roach, Gerry. 2. Mountaineers--United States--Biography. I. Title.
GV199.92.R612A3 2004
796.52'2'092--dc22

2004015484

ISBN 1-55591-471-3

Printed in the United States of America
0 9 8 7 6 5 4 3 2 1

Cover Design: Jack Lenzo
Text Design: Nancy Duncan Cashman
Cover Image: Gerry Roach, Roger Grette, and
Rob Blair (top to bottom) on the Southeast Ridge of Mount Blackburn
in Alaska, 1977 (Courtesy of Barb Roach)

Fulcrum Publishing
16100 Table Mountain Parkway, Suite 300
Golden, Colorado 80403
(800) 992-2908 • (303) 277-1623
www.fulcrum-books.com

For Shirley

I prefer to believe that she transcended.

contents

foreword

In 1963 American mountaineers succeeded in making what in those early years was only the third ascent of Everest. They were also the first Americans to reach the summit, but as late as the mid-1970s no American team had repeated the feat. At that time the Tibetan side of the mountain was still closed, and Nepal allowed only one expedition per season. As a consequence Everest was booked for years in advance, and for most climbers getting a chance at the world's highest mountain seemed as likely as getting invited to go to the moon.

But in 1975 a French team that had the permit to launch an expedition the following year suddenly dropped out. Phil Trimble, an amateur climber of only modest experience, learned about the unexpected vacancy and applied for the opening. A few months later, to his surprise, he was awarded the permit. With only six months before departure, Trimble had to assemble a team capable not only of climbing Everest but just as important of organizing the tons of supplies and the labyrinth of logistics that in those years were part of nearly all Himalayan expeditions to 8,000-meter peaks.

Trimble sent a friend and fellow climber, Arlene Blum, to the annual meeting of the American Alpine Club to scout for candidates. One of the first she considered was a lean and obviously strong climber then in his early thirties named Gerry Roach. Gerry wasn't famous, but in the tight-knit world of climbing he had a reputation as a tough and tenacious "peak bagger," someone interested not only in first ascents or new routes but also in getting to the tops of as many mountains as possible, by any route. In 1976 Gerry was making 240 ascents per year. He had been on mountaineering expeditions to every continent, including Antarctica, which in those years was very unusual. Still, Arlene wasn't sure Gerry would be interested in Everest. She had already asked other climbing friends, and most had declined. Everest would be too complicated, they said, too high, too cold, and with too much risk of frostbite (in those years climbers still wore leather boots).

"Have you ever been to Nepal?" Arlene asked Gerry.

"No, but I've always wanted to go."

"Well, a friend of mine has a permit for a big peak over there. We still need some climbers on the team, expedition-types who don't mind all the preparation work."

"What's the peak?" Gerry asked.

"Well, I know this sounds a little absurd," Arlene replied, "but it's kind of the ultimate peak bag. It's Everest."

"Everest!" Gerry exclaimed, and then without pause said, "I'll go!"

▼ ▼ ▼

I was the last climber invited to join the American Bicentennial Everest Expedition, and also the youngest. Like Gerry, I had been surprised—even shocked—when I was invited, but unlike Gerry, climbing Everest for me was something I had never considered. It was so high, so remote—so mythical—that it seemed beyond the pale of possibility. Gerry was different. He had dreamed of climbing Everest since boyhood, when the news arrived that Hillary and Tenzing had reached the summit, and of the twelve of us who made up the Bicentennial Expedition, we all gave Gerry the best odds of reaching the top.

In those years to reach basecamp we had to walk 175 miles, beginning at a trailhead a short distance outside Kathmandu. We had more than 600 porters to carry our twenty-six tons of supplies. I spent most of the time hiking with my climbing partner, Chris Chandler. Including the Sherpas, there were so many people on the expedition that even after we reached basecamp I still hadn't talked to Gerry very much, and I didn't know him that well. Even as we started up the mountain, Gerry and I were always on a different rope team. That suddenly changed, however, about a month into the climb, when Trimble, who was the leader, chose the summit teams. I had been high on the mountain carrying a load of supplies while Chris, my usual rope partner, had been taking a rest day. Reasoning that I needed to rest, Trimble decided to assign Chris and another climber to make the first attempt at the summit, and I would be paired with Gerry and a third climber to make the second bid. Trimble reasoned that with Gerry on the second team, if the first attempt failed the second would have an even better chance of getting to the top, since Gerry was physically the strongest climber.

Those of us on the second attempt followed the first team by two days. As we climbed slowly up the Lhotse Face we could see the famous wind plume boiling off the summit ridge, and when we stopped we could also hear it, like the constant roar of giant surf on a distant beach. The previous evening we had received a radio report from basecamp that Chris and his partner had reached the summit, and soon they passed us on their way down. They told us that just below the summit the hurricane-force wind had kept their climbing rope suspended in the air, nearly pulling them off the ridge, and now, as the wind seemed to be increasing even more, they weren't sure we could make it. Personally I wasn't sure I could make it either: the wind notwithstanding, I had a cough and pain in my lungs I feared might be the beginning of pulmonary edema.

We decided to retreat, but Gerry would tell me later he was absolutely confident he would regroup and make another attempt. At our advanced basecamp, however, we learned the Sherpas wanted to go home, and as the wind was unabated, Trimble decided to call an end to the expedition. Gerry was shocked. A few days later, in an interview with our camera crew, he said, "We had a hundred oxygen bottles, a good three weeks' food remaining ... we should have gone at it again."

▼ ▼ ▼

For me, I was ready to go home. We had started our trek to basecamp in late July; it was now early October. But for Gerry, his boyhood dream was shattered and his disappointment was palpable. At the time I assumed this was a reflection of the depth of his dedication to the mountains; after all, Everest was the ultimate on anyone's tick-list. But now, twenty-eight years later, as I write this foreword to Gerry's most recent book, I realize that his disappointment in 1976 was much more complex than missing the biggest notch of all on his climber's belt. As I said, on the Everest expedition Gerry and I never talked about our deeper motivations that spurred us to climb the high peaks, but after reading *Transcendent Summits* I feel now I have finally heard from Gerry the full story behind his passion.

Everyone I know who has pursued mountaineering as a lifelong devotion has brought down from the high summits lessons they have applied to their lives at lower elevations. I think you will find it interesting, as I did, to read Gerry's description of how climbers in the 1950s taught themselves risk assessment, how they did their homework before a climb, but then how, if they didn't have all the answers, they committed anyway. Gerry also describes the shocking awakening when—and this happens to everyone I know who pursues the sport long enough—your first close friend dies. Gerry explains how you rationalize the accident, identifying the mistakes your friend made, vowing never to make the same errors yourself. Gerry also writes about the inevitable next phase, when finally one day you get yourself in a situation where later you realize you survived in part because of luck, and you have to acknowledge that things could have gone differently. Finally, you have to reconcile your mortality, realizing that no matter how careful you are and how skillful you have become, you are still in a game that could kill you.

▼ ▼ ▼

Gerry builds these stories one on top of the other, one experience—one summit—transcending to the next. When I finished this book I shouldn't have been surprised by the depth of lessons Gerry has brought down from the high peaks. There is a list of them that he sums up in an acronym he calls "WHO CLIMBS UP," where every letter represents a different lesson. There was one lesson, represented by the letter "P," that didn't surprise me, however, because it stood for an attribute that Gerry learned early in his climbing career that I had observed firsthand. Seven years after Gerry was forced to turn back on the Bicentennial Everest Expedition, I landed a job filming another expedition to Everest, and Gerry was again on the climbing team. I hadn't seen him much in the intervening years, but he still had the same intensity in his eyes and the same set to his smile. It was a smile that broadened and was accompanied by a firm and confident nod when, near the end of the expedition, I interviewed him, asking him what it was like when he finally made those last steps to the highest point on the planet.

For Gerry, the "P" in that lesson stands for "Perseverance."

— Rick Ridgeway
author, *The Last Step: The American Ascent of K2*

chapter one

the classified kid

My First Expedition

my first awareness of nature was that the smog-infested air hurt
my five-year-old lungs. Living below the shadows of the San Gabriel Mountains, it
hurt worse when I inhaled—precisely when I most needed the air. As soon as I was
able, I looked above the smog at the mountains and imagined that they would offer
a better place for my lungs to be. However, the San Gabriels seemed impossibly
high and ridiculously far away, floating above the Los Angeles pollution like some
cosmic candy. All I knew was that to taste this candy, I would have to go on my
own, since I could not ask my father to drive me and my sisters. I couldn't ask since
my father's bomb lab was somewhere in the mountains, and I had learned to keep
my mouth shut about his bloody bombs. But when we took a family trip to see
some cousins who lived in Altadena, I saw my opportunity.

My relatives' home in Altadena was closer to the mountains than our home in
Pasadena, so I was halfway there. As the families sat in the house chatting away, I
went outside to play, as I usually did. I didn't know much, but it did seem to me
that these family conversations avoided serious topics such as bombs and mountain
escapes. Nevertheless, I liked these visits to Altadena; the smog was usually not
quite as bad here, so my lungs felt better. Smog or no smog, I preferred to be outside dreaming and scheming. After taking my customary lap around the lemon tree
in the front yard, I looked up at the mountains. They still looked impossibly high,
however today they looked especially clear and crisp. I saw trees etched against the
sky, branches extended as if they were there to hold mountain and sky together. I
saw boulders that vacillated between pink and white, whose purpose seemed to be
to keep the trees in the sky. The mountains were a better place! This was it then—I
had to get there.

I knew that these family visits usually lasted for several hours, so with a little luck I could sneak away, climb the mountain, and get back before I was missed. I also figured that I would need some speedy transportation for my assault. My Red Flyer wagon was back in Pasadena, so with a surge of five-year-old energy, I rolled my cousin's bicycle out from the back of the garage and bumped it across the cracks in the driveway. The rear wheel squeaked, one pedal was lopsided, the handlebars were not even, and the front wheel wobbled. Ignoring these minor defects, I pushed my freedom machine forward across the sidewalk and into the street with all my might. With my left foot on the pedal, I slung my right leg over and vaulted up onto the seat. I had never been on a bike before but had watched my cousin do it once. It hadn't looked that hard, but as my escape machine rolled quickly down the hill away from the house, I was not so sure.

This was it then—
I had to get there.

My newfound freedom and speed were heady, and for a few brilliant moments, the wind was in my face as I accelerated toward my lofty goal. I was in charge of my destiny and the commander of a mighty machine. Then, I realized that my feet could not reach the pedals, which quickly proved to be a mighty miscalculation, since the coaster brake was in the pedals. I could steer, but I could not stop. Terror quickly replaced my euphoria as I saw the hill drop steeply in front of me for several blocks.

I was already in grave danger, and it became worse with each passing second as my monster machine continued to accelerate down the hill. I knew I was a goner, since the yards all had rock walls next to the sidewalk. Worse, beyond that was a maze of curbs, signs, cross streets, traffic, and in the next block, a large crouching dog waiting to chase me. As the houses sped by, my terror threatened to paralyze me, but just before it succeeded, I exercised the one control that I had. Spying my salvation, I lurched the handlebars hard to the left and aimed for the one hedge that the neighborhood offered.

However, I had miscalculated again, since before I could hit the hedge, I had to jump the bike over the curb. I was definitely not equipped for this maneuver and just rocketed toward my doom with a grim determination that the curb and hedge were a better fate than the street's lower horrors. Commanding my mission to the end, I kept my eyes open.

I hit the curb at speed, arching forward away from my massive missile. For a split second I thought that I might actually fly over the hedge to an unknown ending in the yard beyond. Fortunately it was a high hedge, and I crashed into its upper reaches with a crunching whoosh. I was badly tangled in the twisted twigs, and it took several minutes to climb out and down to the sidewalk. My shirt and pants were torn, and I was scratched from neck to scrawny legs, but I didn't seem to have any broken bones. Thanking the hedge for having done its job, I retrieved the bike from its landing site next to a rock wall at the end of the hedge. The front wheel now wobbled a lot, but with any luck, my cousin wouldn't notice.

Dejected and limping, I pushed my former freedom machine back up the hill toward the house. With my expedition over, I couldn't even glance at the San Gabriels. Trying to hide the blood oozing from my scratches by wiping it on the inside of my shirt, I thought that if there ever was a next time, perhaps I should skip the freedom machine and just stay on my feet. It would take me six decades to reach the summit of those seemingly extraterrestrial mountains, and the enormous journey that lay before me would far surpass my wildest childhood fantasy.

White Mice

After the Japanese attack on Pearl Harbor in 1941, my father, a Ph.D. physicist, moved his family to Pasadena, California, rolled up his sleeves, and went to work for the war effort. There was an opening for the director of a lab, and he snatched the opportunity with enthusiasm. It was dangerous work—the reason that there was an opening at the lab was that the previous director had been killed. My father refused to talk about his work, even with my mother. She knew that he was up to something out of the ordinary, but every time she quizzed him about what the lab did, he just replied that they were working with white mice.

On our occasional weekend getaways, we drove to Long Beach, which was even farther away from the San Gabriels. I couldn't see the mountains from Long Beach, so turning my attention to the sand and waves, I tinkered along the shore with my older sisters, Charlotte and Janet, looking for shells and anything else that the ocean offered up. On one occasion, my sisters suddenly stopped and gazed westward across the waves. Janet in particular seemed to be looking beyond the water.

Clutching my hand tighter than usual, she pointed west and said, "Look out there, Gerry. There's a war over there."

"War?"

"That's where people kill each other. It's very dangerous for all of us."

I peered across the water, but since I was too short to see beyond the waves, I didn't see any threat. Nevertheless, I stared at the waves, trying to understand until the incoming tide whooshed around my ankles and the sucking sand nibbled at my toes.

White Light

At 8:15 A.M. on August 6, 1945, while my father was away on a business trip, it was a normal morning in Hiroshima, Japan. At 8:16:02, my dad's white mice became white light, and the world changed. The souls near ground zero were the lucky ones, because they died instantly. In less than a second, the flash reduced people to small bundles of smoking char, while birds and insects simply sparked in midair. Squirrels, frogs, and family pets crackled and were gone. Trees, leaves, bikes, hedges, and gardens vanished. The blast flattened buildings then tore up their foundations. Parents and children alike left family memorials in outlines etched in riverbank granite, facial expressions gone, echoed postures often looking upward, arms outstretched.

The white light came first, then the heat, then the blast. These stages were only of interest to scientists; the reality on the ground was not so simple. Formerly energetic friends staggered about with their charred clothes dragging from their blistered bodies like rotten rags. Their hair was gone, and their burned faces were often unrecognizable. More often, one could not tell male from female or even front from back. With scorched skin hanging from their faces, arms, and fingertips, thousands walked with their arms outstretched, hands pointed downward, in a vain attempt to cool their remaining tissue. They had a special way of walking: they walked very slowly. These souls were not survivors; they were walking dead.

What remained, burned. After the great blast came heat, flames, and smoke black enough to scorch the heavens. The morning sky turned to twilight, while some arm-outstretched wanderers staggered into the flames to more quickly end their torture. As the firestorm took over, those lucky enough to only be trapped in collapsing buildings now burned. The walking dead shuffled among the dead. Frightfully injured forms beckoned, then collapsed. In some places, there were so many dead people that there wasn't enough room for the living to fall.

Night brought black rain, then ashes. Later, radiation poisoning laid waste to the blast survivors. By the end of 1945, 140,000 of Hiroshima's souls had moved into the world of the dead. But the dying continued. In the end, more than 200,000 people died from this one blast, and that many again were scarred for their now shortened lives.

It was not just people, animals, and plants that died that day. The blast also took restaurants, laundries, theaters, books, gates, gravestones, temples, heirlooms, radios, clubs, clothes, markets, medicines, phones, letters, cars, sidewalks, scrapbooks, businesses, clocks, signs, works of art and history. One bomb had destroyed a society.

This is the way war really looks. Three days later, on August 9, the United States dropped a second, more powerful atomic bomb on Nagasaki. Together, these two blasts killed more than 300,000 people and placed the world in a situation that could no longer be resolved by war.

When my father returned from his "business trip," my mother stood in the doorway with her arms folded. All she said was, "You and your damn white mice!"

My Simple Question

As a kid, I wanted to know how big the A-bomb was, so I asked my father. I figured he should know, since he and his white mice had worked on it for several years now. Walking into our living room where he sat reading the evening paper, I cupped my little hands and asked, "Daddy! How big is the bomb? Is it this big?" At first, my dad ignored me, keeping his eyes on the paper. Holding my arms out, I persisted. "Is it this big?"

Now my dad's eyes left the paper, and he looked at me sternly. "I've told you not to ask these questions."

Never tell a youngster to not be inquisitive. Recupping my hands, I tried again. "Daddy, is it this big?" Then spreading my arms, "Or this big?" Sweeping my arms wide, I ended with, "Will it fit in this room?"

My father set the paper aside, removed his glasses, and replied with a sternness that only thinly masked a deep frustration. "Gerry, I can't and won't answer these questions. Now go outside and play."

"Daddy, don't you know the answer? You *do* know the answer! You know about this bomb. It's *not* white mice."

Now my dad roared. "Get out of here! I'm trying to relax!"

Hearing the commotion, my mom rushed into the room. "Franklin! Show some civility! He's just a child, and his question is a good one."

Fidgeting with the paper and smacking his lips in frustration, my father replied in a breaking voice, "You know I can't talk about it. Not here, not anywhere. Those numbers are still classified. Now, leave me alone and take Gerry with you."

I had never seen my mother stand up to my father, but now, as he slumped in his easy chair, she stood near with arms folded and eyed him for a long moment. Finally, she said, "In the end, it doesn't matter how big the bomb is. What matters is that it killed hundreds of thousands. Civilians, for God's sake!" I shrank into a corner and listened in silence as she continued. "The number of deaths certainly isn't classified. The bomb's horrors are well documented. Why not its size?"

Clearing his throat and dropping into his terse lecture voice, my dad defended himself with, "The bomb shortened the war by six months and saved many American lives."

My mom continued quickly, "Oh stop parroting that party line. The war was just about over anyway! How many deaths will satisfy the labs? A million? A hundred million? I understand that you are now working on a superbomb that will do just that. It's bad enough to commit murder, but it's even worse to justify it. Franklin, your blessed science has created a death machine!"

Still defending, my dad snapped, "Science did not invent nuclear fusion and fission, Eloise. They are facts of nature. What is wrong with seeking nature's truth?"

Undaunted, my mom continued. "Bomb versus bigger bomb. Where will it end? Instead of guaranteeing sovereignty, this bomb will create a *reductio ad absurdum* of sovereignty."

"Politicians make those choices, not scientists."

"Good grief, Franklin. Do you expect all nations to be restrained and reasonable for all time? The A-bomb has shorted out sovereignty. That's a new fact of nature, and everyone, Gerry included, has a right to be curious about it."

Storming from the room clutching his newspaper, my dad retorted, "It's also a fact that the war is over. Now let's get on with our lives!"

My mom dashed to my corner, scooped me up, and rushed with me into my room. Assuring me that it would be all right, she stayed with me for a long time, but her trembling told me that it was not all right. Still tremulous, she returned to her dinner duties. That evening, the family ate in silence.

The Great Wall of Paris

In 1950 my father did make a move away from war work. He accepted a Fulbright fellowship to work for a year in Paris on his ongoing astronomical research in collaboration with his French colleagues. When we docked at Le Havre after a five-day crossing from New York on the classic liner the *Ile de France*, my family panicked when they could not find me. However, I was safe and sound high in the ship's ropes, where I had climbed to get a better view of the exciting docking.

My older brother, John, who was thirteen years older than I am, already had a family of his own, and he had not joined the rest of us on this year abroad. Thus reduced to a family of five, we lived in a narrow, coal-heated apartment at the edge of the city at 33 Boulevard Mortier. On sunny Sundays we visited parks and castles, and when it rained, we visited museums. At age eight, I logged enough hours in castles and museums to last me a lifetime. On one of our many visits to the Louvre, my mom parked me in front of Leonardo da Vinci's *Mona Lisa* for an hour while she perused the nearby paintings. I was under orders to study Mona's expression carefully. Forced to gaze at her, Mona Lisa became my first girlfriend.

When my mother returned, she asked, "Well, is your Mona sad or happy? Did you see her expression change?"

Standing and stretching, I replied, "No changes—she's obviously just sad. How about a painting with more action?"

This time I got my wish. The next Sunday my mom parked me in front of a huge Rembrandt for an hour and a half. This painting depicted a desperate struggle at sea, and it held my interest as I let my imagination roam free over the waves. At the end of my study session, my mom asked, "Well? What do you think those people are thinking?"

"That next time they should skip the ship and just stay on land! Can we go outside now?"

There were no mountains visible from Paris, but I did go on long exploratory walks by myself on Saturdays. I delighted in the Arc de Triomphe and walking along the Seine near Notre Dame. I also liked hiking up the long stairs near Montmarte. With my sisters' help, I figured out how to use the Metro, where my main memory is having my face squished against a coat smelling of wine, smoke, and urine. Nevertheless, the Metro extended the range of my excursions, and they became more ambitious. On my more-extended outings, prostitutes occasionally propositioned me, but I was far too shy to help them out.

On one of my ramblings, I discovered a wall that I thought I could climb. It was a constructed retaining wall about fifty feet high between two adjacent streets at different levels. The wall was tilted up at the heady angle of forty-five degrees and paved with rounded cobblestones that had gritty mortar between them. The wall was definitely steep enough and high enough that I would die if I fell off its upper reaches. There was a second wall a block away, but I immediately discarded all thoughts of climbing that one, since it was even higher and steeper. If the first wall could kill me, then the second one could clearly do so quicker.

On my first attempt, I chose a tough section of the lower angled wall, climbed up twenty feet, and with my feet skidding spastically on the smooth cobbles, panicked. Without thinking about how to do it, I climbed back down to the sidewalk's safety. I had seen enough of the contrived and illusionary adventure depicted in the Louvre's paintings. While not as grand, this wall was real, and its adventure was mine, not someone else's. I paced back and forth along the sidewalk at the wall's base feeling the cobbles. The lower ones were smooth and oily from decades of passing Parisians, and I imagined that bums and lovers alike must loiter here in the night shadows. Above street level, the cobbles had more texture and gave my palms a better purchase, so I chose the center of the wall and started back up.

Sometimes the cobbles were nicked, and I crammed a finger into a tiny hole for extra security. Occasionally, I could rub the mortar with my fingers, remove some of it, and produce a deeper space for my hands, and, two moves later, my feet. The trouble with this tactic was that the excess mortar fell down onto my next footholds, and I had to scrape it away with my foot before using the hold. Of course, there was also the possibility that I could weaken a cobble's support to the point that it would fall out, so I added this disaster to my mounting concerns. When I found myself spending more time excavating and cleaning my footholds than climbing, I tried harder to use the holds as I found them. On this attempt, I climbed up thirty feet before I got into trouble. I hadn't noticed that the upper half of the wall was steeper than the lower half, and my breath frosted the zipper of my plaid jacket as my school shoes started to ooze off the rounded cobbles.

My fear found me again, but this time I looked down to analyze my impending doom. All my excavating had showered my lower footholds with grit, thus a direct descent would result in an immediate death. I looked about for a slower demise. To my right was the harder route that had already defeated me, and I again discarded the direct ascent above me as too terrifying. It was not too difficult or too dangerous, just too terrifying. I knew that there was a difference between these elements, but was in no position to analyze it further or to overcome my fear. My breath had now frosted both the zipper and the collar of my jacket, so I pursued my remaining option and traversed to the left.

The wall was gentler here, and my breathing slowed. Since it was easier to climb up than down, I looked up for salvation. The remaining wall above me looked more climbable, but my fear was still in command. Worse, my lower legs were starting to tremble, and my fingers were raw from my earlier excavations. I glanced down, realized that the cobbles below me were gritless, and again climbed down to the sidewalk's sanctuary.

Another boy might have walked away at this point with their adventure complete. Still others might have gone searching for another look at the prostitutes. I did neither. In the advancing afternoon light, I prowled the sidewalk once more studying the wall even more carefully. Now I could see how the wall's angle varied from bottom to top and from side to side. I noticed where there was grit and where the cobbles seemed more solid. I spotted several cobbles that had significant nicks in them. It was now obvious that the left side of the wall offered the best route. I had just climbed down its lower half, and as my breathing calmed, I once again considered the upper half. It looked easier from the sidewalk than it had from on high, and I started back up. I was only eight, but I reasoned that if I was going to die, then I might as well die trying.

When I reached my previous high point, I held my fear at bay long enough to observe that there were sufficient holds for the remaining ascent. Then, I instituted a style that was to be with me for many years. As my fear screamed at me to quit, go down, even die rather than proceed, my hands and feet calmly went about their business of climbing the rock. After reaching the upper sidewalk, I crawled away from the edge, then collapsed on the concrete. After pinching my arm to assure myself that I was alive, I realized that I was also safe on top of the climb. Thus, at age eight, I learned the meaning of the expression, "Climb through or die." After brushing off some of the leftover mortar, I pulled myself up. My ragged breath did little to calm my wobbly legs as I walked along the top of my wall toward the nearest Metro station. Today's adventure was over, but I knew that I would be back.

The wall became a favorite stop on my Saturday outings, but of course, I could not talk about it to my sisters or parents. I could more easily tell the story of being propositioned than the story of my wall climbing. I learned to study my wall from both the top and the bottom, then compare my visual notes. Sometimes I could spot a hold from above that was unseen from below. With practice I learned to spot these holds from below first. After several outings, I had climbed the wall's center and right sides and delighted in climbing its easiest left side. I also practiced climbing down the wall. No one ever took notice of my climbs, except an occasional young woman promenading by on the lower street. Coming and going from the wall, I just waved to the prostitutes, who always waved back while cooing enchanting encouragement. With husky voices, they always called me "chéri." Then one day, my feet took me to the base of the other wall.

This was the wall in the next block that I had dismissed as impossible, since it was higher and tilted up at the dizzying angle of sixty degrees. Using all my new-found skills, I surveyed the wall for a long time from all angles until I spotted the easiest route, which was on the right side this time. Figuring that I could retreat if it proved too tough, I no longer expected to die and started up.

The first thirty feet went smoothly, but once again, the final twenty feet were steeper than anticipated. Now, too late, I realized my error. I had no experience in climbing down a wall this steep, and I was already past the point of no return. Reasoning that I had to climb to the top or die, I continued up until I was only five feet below the upper sidewalk, but here another problem presented itself. The top of this wall was near a bus stop, and Frenchmen had been using this spot as an impromptu *pissoir* for years. I struggled with the stinky, slimy cobbles for several minutes, but could not make further upward progress. My shoes would only last for a few seconds on the coated cobbles before they oozed off, so I had to change footholds every few moments. As time passed, the bottom of my school shoes built up their own coating, and the time between my foot shuffles decreased. All the fears that had tormented me on the lower-angled wall were nothing now. I no longer just thought I was going to die, I *knew* I was going to die. My aching fingers knew it, my slimy feet knew it, and most of all, my useless brain knew it.

When a stream of angry French rained down on me from above, it did not sound like salvation. I looked up to see a fat lady draped in heavy, drab clothing and covered by a great coat that threatened to chafe her ankles. She carried two full shopping bags, one in each hand, and my upward glance toward her black stockings only launched a louder tirade. I had learned a little French during the previous year, but this was no time for a language lesson. I had no idea what she was saying and no brainpower left to form a reply, since I was fully occupied with my now rapid-fire foot shuffle.

When I looked back up for what I assumed would be my last look at the sky, I saw the lady put one of her shopping bags on the sidewalk then extend her hand down toward me. I still had to make two upward moves to reach her hand, but these were the moves that had stopped me in the first place. However, I was now desperate, so with both hands and feet slipping, I made one of the moves, then started sliding back down.

Suddenly I heard some angelic voices cry, "Allez, allez, chéri! Vite! Vite!" It was the prostitutes on the sidewalk below cheering me on. When my would-be rescuer spotted the ladies of the night, she stiffened and withdrew her extended hand. While I continued my now frantic spinning, my friends in the shadows below let loose with a volley of French that far surpassed the shopping lady's first salvos. Their tirade was intended for the shopper, not me, and their meaning was abundantly clear to all within earshot.

After setting her second shopping bag down, the shopper stooped as best she could, lowered her pudgy hand one more time, and shook it hard with an insistence that needed no translation. I surged up the final moves, clutched her great paw, and let her haul me to the safety of the upper sidewalk, where she immediately leveled more scolding French at me. I was impressed with her strength and amazed that someone so fat could be so strong. As she bent to retrieve her shopping bags, my ladies below sent up a chorused "Bravo, chéri! Bravo, mon ami!"

Gerry near his grandmother's home in Larvik, Norway, in 1951.

Hearing this, my savior stomped away, but not before she hurled a large wad of spit down toward my lovely friends. The spit landed on the already well-greased cobbles and oozed toward the prostitutes. After I collected myself a little, I wobbled off into the dusk, but not before waving one more time to my lusty ladies of the heights. I was a mess, but I had made it up the wall, albeit with a little direct aid from two disparate departments. The wall had taught me a lot, but I clearly still had a lot to learn. The next week my family left on our scheduled vacation drive around Europe, and I never got a chance to return to my Great Wall of Paris. As we drove north toward Scandinavia, my main memory of France was the smell of urine.

The B-TV Traverse

Returning from Paris in 1952, my father moved the family to China Lake in southern California's Mojave Desert. He wanted to continue his photometric research of the upper atmosphere and needed clear night skies for an observatory. The Mojave provided these, and he inked a contract with the Naval Civil Service, which funded research projects that were not strictly military in nature. This was one of the navy's enlightened post-war programs. Soon Dad had data rolling down from photometers on top of Cactus Peak, which was on the northern perimeter of the Naval Ordinance Test Station, or "NOTS" as we called it.

The fact that my father was now doing pure research was a fine point that was lost on me, since I was living on a military base. On special weekends, the family attended air shows, a roar of speedy fighter flights, bombing runs, and most important, firings of the deadly sidewinder missile. Never mind my dad's research, it felt like the death machines had me surrounded.

Yet the air here was clear, and my lungs no longer hurt with each inhalation. Breathing deeply for the first time in my life, I quickly found alluring adventures out in the desert. It was easy to get to, since all I had to do was cross the street and walk into it. Along with a group of like-minded buddies, I spent many hours chasing horned toads, scorpions, black widow spiders, and even the deadly sidewinder rattlesnake for which the mighty missile was named. We must have looked like a sidewinder missile to a horned toad as we chased it under a brittle-bush, surrounded the bush, then tried to pounce on it. We captured scorpions by turning likely rocks over until we found one, then carefully scooped up the tiny terror with a piece of cardboard. I found black widows mostly in the garage and under the house, however the sidewinder rattlers were another matter. Finding them was hard, and actually capturing them required either great bravery or a special snake stick, neither of which we had. Mostly, we just danced around the buzzing viper in a Mojave standoff. It was a dance of mutual respect.

Of course, my terrorization of the desert creatures was not environmentally wise, but it seemed insignificant compared to the damage the navy's bombs did when they slammed into the desert. The reason a navy base was in the desert in the first place was so they could test powerful and dangerous explosives far from populated cities. With distant bombs booming in my ears, I sensed that I was not yet in command of my future.

At least on my desert rambles I was the master of my own discoveries. If I ran into a cholla cactus, it was my own stupid fault. If a catclaw bush raked my arm and made it bleed in long red lines, I had no one else to blame. If I twisted my ankle in a creature's hole, I limped home knowing that I had to be more observant of the desert floor and its residents. Slowly, I also learned that if I didn't bother the desert's dangerous creatures, they wouldn't bother me. Soon, I navigated across the Mojave with aplomb, and my rambles became longer.

One of my favorite desert games was tire rolling, and as unlikely as it may seem, it taught me a lot about dealing with the forces of nature. The best place to roll tires was on the dry lakebed of China Lake itself. I had never seen water in this "lake," and for my navy-brat buddies and me, it was just a large, flat, barren playground. Old tires were easy to come by, then we drew a long launching line out on the lakebed. After sprint starts to get our tires rolling, we let 'em rip at the line, and of course, the longest roll won. The lakebed, which was miles across, consumed our longest roll with ease, and for longer rolls we learned to go out on windy days. We always measured our rolls by pacing and counting.

Then one cold winter day, a raging wind howled down from the Sierra to the northwest bringing volumes of sand and dust with it as the huge storm rolled across the Mojave. The sky smelled like rain, and even the brittlebush bent in submission. Instead of hunkering down in the house, three of us dashed out to the lakebed for the roll of our lives. This was not a competition between us, but one big roll for the books. Instead of our usual sprint start, a gentle push got our tire rolling, then the wind did the rest. As the tire accelerated away from us, we sprinted downwind trying to keep it in sight while the sand-filled wind chewed at our ankles and elbows. If we didn't see where the tire fell, we couldn't measure the record roll. To our amazement, the tire raced away from us and disappeared into the maelstrom.

With the tire lost, we turned back into the storm just as the rain started. Within seconds sand-infused water filled our hair, eyes, noses, and clothes. We stumbled along in our soggy shoes as the lake began to fill. Could it actually consume us? We didn't know, and bent to the task of escaping China Lake's rising waters and shoe-sucking mud. We had run downwind farther than we realized, and our slow upwind slog surprised us. We could not raise our eyes to see forward, so we just kept pushing into the wind and water. The muddy water filled our shoes then lapped at our ankles.

With our arms doubled over our heads, we sloshed onto the shore and squished back to town. The storm raged for three days while we paced past our windows, wondering where our tire was. Had the waters floated it away? We knew that our record roll was out there somewhere just waiting to be measured, and we knew that we had to find it. Even after the storm was over, we had to wait for the lake to dry up again. Three weeks later, we had our chance.

At the lake's edge, we scanned the barren bed for any sign of our tire. Seeing nothing, we marched out to find it. To our dismay, the lake was not really dry—it was still muddy in the middle. After making a mess of our shoes, we circumnavigated the center of the lake. An hour later we reached the far shore, a no-man's land we had never investigated before. After walking along the foreign edge for twenty minutes, we found our tire tangled in a cholla fifty feet inland from the lake. It had not only rolled all the way across the lakebed, it had blasted fifty feet beyond. We whooped in a victory dance around the cactus-tire combo, but in the end, left it untouched. We could not separate the tire from its embracing cactus, so we left it as a monument to our great record and started our long trek home. There was no point in pacing this one off, and with our detour around the lake's muddy middle, the measurement would not have been accurate anyway. Our world-record roll was simply China Lake plus fifty feet.

My life in the classroom was very different from my desert rambles, and after spending a year in French schools, I felt out of step in the China Lake elementary school. One day our fourth-grade teacher set us up for a big IQ test to find out who were the gifted ones and who were the dunces. She first passed out a test booklet full of questions, then an answer sheet, complete with a number 2 pencil. She went on to carefully explain that we were to indicate our answers by filling in our chosen oval. I had never seen such an answer sheet, but was smart enough to know that the page full of empty ovals looked like trouble. I carefully penciled in my answers, then after finishing the last question with twenty minutes to spare, I spent the rest of the hour looking out the window and fidgeting. Of course, the teacher noticed this transgression. At the end of the hour, I dutifully handed in my nicely marked answer sheet, not knowing that while the questions had been easy, I had indeed made a grievous error.

The next day the teacher made a flourish of presenting the results and explaining the score brackets with their usual 70, 80, and 90 ranges. Then walking up and down the aisles, she handed back our answer sheets with our scores marked and circled in red. When she got to me, the teacher paused and gave me a look of pity that has been forever framed in my mind. She gently set my answer sheet down and moved on to the gifted kids. I turned the sheet around to see my number, and the blood drained from my face. My circled red score said 22. Now I knew why the teacher had looked at me with such pity; I was not just a dunce, I was an idiot.

Struggling to understand, I turned the answer sheet back around to check my answers. There were all my little marks, right where I had left them. The questions had not been that hard, so what had gone wrong? I studied the sheet carefully to see if I had been off by one row or column. Then, the blood rushed back into my face when I realized that I had filled out the entire sheet upside down! I was far too embarrassed to point this out to the teacher and sat there considering my interesting result: recorded upside down, my random marks still produced twenty-two correct answers. I soon realized that this made sense since there were four choices for each question, and that even upside down, I had one chance in four of guessing the correct answer. As I struggled to summon the courage to explain the source of my idiocy to the teacher, who now eyed me nervously, a shrill siren went off in the playground.

This was a bomb drill, so I quickly forgot about the test and listened to a new set of instructions: how we should crouch under our school desks, bury our heads between our knees, and cover the top of our heads with our interlaced fingers. Since the most probable direction of a Russian attack was from the north, the teacher told us to face south. Bent under my desk with my little rear raised toward the impending A-bomb blast, I really did feel like an idiot. The Cold War with Russia was underway, the Reds were coming to destroy us, and with my head where my feet should be, I knew that my mom had been partially right: the A-bomb had not just shorted out sovereignty, but our sanity as well.

That evening at dinner, my father surprised us all by asking, "Who wants to watch an amazing sight tomorrow morning? If you want to watch, I'll wake you in time. Otherwise, you can sleep through it." I immediately thrust my hand in the air to signal assent.

Full of anticipation, my older sister Janet asked, "What is it? A meteor shower?

A lunar eclipse?"

"I can't tell you."

Janet's eyes fell, and her enthusiasm fled, "Oh, *that*. Is it safe? I'm not sure I want to see it."

To relieve the now familiar dinner table tension, my other older sister, Charlotte, tried to look cheerful and said, "I'll watch it with Gerry. It's time to learn." Expecting an astronomical wonder, my arm remained rigid in the air.

My father woke the three of us at 2:50 in the morning, then ushered us into his study. Arranging three chairs to face the large window, he just said, "Watch those mountains to the northeast. It's scheduled for 3:00 A.M."

Janet said, "Dad, aren't you going to watch and explain?"

"I'll watch in the other room with your mother."

Staring out the window, we sat at attention, waiting for some miraculous sight. When 3:00 came and went, I wondered aloud, "There's no moon, so it can't be a lunar eclipse. Maybe it's a new comet."

All Janet said was, "It's late."

"How can a comet be late? This is science!"

As the minutes dragged on, I started to fade, but I struggled to stay focused on the northeast horizon. I studied the ridgeline wondering what was beyond. Right after I jerked up from a nod of sleep, it happened.

Starting from a point, the light spread across the sky with a speed and intensity that none of us had ever experienced. In less than a second, the sky was brighter than a week. Still at attention, we sat bathed in the great light, while our long shadows etched the bookcase on the back wall of dad's study. The light gripped the sky and us for a monstrous moment, then as fast as it had come, it retreated to its starting point. Our night vision shattered, we sat dumbfounded in the dark's resurrection.

Breaking the silence, I whispered, "That was no comet!"

Wise beyond her years, Janet said, "Gerry, that was a different kind of science."

Charlotte muttered to herself, "I had no idea it was *that* big!"

Blinking back toward the northeast, I stammered, "That's the bomb! They're testing them over in Nevada right?"

Janet just nodded in assent. Not knowing what to do and expecting an explanation from Dad, we remained at attention. After I pondered the event for another minute, I realized that it was a long way to Nevada, so I asked my sisters, "Is this the A-bomb or that new superbomb?"

When Janet was silent, I continued, "It's the super isn't it? Whadda they call it? H-bomb?"

Janet rose and said, "Yes, they're working on it. It takes an A-bomb to set off an H-bomb."

"Is Dad working on it?

The Classified Kids. Gerry, Janet, and Charlotte in the Mojave Desert near China Lake.

After wiping away a tear in her eye, Janet nodded once, then left the room. After pondering for another minute, I asked Charlotte, "We can't ask Dad about this, can we?"

Charlotte dropped her eyes and replied, "No. Don't bring it up. This new one is even more secret than the A-bomb."

"Because it kills a lot more people, right?"

Now it was Charlotte's turn to be silent. When it was clear that Dad was not coming back to explain what we had just seen, Charlotte and I rose and returned to our rooms to sleep. Restless, I stood at my window gazing northeast until the sun broke the horizon. When I could see the mountains clearly, I crumpled onto my bed for a nap.

That day in class, I asked my teacher if she had seen the bomb blast, but she just gave me her sorrowful look. No, she had not seen the blast and knew nothing about it. I went on to offer my opinion that, based on what I had heard, crouching under our desks was a useless action in the face of a real A-bomb, since we would just crackle and be gone. Putting our rears in the air would only ensure that our etched memorials captured our cowering. Perhaps if we could disappear into a deep basement, we might survive the blast, but then we still had to deal with the heat, fires, and radiation. I don't think my teacher had ever considered the bomb's realities, and with her conviction that I was an idiot, she dismissed my opinions.

▼ ▼ ▼

In the early spring of 1953, my dad's brother arrived for a rare visit. By his choosing, Uncle Laurence was a family outcast who lived a secret life in Alaska. Apparently, the Alaskan winter had driven him south. He took one look around at China Lake's mountain backdrop, then did something no other family member ever did: he took me for a hike.

We drove out of town and immediately started up the west face of B Mountain, so named for the large "B" painted on it by Buroughs High students. I was surprised at how fit Uncle Laurie was; I struggled to keep up as he stomped straight up the steep slopes that were covered with loose, crumbling rocks perched precariously between cactus traps. In past explorations I had learned much about the Mojave's cactus and steered through them with only occasional disasters, but this steeper slope definitely proved harder than my flat rambles. Skirting the great B, we climbed steadily to the summit as fast as my legs would go. On top I was puffing mightily, but Uncle Laurie was not. All he said was "Good job, sport! We gotta get that smog out of the bottom of your lungs. Now sit down and look at the view."

Uncle Laurie made me sit in four different directions while he pointed and talked about what he saw. I was amazed that my uncle could swoop in from parts unknown and know so much about his surroundings so fast. Gazing northwest he said, "There! That's the Sierra."

Only half looking, I replied, "How on earth can you know that?"

"Cup your hands over your eyes to cut the glare and take a better look. You can just see the snow."

Cupping and squinting, I took my first long look at the Range of Light. "Oh! I see it now. How do you know that it's snow?"

"'Cause it's white."

"Is there a lot of snow in Alaska?"

Chuckling heartily, Uncle Laurie replied, "Yes—a lot! Especially this time of year."

"Do you have mountains like the Sierra in Alaska?"

"Oh yes. Except that they are much bigger, higher, and colder than the Sierra."

"How do you know?"

"'Cause I've seen 'em."

"And they're white, right?"

"Completely—even in summer."

"In summer? How can that be? Hey! Where are you going?"

Uncle Laurie didn't respond immediately as he strode north to the summit's edge and stood cupping his hands against the glare. Then all he said was, "OK, sport, follow me."

"Where are we going? Back to the car? We just got here." While I protested, my uncle strode off down the north face of B Mountain. I had assumed that we would return to the car via the west face, which we had come up, but when it was clear that Uncle Laurie was not looking back, I followed. Uncle Laurie hiked even faster now, and I half trotted to keep up. My dry lakebed sprints were coming in handy, since we reached the bottom of the slope quickly and continued nonstop to the north. It was now clear that we were not heading for the car.

Without breaking stride, Uncle Laurie started up the opposite hill and did not stop until he was on top of the next peak. Lagging farther and farther behind, I still followed with an untiring enthusiasm. Half crawling over the edge, I found Uncle Laurie poking around the towers perched on this next summit. Curious, I asked, "What's this mountain, and what are all these towers doing here?"

"I'd just call it TV Mountain, sport. These towers let you watch Lawrence Welk on your television."

"We don't have a television because daddy won't allow one in the house."

"A wunerful, a wunerful! At least Franklin got that one right!"

"What's a wunerful? And whaddaya mean right? And why don't they put the towers somewhere else?"

"Towers and observatories always end up on summits, but hey, it's still a summit. Look, you can still see the Sierra.

While I cupped and squinted, Uncle Laurie strode off. I hollered after him, "Hey! Now where are you going?"

"Back to the car. Follow me."

On the desert floor below both peaks, Uncle Laurie plopped down and stretched out on the sand. "What are you doing now?"

"Go look for snakes, sport. I'm gonna take a nap."

By the time I started to protest, Uncle Laurie was snoring. I figured that he had placed me on snake guard duty, so I made the rounds to keep any vipers from my strange, sleeping uncle. As his snoring rose into the air, I pondered what I had just seen. Climbing these peaks was certainly tougher than chasing tires across dry lakes and even tougher than my flat desert explorations. From the mountain summits I could see things that I couldn't see from the desert floor, and I could see in all directions at once. This by itself more than compensated for the extra effort that the peaks required. My lungs had happily flushed away the city's sins, my eyes had taken in a feast, and my legs had received a workout far beyond any activity that I had experienced. If I could just get my legs in shape, I felt that I could learn as fast as I could climb. Excited, I pitched twigs at lizards headed for my sleeping uncle and resolved to ask him more about Alaska.

As quickly as he fell asleep, he woke up. Sitting up and stretching, he said, "Oh my. That sand nap made my whole trip worthwhile! So, sport, catch any snakes?"

"No. Just saw some lizards."

Jumping up and shaking the sand out of his pants, Uncle Laurie again said, "OK, sport, follow me."

Uncle Laurie left the next day, and I never had a chance to ask him any more questions about Alaska. After all, his life up north was a secret, but to me, his secret seemed vastly more interesting than my dad's classified bombs.

Two Men as One

My parents, as most people did in those days, subscribed to *Life* magazine, and when the July 1953 issue arrived, it caused quite a stir. The cover held photos of two men in funny clothes, and inside was a long article about how they had just climbed Mount Everest. I found the magazine on the end of my parents' bed and sat in the dim room reading the story until my mom came in, flipped on the light, and said, "Ah, there you are. That's quite a story, isn't it?"

Even though it was just a magazine, anything that I picked up in my parents' room was potential trouble, so I asked, "It's not classified, is it?"

Laughing, my mom replied, "Oh, good heavens, no! Bring the magazine to the kitchen table where the light's better so you can enjoy the pictures. These men have gone where no one has gone before."

"How do I know that they are telling the truth?"

My mom always nodded her head toward me when I asked a good question. "First of all, take a good look at the pictures—you can't fake pictures like that. More important than the pictures, though, is the fact that mountaineers are men of honor."

"What does that mean?"

Nodding again, my mom continued. "It means that they cannot lie about something as important as reaching a summit—especially the summit of Mount Everest."

"So even if there were no pictures, we would have to believe them if they said that they reached the summit?"

"That's exactly right."

Deciding to test the theory, I said, "Uncle Laurie and I reached the summit of B Mountain and TV Mountain!"

Smiling, my mom answered, "Yes, I believe you!"

Looking at the photos again, I blurted out, "Someday I'm going to climb Mount Everest!"

"I believe that you will certainly be strong enough to try. Now come to the kitchen; dinner's almost ready."

When my dad came home from work, he found me sitting at the kitchen table still poring over the story while my mom prepared dinner nearby. As he often did, my dad reached right into my world and asked, "So, Gerry, do you believe that Hillary and Tenzing really made it to the top of Mount Everest?"

"Yes! Look at these pictures—you can't fake stuff like that!"

"That's right. I believe that they made it too, but there is a controversy about which man stepped onto the summit first. The newspapers want to know which of the two was the *first* man to climb Mount Everest."

Flipping to page 136 and pointing, I said, "Isn't *Life* magazine better than a newspaper? Look, I just read Hillary's account and it says right here, 'A few more whacks of the ice ax in the firm snow and we stood on the summit.' When he says 'we' that means that they reached the summit together, doesn't it?"

"Yes, it does. Even if one man stepped up to the highest point a few strides ahead of the other, they still reached the summit together."

Curious, I asked, "Why do you believe that?"

Nodding at me again, my mom also nodded at him to answer my question. "Well," my dad began, "I think that the whole debate about which man was first is utter nonsense. When two men are joined by a rope, they are as one."

Never satisfied, I asked, "How do you know that they were joined by a rope?"

"Ah, that one's easy—flip back a few pages." After I turned back to the two-page photo spread on pages 126 and 127, my dad pointed at the already famous photo of Tenzing standing on the summit of Everest and said, "There—you can see the rope in the photo."

Happy that my parents were really talking to me and that this new subject was not classified, I asked, "How do I know that Hillary took this photo and that he is really tied to the other end of the rope?"

Now my mother took over. "These are men of honor, remember? This is a true story about a great triumph. Never mind the details; they made it, and that's inspiring for the whole world. Now wash your hands and set the table. Dinner's ready."

As I became one with my mom's meatloaf, mashed potatoes, and peas, I noticed that there was far less tension at the dinner table that night. I felt like Hillary and Tenzing had marched right into our kitchen with their rope to calm us. Later, I pored over the pictures again, trying to understand the great triumph. I was inspired and wanted to know more about this strange activity that could make men act as one with something so simple as a rope.

n a s c e n c e

Classified Climbs

pointing across town, my mom said, "Those are the Flatirons, Gerry. They make Boulder famous."

"What are the Flatirons?" I asked.

"They are big, uplifted sandstone slabs. Some of them are a thousand feet high."

Cupping my hands over my eyes and squinting across town for a better look, I asked, "What good are they?"

My mother, as usual, had a meaningful answer. "Oh, they are beautiful to look at, and they grace the horizon. To touch such a rock is to touch Mother Earth directly." I was not immediately convinced, but I secretly decided to find out for myself what the fuss was about.

In a major, life-changing move, my family was now in Colorado. In 1954 my dad moved his research program to the National Bureau of Standards in Boulder. It was the mountains that had brought us there. In a time long before satellites, he needed clear night skies for an observatory to study the airglow, which is a southern cousin to the more famous aurora borealis. The airglow had not been observed from the midlatitudes of the Rocky Mountain region, and the NBS observatory was part of a growing worldwide network of photometric observing stations. For his observatory, Dad selected a small 9,000-foot mountain in the foothills west of Boulder that we called "Fritz Peak." I was now a long way from the San Gabriels, but I had many other mountains to look at and ponder.

My father was leaving the war further behind to move on with his life, and his life example was poignant: in times of need, serve, but beyond that, follow your heart. Now, instead of watching bomb blasts in the California desert, I spent many nights on top of Fritz Peak feeling the wind in my face and watching hard-edged snow clouds whip across the Continental Divide. The war was now long over, and laughter surrounded our dinner table.

Reasoning that Hillary and Tenzing were still helping me, I resolved to learn more about them. In the spring of 1956, I was a seventh-grader at Baseline Junior High in south Boulder and found myself in a study-hall period for an hour a day. During my study hall, which was held in the library, I was supposed to do my homework, but I soon had a better idea. Acting studious, I roamed up and down the aisles tracing a single finger along the bindings looking for books on Everest. Of course, the librarian came to my aid, asking, "What book are you looking for, Gerry?"

I was just old enough now to invent a simple subterfuge. Pulling my father's astronomy textbook out of my book bag and opening it, I said, "I'm doing research on the red shift of receding galaxies. I know you don't have any books on that specific topic, so I'm just looking for related materials in other fields." The truth was that I was indeed reading my father's astronomy book and had often discussed the spectral red shift of galaxies with him. The key question that we talked about was whether the observed red shift really indicated a velocity or was just the result of "tired light," as my dad called it, which only indicated the density of interstellar gas and dust that the light had passed through on its journey to Earth. However, I never got this far into the conversation with the librarian, and she soon let my tracing finger roam the library freely. I soon found an Everest book, in the back, out of sight of the librarian. To my surprise, it said nothing about Hillary and Tenzing.

My new tome talked about the much earlier 1924 British expedition to the north side of Mount Everest. After quickly thumbing through the volume, I realized that there was another enormous chapter in Everest's climbing history that had nothing to do with Hillary and Tenzing. Leaning against the corner shelves, I began to read. After skimming over the planning, approach, and first half of the climb, I found myself at 26,000 feet on Everest's northeast ridge. It had been relatively easy to get here, but the real challenge was the last 3,000 feet to the summit. The upper part of the 1924 route followed the northeast ridge past the first rock step then on up to the more difficult second step. Above this, no one knew what to expect, since no one had ever made it above the barrier cliff. Flipping the pages as fast as I could, I discovered that Mallory and Irving were going strong for the summit with oxygen, but then they disappeared into the mists near, or perhaps above, the second step. Astoundingly, they were never seen again. Thus one of mountaineering's great unanswered questions penetrated my youth like an arrow. What had happened up there? Presumably they perished, but did they make it to the summit first and die on the descent? Did Mallory and Irving beat Hillary and Tenzing to the top of Everest by a whopping twenty-nine years? Just as my mind prepared to climb up after the pioneers to see for myself, the bell rang, sending me to algebra class.

The next day I got an early start, and after sneaking to my corner, I quickly found myself above the first step. Staring at the pictures, I became a high-altitude sleuth, and went looking for Mallory and Irving.

▼ ▼ ▼

When I pulled up to the top of the second step, Mallory and Irving were well ahead of me, but I could still make them out through the mist. As I struggled in the rarefied air to catch up, I caught glimpses of them creeping closer to the sharp summit. Following in their tracks, it seemed like I would finally answer the riddle of their disappearance. I faintly heard a bell but ignored it, since I was too close to the summit to worry about algebra.

I huffed and puffed up the last few feet expecting to surprise them on the summit, shake their hands, and congratulate them on their first ascent of Earth's highest peak. Instead, I was the one who was surprised, since they were not there! They had only been a few minutes ahead of me and had not passed me in descent, so where were they? Knowing that I could not stay long, I quickly looked around. I was definitely on top of Mount Everest, and their tracks led right up to the highest point, but then stopped. They couldn't have gone down without my seeing them, and there were no descent tracks in any direction. Where on Earth could they have gone?

A waft of breeze made me look—up! Mists swirled and boiled through the view-blocking clouds, but I willed them to part. As I stared beyond the summit, the breezes gently pulled the clouds apart. I stared hard, and there they were! High above Everest, Mallory and Irving were climbing through the mists, their legs pulsing to an unknown beat. As the mists closed in a final embrace around the Transcendent Climbers, the second bell sounded, forcing me to descend.

▼ ▼ ▼

I lurched out of my corner and left the library under the librarian's inquisitive gaze. My transcendent ending to the riddle defied gravity, but if astronomers could discuss a "tired light" alternative to a long-established assumption, then perhaps there was a shred of plausibility to my "discovery," at least for Mallory and Irving's spirits. In any case, this was my first brush with a Transcendent Summit, and it would make more sense a decade later. Thus inspired by Mallory, Irving, Hillary, and Tenzing, I soon found my way into the Flatirons to climb the rocks and touch the sky.

▼ ▼ ▼

Gently waving tree branches filtered the streetlight, creating dancing shadows on the lawn. In silence, I tiptoed across the shadows to the back of the Wheeler household. According to plan, the string that hung out of Geoff's bedroom window was attached to his toe. I tugged the string gently, but with enough power to wake Geoff. Without a sound, Geoff retrieved our pack from under his bed and passed it out the window, then climbed out to join me on the grass. We slipped away into sly shadows, not speaking until we were past all the houses and on the trail. Convinced that our parents would stop us, Geoff and I were engaged in stealth climbing on the

Flatirons above Boulder. My dad had kept secrets from me; now I kept secrets from him. For fear of reprisal, I simply couldn't talk to him about what I was doing, so my climbs had become classified.

While I knew that Hillary and Tenzing had been tied together with a team-bonding rope, I had no idea what they did with the rope to make their climb safer. Basically, the only thing that Geoff and I knew about high-angle rock climbing was what we had seen in crude cartoons. A useless rope dangling in space always joined two climbers, and they carried a pick tool at the ready for some unknown action. We couldn't find a long enough pick in either of our dads' toolboxes, so we forgot about that part, but we did have the required rope. It was the twenty-foot-long Wheeler clothesline. Threatening to trip me, the limp cotton twine draped down around my feet as I climbed. Ironically, our "act-as-one" rope that Hillary and Tenzing had prescribed, nearly hastened my demise. After each sneak ascent, the rope silently reappeared between the backyard poles, and we always claimed that we had just gone hiking. We could only borrow one of the four clothesline strands lest Geoff's parents spot the transgression, and of course, our clandestine climbs were always scheduled for nonlaundry days.

On a hot tip from a University of Colorado student, we found our way to 1215 Grandview where Alice Holubar ushered us into her basement, which was the original Holubar mountaineering store. Alice almost certainly saved our lives. She threw a fit when she heard our climbing stories, then lectured us about how we needed pitons, carabiners, a hammer, a nylon rope, and the book *Belaying the Leader*. We replied meekly that we couldn't afford all that. Nevertheless, she kept us in the house until we emptied our pockets, bought one piton, one carabiner, and the book. Since we couldn't afford a fancy nylon rope, she also extracted a promise from us that we would at least buy a better one. It's a good thing that we had no clue about what to do with the clothesline, because it broke when we tested it on my flagstone chimney, dumping me ungracefully into my mom's flowerbed.

We silently revisited my dad's tool chest to borrow a hammer, and since it was a claw hammer, we finally had the required pick tool. Then, after raiding our paper-route piggy banks, we walked downtown and bought eighty feet of Orlon rope at the surplus store. We reasoned that Orlon sounded like nylon, therefore it must be just as good, and it certainly was cheaper. It was a Friday. Naturally, we had a climb scheduled for Saturday morning, so only one of us could read the belaying book before the climb. On the walk home, Geoff and I stopped a block from the Wheeler household to hide the rope in Geoff's book bag and flip for the book. Geoff won the flip, and he read the book under his covers late that night with a flashlight.

At the base of the Second Flatiron the next morning, Geoff tied our new rope around his waist, told me to feed it out, then rapidly climbed upward, disappearing around a corner. When Geoff hollered for me to follow, I tied the rope around my waist with the bowline that I had learned in the Boy Scouts, and after climbing around the corner, I saw Geoff pulling in the rope around his waist. Dumbfounded,

I soon found my way into the Flatirons to touch the rocks.

I hollered, "What in the heck are you doing?"

Geoff replied proudly, "I'm *bee-laying* you!"

"You look silly doing that." I replied.

"I read the book. When you fall, I hold you on the rope."

"Good grief, Geoff, I'm not going to fall off just for the book's sake."

"No, no, don't jump! It's only in case you fall unexpectedly."

"Oh."

It was a bit spastic, but we were on the right track. We pricked our fingers, clenched them in a bloody handshake, and gave birth to the Summit Club. As our paper-route money allowed, we bought more gear from Alice, adding each new piton and carabiner to our sacred collection with much fanfare. We hid our growing book bag full of gear under Geoff's bed, since he had a bedspread that went to the floor and I did not. After making our shadowy getaways from home, we pulled the rope out of our bag so that one of us could carry the rope and the other the "pack," as we preferred to call the book bag.

Alas, one cold morning Geoff's mom, Catherine, woke from her slumber and heard the soft clump of our escaping boots on the pavement in front of the house. Not realizing that this detection had occurred, we exposed our rope earlier than usual. Three blocks from the Wheeler house, Geoff's dad, Harry, caught up to us in the family Buick. Still in his bathrobe and slippers, he rolled down the window with great dignity. "Where are you boys going at five in the morning?" he asked.

At first we said nothing, but Harry leaned toward the open window expectantly. When we could no longer ignore his gaze, we stammered, "Uh, we're just going hiking!"

Harry eyed us keenly, then replied, "With a rope?" We couldn't wiggle out of the fact that our sacred rope was over my shoulder, so we were busted. Our parents forbade any further climbing; ironically it was our act-as-one rope, which the masters Hillary and Tenzing had prescribed, that lead to our demise.

Hillary and Tenzing had filled me with *Inspiration*, and without my knowing it, had taught me the "I" of an acronym that would grow for many years. My "WHO CLIMBS UP" acronym would eventually headline my hard-learned tenets of mountaineering. However, right now I was busted, sadly lacking in knowledge, and assumed that my climbing career was over. My answer to "WHO CLIMBS UP" was simply, not I. However, I had enough inspiration that I still tingled when I thought about the mountains, and my imagination still soared. With a flick of a mental switch I could instantly be on Everest's summit ridges feeling the texture of the nearby rocks, enjoying the crunch of the snow at my feet, reveling in the thin wind, and carefully studying the route ahead. I invented scenarios in my mind that, no matter how desperate the struggle, always left me on the summit. Occasionally I would fly above the summits looking for clues there as well. However, the real summits that lay ahead of me were far beyond my wildest fantasy.

The Lay of the Landscape

After pondering our fate for a few weeks, our parents announced that we could continue climbing, but only if we received proper instruction. With an introduction from Alice Holubar, Geoff met Prince Willmon and Jonathan Hough, members of the Rocky Mountain Rescue Group, and they took him on a climb of the Third Flatiron. At first I was jealous of Geoff's conquest, but soon enough the Rescue Group took me under their wing as well, and that made all the difference.

There was a big age gap between the Rescue Group members and us, since Geoff and I were in junior high and most of the group members were students at the University of Colorado. At first we went on training missions where we practiced search techniques and team organization as well as basic skills such as how to use a map and compass. As our knowledge improved, we went on rock climbs with group members. With our head start, Geoff and I quickly demonstrated that we could take care of ourselves on a rock, and we started going on the group's more technical climbs where we practiced litter evacuations on vertical cliffs. We discovered that there is a huge difference between cotton and nylon and how close to disaster we had been. With our new nylon ropes, we learned all the requisite knots. We relished speed-tying competitions where the time to beat for a double fisherman's knot was six seconds. We learned how to tie knots one-handed and even practiced in the shower with our eyes closed, as we progressively made the shower colder to simulate a desperate situation in a deepening storm. Jonathan Hough was a stickler for details, and he insisted that we should be able to do all that with one hand behind our back while hanging upside down.

Geoff and I worked hard to close the age gap between ourselves and our mentors. We had many vocal wall-sitting competitions where we propped our backs against a wall and lowered into a chair position, but sat unsupported without a chair. At first I could only manage five minutes of the quad-killing exercise before sagging to the floor. Going into secret training, I learned how to wall-sit for more than an hour, which even impressed Hough. I also practiced holding my breath. In the privacy of my bed, I held on until the two-minute barrier loomed, then three. Passing out on occasion, I learned about limits until I could hold my breath with some aplomb for more than four minutes, and years later I extended this time to more than six minutes. Geoff and I also had a pact that the first thing we would do upon opening our eyes in the morning was roll onto the floor and do fifty push-ups. We also trained until we thought nothing of doing 1,000 sit-ups.

I soon had a chance to strut my stuff on the Rescue Group's spring 1957 trip to Arches National Monument in Utah. Unfortunately, Geoff was unable to go on this trip. Our exploration of the monument started as many do, with a hike to Landscape Arch. It spans 306 feet and is touted as one of the longest freestanding rock spans in the world. The arch is not only longer than a football field, it is also very thin, only about twelve feet thick at its thinnest spot, and the rest of the arch is not much wider. Landscape's most breathtaking spectacle, and the one that impressed me the most, is that, unlike many arches, it is far from any other rock-face, hence is surrounded by a great deal of air. The ground is about a hundred feet below the arch—the height of a ten-story building. However, the trail from which most people view the arch is at the bottom of the sloping basin below the arch, more than 200 feet below it. Landscape Arch is also fairly flat—the classic arch shape is barely there. If modern engineers had to build a similarly shaped bridge from steel, they would likely fail. Landscape Arch is like a suspension bridge without any suspension cables.

After marveling at this freak of nature, we hiked north past other arches and finally made camp in one of the many convoluted canyons in the northern wilderness of Devil's Garden. The stated purpose of our trip was to find the elusive Hidden Arch, but I didn't care much about that, since I was happy just running around on the slickrock. This was my first trip to Utah's canyon country, and used to Colorado's greens, blues, and whites, I was agog at the subtle shades of pink, red, and vermilion that adorned the vertical sandstone walls. Scuffing through the sand below the rock walls, I also knew that this desert was very different from China Lake's Mojave, and I loved this addition to my rapidly growing collection of sights.

All day one of the group members, Bob Farley, had been sprinting ahead of the group, but then stopping to do a push-up down to a flower. That evening, Bob had a different idea. Surprising everyone, Bob announced, "Uh, there's a party going on back at the cars. Anybody want to join me?"

Always quick on the uptake, Hough replied, "Bob! You backpack all the way out here for some communion with nature, and now at 9:00 P.M., you want to hike back to the cars for a party?"

Bob, who had clearly thought about this, said, "There are girls there, and I'm going. Anyone with me?"

To everyone's astonishment, I jumped up and said, "I'm going too!"

Hough just laughed and said, "Gerry, you're only thirteen! You can't even spell girl much less do anything about it, and even if you did know what to do, these party deals usually don't work out. Anyway, I can't believe there really are girls just waiting back at the cars. For Pete's sake, go to bed and get some sleep! We have a big day tomorrow."

Bob had already marched out of camp on his mission, and to everyone's continued astonishment, I followed him into the moonlight. It was true that I knew nothing about what to do with girls, and I didn't expect that there would be any at the cars, but I could not pass up a chance for a mysterious midnight hike. Bob had a light, but we did not need it to find our way in the moonlight, and we made good time across the slickrock. When Bob, who was many years older than I was, broke into a trot on the easier sections, I knew that he knew more than I did and was indeed on a preplanned mission. Passing underneath Landscape Arch again, I marveled at how distant and aloof it appeared in the moonlight. When we arrived in the parking lot, the moonlight gleamed on our cars' silent bumpers, but there was not a soul in sight. The hike had been marvelous, but with the girl mystery solved I assumed that we would just head back to get some sleep. However, Bob was agitated and still seemed convinced that there was a party somewhere. When he marched off down the road on his continuing mission, I said, "Bob! Enough already! Never mind girls, there's *nobody* here! Hey, it's almost 11:00 P.M. I'm heading back to camp."

Without looking back, he replied, "OK. Suit yourself."

Leaving Bob to his mission, I hiked back along the trail, then heard some stifled giggles coming from the rocks. True, I was only thirteen, but I knew that it was not the rocks giggling at me—those giggles belonged to girls. Standing stock still, I listened for more clues. The giggles, now rising to chuckles, echoed off the walls that rose above me in an astonishing sweep that easily blocked the moonlight. The girls no longer seemed to be chuckling at me, but rather they seemed engaged in, well, a party. The sound seemed close, but with the echoes, I could not locate its source. With the sand muffling my footsteps, I moved silently forward along the trail, pricking up my ears. The laughter was louder for a while, then faded. Looking at the towering walls on both sides of me, I was completely baffled, since the sound still seemed to be coming from the rock, but how could there be a party on a vertical wall? Determined to at least figure out the party's location, I retreated, paying close attention to the far wall's features. When the now animated voices seemed loudest, I stopped to look more closely at the rock. I took a few strides toward the wall, then stared up an impassive, blank sweep of sandstone. There was certainly no party directly above me, but turning back to look at the opposite wall I saw it.

Partway up the far wall was a large, dark shadow that held the voices. I assumed that the black shadow was some sort of an alcove in the otherwise vertical cliff and that the girls had climbed up into it somehow. From my position, the wall below the alcove looked smooth and impassable, but if the girls had made it up, there must be a way. Crossing the narrow slot and the trail, I scampered up a sandy slope to the base of the smooth wall, and from here, I could just see a few features in the rock. It was not completely smooth. The now impassioned voices were only twenty feet above me, and my curiosity was past the point of no return. In one of the cleverer moves of my youth, I exclaimed in a heavy stage whisper, "PSSSSST! Hey! It's me!"

After a shuffle and more broken giggles, a dark figure appeared at the entrance to the alcove and a shaky male voice said, "Hey, Bob! That you?"

Without hesitation, I pressed on. "Uh, yes! It's me! How do I get up there?"

As a new flurry of giggles pulled the mystery man back into the alcove's deeper shadows, he left me with, "Jus comon up! You cun figure it sout. Slurry! Jane's up here waitin' fer you!"

The guy seemed drunk and preoccupied with his own date, but I understood his message. Perhaps Bob had a blind date who would not know what he looked like. If I could just make it up the rock, I might learn a little more about the spelling of the word girl. Highly motivated, I moved up on the wall, and by feel alone, worked out a devious combination of side pulls and downward palm press-es, then triumphantly pulled up into the alcove to face Bob's date and my fate. Since it was pitch dark, I couldn't tell if she was beautiful or not, but it didn't mat-ter, since Jane did indeed think that I was Bob. Her first words were, "Oh, Bob! I've been waitin' for you! What took you so long?"

Puffing from excitement and my effort on the wall, I plopped down onto the sand next to her and stammered, "Oh, Jane! I ran all the way!"

Taking my hand and giggling like a pixie, she said, "I'll bet you're very strong, Bob!" Then, putting a glass bottle into my hand, she added, "Here, try some of this!" I took a big swig, expecting a beer, and too late discovered that it was not beer. Sputtering, I spewed my fiery mouthful into the darkness. Feeling for me in the dark, Jane said, "Bob! Are you all right?" I inhaled to respond and some of the booze went down my windpipe. Coughing badly, I could not speak for three min-utes, but it was not a total loss, as Jane kept patting and rubbing my back. Not waiting for my coughing to fully subside, Jane said, "Lie down, Bob. You'll feel better, I promise!"

Just as Jane tugged at me to lie back, I heard Bob at the bottom of the cliff. "PSSSSST! Hey! It's me!"

I had hoped that Bob would not discover the party, but now, knowing that I would have to face Bob sooner or later, I decided on sooner, but could not relin-quish my position without a little fun. Crawling to the edge, I called down in my stage whisper, "Hey, Bob! That you?"

Here, Bob departed from the script. "Of course! Who else would be here at midnight? Say, how do I get up there?"

Suppressing a detailed description, I just whispered, "You can figure it out!" Then I watched Bob's shadowed form start up the rock. Turning back toward the alcove, I couldn't see what was going on but heard much slurred giggling and the clinking of glass bottles.

After two minutes, Bob still had not appeared, then I heard his shaky voice, "Hey! This is hard. I don't think I can make it. Do you have a rope up there?" Looking back down, I saw Bob at the crux, which was just a few feet below me. Now I was trapped between Jane and Bob.

Since Jane seemed preoccupied by the bottles for the moment, I whispered, "Yes! Just a minute." Then I whipped off my belt, crawled to the edge, and held it down at arm's reach. Maintaining my whisper, I continued, "Here, grab this."

Instantly grabbing my belt, Bob pulled up so hard that I thought we were both heading for the bottom, me headfirst. Hanging on to my belt with my right hand and clawing at the useless sand with my left, I slithered inexorably from the alcove toward a dark doom. However, Bob was as excited as I had been to reach this special spot, and he arrived quickly by doing a belly flop over the edge. Puffing, he said, "Thanks, Mike! Where's Jane?"

Since it was still pitch black and Bob hadn't recognized me, I now saw my chance for escape. Barely maintaining a whisper, I coughed out, "Back there, Bob! Hurry! She can't wait to see you!" Without looking at me, Bob plunged into the shadows. I sat on the edge, closed my eyes against the darkness, took a big breath, clutched my belt against my chest, and rocketed down the rock into the dark. When my feet hit the sand slope below, I pitched forward, did three rolls, and ended up sprawled in the middle of the trail. Smelling freedom, I jumped up and sprinted toward camp clutching my pants with one hand and my belt with the other. The last thing I heard was Jane's slushy voice saying, "Oh, Bob! You're back! What was that all about?" As I sprinted away from the rising laughter, it dawned on me that, depending on the outcome of Bob's date, I might never know what Jane looked like.

When I reached the open territory below Landscape Arch, I stopped my sprint to catch my breath, check for injuries, shake the rest of the sand out of my pants, and put on my belt. With those chores complete, I looked up at Landscape. The surreal span soared far above in a starry universe all its own. The moon was now close to the arch, so I moved up until the orb appeared between the span and the wall behind it. I sat in this position for a minute pondering the party, but then the power of my current surroundings took over, so I lay back on my elbows and took in the silent, motionless desert. Without the arch, the basin I was in would be an enchanted place, especially right now. But with the impossibly narrow span of rock completely crossing the basin, the whole place took on another quality. Even the air under the arch seemed charged. I felt like I was in a church, but one unlike any I had ever been in, and I had toured Europe's finest cathedrals. Suddenly an idea popped into my head. My crew cut tingled, and I sat back up.

Looking at the moon shadow below Landscape Arch, it occurred to me that, while I would never be able to walk on top of the great span, I could at least walk across the desert in its shadow. Rising, I moved beneath the arch, turned south, and walked along in the shadow toward the basin's wall. It was rough going in spots, but I did not leave the shadow. When I reached the wall, I looked up at a steep sweep of impossible looking sandstone, then, looking back, I saw the arch's shadow extending completely across the basin in a graceful arc of its own. If the basin itself was sacred, then I somehow knew that my *motion* here would add to the arch spirit—and thus honor it. Touching the basin's south wall, I turned and hiked north in the shadow, this time going all the way to the basin's north wall. En route, the true length of Landscape Arch surprised me, and I realized that merely looking at it had not been enough to understand its power. When I touched the far wall, I felt the arch spirit enter me. With my shadow journey complete, I struck out across the dark desert toward camp.

As I wriggled into my chicken-feather sleeping bag at 2:00 A.M., Hough stirred and said, "Is that you, Farley?"

"Uh, no. This is Gerry."

"Where's Bob?"

"Well, if he's not here, then he's having a great time with Jane."

"Jane? Oh jeez, just tell me about it in the morning. Now get some sleep!"

In the morning, we found Bob curled up, softly snoring in a sandy spot next to a flower. As was often the case among men in those days, a man's private life was private, and the subject of Jane's Alcove, as I have always called it since, did not come up at all. So I never did find out what Jane looked like.

After the sun warmed us, we launched on our search for Hidden Arch. We spent hours tromping and romping up and down alleyways between myriad sandstone fins, but we could not find the well-named arch. Finally, disappointed, the crew packed up and started back toward the cars. Partway back along the now well-known trail, Hough paused, let the rest of the group continue ahead, looked at me, and said, "I think we can get on top of it. Let's give it a try!" When I realized he meant Landscape Arch, my hair tingled and my face flushed. The mere thought of being on top of Landscape was enough to fill me with both terror and desire.

Bob, who had been following behind in a fog all day, caught up to us and joined our impromptu discussion. When he heard Hough's idea, Bob asked, "You mean get above it and look down on it, don't you?"

Hough replied, "No. I mean let's walk across it." Bob was skeptical, but this was Hough's moment. He continued, "Look, I have a plan. I've got the rope. Gerry, grab your rappel sling, some biners, your prussik slings, and leave the rest of that crap here. Come on, Bob, let's at least try. Worst case, we'll look down on it." Ready in two minutes, Hough and I started toward the end of a fin with our slings wrapped around our waists and the coiled rope over Hough's shoulder. Bob, still skeptical, followed with nothing.

We could not see the arch from here, but Hough had clearly thought about this and he knew which fin to attack. Scrambling up some easy initial slabs, he came to a steep move near the top of the fin that required a moment's thought. After Hough solved this problem, he disappeared onto the top of the fin and it was my turn. Since I'd scrambled around on the slickrock for many hours now, I felt good on the friction moves that this place requires, and I scooted past the barrier move as well. Eager to catch Hough, I moved up but then remembered Bob. Looking down, I saw Bob struggling with the crux move, and without thinking, I said, "Let's go, Bob. That's no harder than what you did last night!"

Bob, in distress, fumbled with the move for another moment, then said, "Yeah, but it was dark last night. Now I can see all the air." Then, looking up and giving me the strangest look, Bob said, "Hey! Wait a minute! How do *you* know?"

I replied, "Bob, if you're still thinking about Jane, maybe you should stop here. Besides, you didn't bring your slings. Now make up your mind. I've gotta catch Hough."

After making a last feeble effort to figure out the move, Bob said, "Yeah, I am. Thinking about Jane, I mean. OK, that does it. I'm heading back down." With Bob now out of danger, I moved up onto the top of the fin and hustled along it looking for Hough. Now out of sight, I heard Bob holler from below, "Hey! How do you know her name?" I paused and grinned, but turned back toward Landscape Arch without responding.

I realized that we might walk on top of this fin all the way to Landscape, and I now understood Hough's plan. But after 100 easy yards, I came to the top of a nasty notch. Hough was already down on the other side of the notch and said, "Oh there you are, I didn't know if you were coming or not."

"Bob turned around."

"Well then, Roach, it's you and me. Now this next move is tricky. Let me get in position, and I'll spot you down." It was my turn to look at all the air. I still couldn't see the arch, but just knowing that it existed and that we were heading toward it with intent stirred my soul and my stomach. Growing impatient, Hough continued, "Come on, Roach. How many times do I have to tell you? Forget the fall and focus on the rock. The air won't kill you unless you fall through it, so spend all your energy on not falling. Now lean out and look at this hidden foothold under the overhang. That's the key." Following Hough's directions, I focused on climbing down the overhang until I could stretch my gangly leg across to safety on the other side of the notch. Hough commended me with, "Good job, Roach. Now let's move out!"

After another 100 yards of easy fin-top walking, we came to the end of the fin and there it was. The view made me feel like I was standing on the edge of the universe, and if you believe that Landscape Arch is in another universe, then indeed I was. Once again, the air rushed into my brain's inner sanctuary and commanded me to pay attention. Some would say that it was just fear, but I felt more than that—it was a combination of fear and awe.

Hough was already busy looking for a route down, and he hollered, "Roach! Get down here. I've found a natural anchor!" Scrambling down to the east, I saw that Hough had already uncoiled the rope and was busy threading it through a hole in the rock. All he said was, "This thread is amazing, and it answers my biggest question. We might actually be able to do this, Roach! Now pay attention."

Seen from above, Landscape Arch with its echo shadow inspires a combination of fear and awe.

"Hough, I've been paying attention for quite a while now."

With the rope tied in place through the thread, Hough let it out down the vertical wall to the east. Several hundred feet below, I saw the trail and the shadow where I had been last night, but that was unimportant now as I was totally focused on the task at hand. Facing the rock, Hough wrapped his long sling around his waist and legs like a diaper, clipped a biner to it in front of him, clipped the rope to the biner, put the rope over one shoulder, grabbed it behind his back with the opposite hand, and rappelled down in our standard diaper-sling rappel. Before he disappeared over the edge, he reminded me, "Bring your prussik slings so you can get back up this pitch." Then he slid down out of sight.

When I heard him holler, "Off rappel," I repeated his maneuver and, appreciating my many hours of practice, slid over the exposed edge into Landscape's universe. Forty feet below I found Hough squatting on his haunches on a ledge, looking south across the arch. All he said was, "We've got it! Now, don't forget to breathe, Roach. Let's go!" Then he rose and trotted toward our prize.

Following at a walk, I felt my crewcut tingle soon after leaving the security of the last ledge. Moving out onto the top of Landscape Arch, I knew that each foot of slickrock was more sacred than the last, in part because the loss of any segment would eliminate the entire arch and release the arch spirit. The first part of the traverse was easy, then the top narrowed into an edge with only three steep feet of rock to the right, below which was air. To the left were six feet of rock, then air. The only place that was not air was precisely where I placed my hands and feet, and for my disoriented brain, I might as well have been walking on air. Turning sideways, I put my hands on the edge and sidestepped along on the wider left side. Midway across this traverse, the enormity of my position hit me like a windmill.

Instinctively I looked up for a handhold, but unlike on a mountain, which always rises above you, there was only air above me here. Then my brain played another trick on me—my tingling feet told me that there was air below me as well. I had never felt like this on a mountain—trapped in midair without wings. As a trickle of sweat wound down the back of my neck, I froze.

I tried to ignore the air by concentrating on my edge-gripping hands. Another drop of moisture trickled down my nose. Mesmerized, I watched it fall to kiss the porous sandstone and spread out like an opening flower. Perhaps as a thank you for the kiss, the rock now helped me move beyond my fear. I straightened my upper body to reduce the chest-crunching crouch that threatened to starve my lungs, took several deep breaths, and had a look around from my sensational perch. With air finally flowing freely through my lungs, I realized that the air itself would not kill me; it was a part of me. Suddenly I knew that I could make these moves, so I relaxed to enjoy the transit. After taking several deep breaths, my now oxygen-rich blood thawed my frozen muscles and my motion resumed. The top soon widened, and I looked up to see Hough running across the far end of the arch.

I stood to walk without my hands, and if nothing else, Landscape Arch taught me that breath leads to balance. I had just learned the big "B" in my "ABC" acronym for rock climbing, which was *Breath*. I had been moving up a gentle incline so far, and reaching midway, I paused to acknowledge my position in the center of the basin. It was only the arch that allowed me to be here—or was it? Moving on, I again realized how long this span really was. Finally, seeing Hough on the far side, I trotted down to join him. Our transit had been so dramatic that we did not need to speak. After touching the wall on the south side, I turned to look back across the span. From here I couldn't see the arch's skinny section, and the rising rock looked like an unsupported, low-angle diving board to nowhere. Hough was already moving back and, feeling my fear returning, I followed. I had been psyched to get here and walk across, but now I had to muster my self-assurance and walk back. We were only halfway.

Back at the high point, I finally saw the narrow, airy section again, and the sight flipped my stomach one more time. Even though our procession was small, my position of last in line was still a privileged one. I was one with the team, but also alone, since I could afford to stop for a moment. Pausing, I watched Hough sidestepping across the airborne arch, which confirmed my opinion from last night that the combination of sacred rock and human motion honored all involved. The exposed edge was tougher going back, since it was slightly downhill and I had more opportunities to understand my tenuous position. Again on the edge, I paused as another drop fell from my face to kiss the arch's most important foot. This one was a tear, since I knew that when the arch did fall, it would fail here. For a moment, I felt as if the arch was unsupported at its ends and that I was flying on a rock rocket headed for the skies.

Perhaps as a thank you for my buoyant thought, the arch remained in support of my passage. I was still an eager, agile kid, and after refocusing on making one move at a time, I completed the return crossing without incident. Back on the relative safety of the ledge below our rope, I looked down at the trail and saw Bob sitting with his elbows on his knees watching us from far below. He was the only witness to our silent journey. Remaining quiet, I waved triumphantly high over my head, then watched Bob rise and wave back—a simple, silent act that connected our two universes. Then Hough and I ascended our rope with our prussik slings and returned the way we had come, leaving no trace of our passage.

I would never make this transit again, but once was enough. It was a powerful, mysterious moment that still stands out in time for me. Even then, it felt beyond magic; later, I would realize that my transit was transcendent. It is appropriate that my first Transcendent Summit was on rock, which is the foundation of all mountains. I find it even more appropriate that it was on an arch, which synthesizes rock and air so eloquently. It also makes perfect sense that my first walk across an arch and my first Transcendent Summit occurred together on one of the longest freestanding rock spans in the world.

Hough and I made only the third crossing of Landscape Arch, and the first by our fin route. The National Park Service later proclaimed the arch off-limits to climbers, and the basin under it became off-limits to hikers after a rock fall occurred from the bottom of the narrow section, eliminating even shadow transits. Today we are left with only the views from the trail and from the higher fin to the west of Landscape Arch. But I have an enduring memory: the feel of the smooth-sided, angled edges along the crest of the narrow section and the rush of all that air embracing my fingers and toes until it became part of me. The freedom I felt that day is something some governments are willing to fight wars to preserve. On that great day I touched God and God touched me, but which came first is not important. The feeling of being suspended in air made me feel powerful enough to leave the rock and fly like Superman. I lived the dream, and my soul still flies free.

Frau Maus

By the fall of 1957, Geoff and I had commandeered a tiny corner of the Wheeler basement, hung our rope and pitons on the wall, and proclaimed it the Summit Club office. During this critical time in our nascence, Prince Willmon was especially interested in our advancement as rock climbers and mountaineers. Prince quickly became our mentor and called us "the Squirrels," a nickname that stuck with the other Rescue Group members. Prince was actually praising us by comparing us to the very agile squirrel, however we thought that the nickname was a bit derogatory. To compensate, Geoff and I came up with a nickname for Prince. We reasoned that a female mouse, while still a good climber, was a stranger creature than a squirrel. Since Prince was a literature major specializing in German, we used "Frau Maus" as our nickname for him. This name also caught on in the Rescue Group, and we had our revenge.

Laughing at our feeble counterattack, Prince made sure that we really knew our knots. He took us on a climb of the Maiden, which is the most ferociously overhanging rock in the Boulder area, most famous for the 110-foot free rappel from its summit. At the base of the climb, Prince had us tie ourselves in then said, "You are perfectly safe, since I have you on belay with this rope and *you tied that knot your very own self!*" Later, Prince went on to explain that climbing was about a lot more than knots and routines. He taught us how subtle differences in technique and rope work can make the difference between life and death. As our ascents went higher, he made sure we understood that we could easily die pursuing this sport. He always reminded us that a momentary negligence could destroy the happiness of a lifetime. But while climbing with Prince, it was obvious that the sport's rewards justified the risk.

One day, acting strangely serious, Prince sat with Geoff and me and said, "OK, Squirrels, it's time to learn something else to go with all your rope skills. Now, repeat after me: *Om Mani Padme Aum.*"

Confused, I replied, "Good grief, that sounds like Greek. I am many pay me, huh? Frau Maus, that mumbo jumbo doesn't make any sense!"

Geoff's first attempt wasn't much better, so Prince patiently continued, "Well, it's certainly not Greek. Actually, the words, *Om Mani Padme Aum* come from ancient Sanskrit, and they are not part of any modern language. Having said that, they are in use all over the world, so for practical purposes, they are part of many modern languages."

Becoming interested, I replied, "Then how come I've never heard these words?"

"You just did. Now listen carefully one more time because the sound of the words is really important, since this is not just a Buddhist prayer, but also a mystic mantra. *Om Mani Padme Aum, Om Mani Padme Aum, Om Mani Padme Aum.* The sound of the words is always important in a mantra, but in a mystic mantra like this one, the sound is even more important than the meaning."

"What's a mantra?" Geoff asked.

"*Om Mani Padme Aum.* Now, say it with me. One, two … "

Slightly embarrassed to speak in unison, I just blurted out, "Oh, Mommy, take me home! Frau Maus, why do we need this mantra anyway?"

"Because, Squirrels," Prince explained, "the Russians just sent Sputnik into orbit. They beat us at something we're supposed to be the best at, and the Cold War has taken a turn for the worse. If the Reds can orbit satellites, maybe they really can lob H-bombs at us. This mantra can protect us. OK now, let's say it together. One, two … "

Then Geoff saved us from further chanting by asking, "So Frau Maus, what does, 'Oh, Mommy, take me home' mean?"

"For the last time, it's *Om Mani Padme Aum.* Translated into English it means 'Hail to the jewel in the divine Lotus, amen.'"

After absorbing this for a minute, I replied, "That's very nice, Frau Maus, but that's just a translation of the prayer. If the sound of the words is important for the mantra, then you are losing that sacred sound in your translation. Don't you need a translation of the meaning that still sounds like *Om Mani Padme Aum*? A translation like 'Oh, Mommy, take me home'?"

Now it was Prince's turn to think for a moment. "Good point, Squirrel, but while 'Oh, Mommy, take me home' sounds like *Om Mani Padme Aum*, it's not the right meaning."

Now Geoff piped in. "Gerry has a good point here, and how come 'Oh, Mommy, take me home,' is not a good translation? It makes sense to me, and frankly 'Oh, Mommy, take me home' is a lot easier to understand than 'Hail to the jewel in the divine Lotus, amen.'"

Frau Maus was always two or three steps ahead of us Squirrels, but now he fell silent for a long time. In all of the Summit Club's meetings with Frau Maus, this was the most pensive that we had ever seen him. Finally Prince said, "Let me think about this and do some more reading. I'll get back to you next week." Then Prince rose to leave.

Surprised by the serious tone of all this, Geoff and I called after Prince in unison, *"Om Mani Padme Aum,* Frau Maus!"

▼ ▼ ▼

Om may be the most powerful word known to humankind, and it is uttered more often than any other word in human language. Om is often chanted alone to reinforce the energy of a creative thought or act. To experience a hint of its power, close your eyes and chant the word, holding the "oh" and "mmm" sounds for the same length of time. Feel the sound reverberate through your head and chest, then settle into your heart.

True to his word, Prince sat down with Geoff and me a week later. Still serious, Prince began, "Squirrels, you got me going this time. There are whole books devoted to *Om Mani Padme Aum*. I can't cover it all, but here is some of what I learned. Each word in the mantra has many meanings, and you can do the math on the combinations. Each culture, language, and belief system takes its own meaning from *Om Mani Padme Aum*, so the complete mantra may have over a thousand meanings. I just about went nuts thinking about only a dozen of them."

Absorbed, I leaned forward, and knowing that it was a crux question, asked, "Were you able to distill all the meanings into one simple one?"

Prince grinned and replied, "I knew you were going to ask that, Squirrel, and yes, I think I've got a handle on it. In my opinion, all the translations of *Om Mani Padme Aum* reduce to 'I seek divine wisdom.'"

Geoff now asked, "That makes sense, Frau Maus, but what about 'Oh, Mommy, take me home'? Is it a good translation or not?"

Grinning again, Prince continued, "OK, Squirrels, I'm gonna give you this one. Yes, it is a good translation, and in fact it may be better than some of the others."

Leaning back, I asked, "You know that I'm going to ask this too. Why is it good?"

"It's not so hard, really, especially if you think beyond the eastern religion mind-set for a minute. After you reflect on it, 'Mommy,' a giver of life, is the jewel in the lotus. 'Oh, Mommy' is an exhortation, or hailing. 'Take me home' is asking permission to return to Mommy's womb, or fount of wisdom. By the way, 'Home' is *Om* with an 'H,' so your translation's sound system is very good. Also, *Aum* is just another spelling for *Om*."

I whistled then chortled, "Wow, that's brilliant! You really thought about this, Frau Maus. OK, one more question. Where is the divinity in my mommy version? We can't just seek the wisdom of the womb, we need to seek *divine* wisdom."

More relaxed now, Prince continued, "No problem, Gerry. Mommy is a giver of *divine* life."

Leaning forward again, I pressed home the last but most important detail. "So my silly Western translation only works if we assume that there is divinity in all of us."

Now Geoff asked, "But we've always known that, so what's the big deal, Gerry?"

"Oh, I just need a logical bridge or proof that it's good. If each of us is divine just standing here, then we are certainly divine when we are climbing, perhaps even more so."

Standing, Prince stretched and said, "Perhaps so, but that's another subject. Come on, Squirrels, let's go eat a wisdom burger!"

Once again, Geoff and I chanted in chorus. "*Om Mani Padme Aum,* Oh, Mommy, take me home! Ohmmmmm belay!"

Thus Prince taught me the pivotal "M" in my "WHO CLIMBS UP" acronym. The "M" stands for *Mantra*. It doesn't matter what the mantra is, how it's translated, or even what it sounds like; what matters is that mountaineers have a mantra to take them out of the moment and let them rest in a higher place.

▼ ▼ ▼

By the spring of 1958, I had climbed dozens of routes on the Flatirons and in the canyons near Boulder. The Rescue Group also introduced me to the high country, where I climbed several of Colorado's fabled Fourteeners. I also took my growing rock skills to the technical routes on 14,255-foot Longs Peak, Colorado's northernmost Fourteener. Longs, which is twenty-five miles northwest of Boulder in Rocky Mountain National Park, is famous among tourists and climbers alike. Climbers know Longs for its great east face, a glacier-carved 1,800-foot-high sweep of rock that challenges the imagination. I started by climbing several traditional rock routes on the lower portion of the face and also the classic Kieners Route, which ascends the entire mountain. Every trip to Longs was like a journey to another planet. And while I couldn't articulate it very well at age fourteen, I already had the answer to the "Why climb?" question in my lap. With that answer and the mystic mantra resonating in my chest, I climbed on toward grander goals. But I had another lesson to learn before I could progress.

Captain Bivwacko

The Creators named the Navajo Diné, which means "Holy Earth People" or simply,
"The People." According to the Diné, they left three underworlds and traveled through
a magic reed to emerge into this, the "Glittering World." Once in the Glittering World,
the first thing the people did was build a sweat lodge and sing the Blessing Song. Then,
they met in the first house, made exactly as Talking God had prescribed. In this hogan
the people began to arrange their world, naming the four sacred mountains surround-
ing their homeland and designating the sacred stones that would become its boundaries.

Mount Taylor, northeast of Grants, New Mexico, represents the turquoise stone and
is the Navajos' religious southern boundary. The San Francisco Peaks, in northern
Arizona, represent the abalone and coral stones and are the Navajos' religious western
boundary. Mount Hesperus, in southwest Colorado, represents the black jet stone and is
the Navajos' religious northern boundary. Blanca Peak, in southeast Colorado, represents
the white shell stone and is the Navajos' religious easter boundary. Blanca Peak is the
highest of the four sacred mountains.

▼ ▼ ▼

In August 1958 Geoff and I sat on the summit of Little Bear Peak eyeing
the mile-long traverse to mighty Blanca Peak with considerable eagerness. The
connecting ridge between these two Fourteeners in southern Colorado is serrated
and precipitous, but to our young eyes, it looked like fun. Geoff and I had been
rock climbing together for more than two years, and we felt confident. I had just
joined the Colorado Mountain Club, so besides having other climbers to go with,
we could now get rides to distant trailheads, since we were still too young to drive.

The beginning of the traverse went well, and we all scrambled along together.
Geoff and I were quite fit, so we naturally gravitated to the front of the procession.

Suddenly, a large rock tower on the ridge blocked simple passage. One glance
at the tower convinced us that we didn't want to climb it directly and that we better
look for a traverse around it. "Check the right side," Geoff suggested.

I took a peek to the right and replied, "Big air. No good."

Geoff had already checked the left side and said, "This will go, but it's exposed.
Let's rope up." With the others approaching, we quickly roped up and belayed each
other around the corner. As Geoff and I coiled our rope on the other side, we hollered
that our route was easy and that the others should follow. Then we sat down to wait.
As time passed and they didn't appear, we kept hollering. We could hear the group
chattering on the other side of the tower, and we were sure that they could hear us.

After an eternity, the leader appeared on the summit of the tower and immediately hurled down insults at us. Ignoring his anger, I said, "Good grief! What are
you doing up there? Didn't you hear us? The traverse on the north side is easy! Go
down and come around!" This logic only drove the leader deeper into his ethos. At

Every trip to Longs
was like a journey
to another planet.

the time, Geoff and I were baffled, but nevertheless, we waited patiently.

The leader spent the next two hours belaying the rest of the group to the top of the tower and rappelling down to us. Now late, we completed the traverse to the summit of 14,345-foot Blanca Peak, which is the fourth highest peak in Colorado and Colorado's highest peak outside of the gentle Sawatch Range. Geoff and I wanted to enjoy the moment, and I stared to the west trying to understand the boundaries of the Navajo Nation. However, the leader would have none of it. Still furious with us, he stomped off the summit leaving Geoff and me to our own devices. After our summit celebration, Geoff and I hustled down, caught the others who were now moving slowly, and returned to camp well after dark, but we never spoke with the leader again. In the language of the time, we just thought that he was a "turkey," however, he was more than that.

A week later, a letter arrived announcing that I had been tossed out of the Colorado Mountain Club. My offense was that I had gone ahead of the leader. At the time, I was devastated: Geoff and I had done the good, right, smart thing, but I was being punished. The leader had clearly made a mistake in climbing the tower, but that was just a mistake, and we all make mistakes from time to time. He had also committed an offense worthy of reprimand, however: abandoning us on the summit. Abandonment is leadership's cardinal sin. If anything, *he* should have been dishonorably discharged from the club for that offense. One thing a fourteen-year-old is quick to recognize is when an event is unfair. My unjust undoing made no sense then, but over time, and for reverse reasons, this incident emerged as one of the best lessons that I received in my first years of climbing.

Usually combinations of errors kill people in the mountains. Sometimes bad events happen to climbers that are largely out of their control. These events are simply the cost of spending time in a danger zone. However, sometimes climbers heap trouble on their own heads, and the usual entry into this personal danger zone is via the ego. If your ego drives you into a bad choice, then you are ripe for trouble. The second, more deadly error is to persist in the first error. This is the worst thing your ego can do to you. The third error, which often seals your fate and eliminates your chances of retreat, is to not recognize the existence of the first two errors.

The leader of our traverse between Little Bear and Blanca in 1958 had demonstrated all three errors. Of course he had heard us. The difference between the ease of our traverse and the difficulty of the pinnacle ascent was so obvious that of course he had seen it. His ego intervened and prevented him from doing the right thing simply because two fourteen-year-old kids had not only suggested the traverse but had also demonstrated its ease. So, he stubbornly created his first error: ascending the pinnacle. When he reached its top and saw us sitting calmly on the other side, his ego noose tightened. He would still have been better off retreating and following our traverse. But he could not admit his mistake and persisted with it, dragging the rest of the group along. That was his second error. Later, he could have abdicated and admitted his bad decision. We were late and the leader had increased the risks to the party, but no physical harm had actually occurred. However, he stubbornly persisted again. Ignoring his errors, he tossed me out of the club. That was his third error. As if that weren't enough, he had also committed leadership's cardinal sin.

When my dad heard about my expulsion from the club, he did an interesting thing. He picked up a copy of *Trail and Timberline*, the club's monthly publication, and read the club's charter. Sitting in his living room easy chair, he said, "Gerry, the club's charter does not say that the club promotes rock climbing or mountaineering."

Confused, I replied, "Huh? What do you mean? It's the Colorado *Mountain* Club."

With his finger on the title page, he continued. "Here's what it says: 'We are organized to unite the energy, interest, and knowledge of the students, explorers, and lovers of the mountains of Colorado.' Now never mind the confusing language, if you distill this to its essentials, it sounds like the CMC is just a discussion group and a casual hiking club. Paraphrasing, the key words are 'To unite the energy of mountain explorers.' Good heavens, if I wrote that line in a grant proposal, I would never get funding for an expedition to climb one of Colorado's hardest peaks! Gerry, I don't know exactly what went on up there, but I do know what you are trying to accomplish, and yes, I do worry. My advice is to use the CMC for information and occasional inspiration but to look elsewhere for leadership and fulfillment. If you climb on your own two feet according to nature's rules, you are more likely to become a leader yourself. Who knows? Maybe someday they will invite you to speak to them about your adventures!"

In the end, the severing of my relationship with the Colorado Mountain Club taught me to be self-reliant in the mountains and not to depend on any club or, especially, on a self-proclaimed "leader." Decades later I traversed the Little Bear–Blanca ridge again and confirmed that the north side traverse is the easiest route past the tower. I just stepped around without roping up. Later still, when I wrote a guidebook to Colorado's Fourteeners, I named the tower "Captain Bivwacko Tower." This name implicitly offers the advice that if you climb it, you will likely bivouac. What I really meant was that, if you climb it, you're an idiot.

In 1958 the only thing that I needed the club for was a ride to the trailhead, and I looked forward to getting my own driver's license. Still scorched from the CMC's fiery sting, I could not understand that I stood at the doorstep of a year that would be full of Transcendent Summits.

Northwest Passage

Like a full moon, you don't have to work very hard to see the light when looking at the Third Flatiron. This beautiful 1,000-foot-high rock is the extant flatiron and the centerpiece of Boulder's backdrop. I had climbed the Third's sloping east face many times, and it remains one of the best easy climbs in the country. However, climbing routes on the Third's vertical west face are another matter. Geoff and I had climbed the test-piece route, Friday's Folly, with Prince. Along with our climbing buddy Stan Shepard, we had even invented a new route next to it that we called Saturday's Folly. Then, the Summit Club set its sights on an even harder route farther to the north called the Northwest Passage. First climbed in 1949 by Tom Hornbein of Everest fame, the route overcomes the huge overhang that guards the top of the Third's large northwest face. Tom used direct aid to reach the overhang, then overcame it with the help of a lasso. The route isn't just an old test-piece, it was a landmark climb in 1949 and remains a trial for all comers today. Triumph was what we were after, but for Geoff and me, the route progressed from a taunt to a test-piece to a trial to a terror.

Our first attempt was with members of the Rescue Group. We climbed the first short but steep pitch and could not believe our eyes as we stared up across a barren slab to the underside of the huge overhang. It looked impossible, since even climbing forty feet above the ground can move a climber into a different universe. We managed to free climb up the finger crack that splits a barren slab called Skid Row. Tom had used aid on this pitch in 1949, but in the spring of 1959 our ability to free climb it was unimportant; it was simply faster. At the top of Skid Row, we crouched under the huge overhang up which direct passage was impossible. We descended down the ramp under the overhang until we could peer up at the remaining challenge. The view was so terrifying that we immediately rappelled back to the ground and went home. I could see the route from Boulder High School, where I was now a sophomore, and it taunted me all week.

Our second attempt was with another companion, and we quickly reached our previous point of failure. This time we continued up a vertical pitch to the horn that Hornbein had lassoed in 1949. Clutching the horn, we had no idea how to overcome the final challenge. It was a five-foot-long horizontal crack across the underside of the great overhang. Tested and stymied, we reversed the horn pitch, then rappelled back to the ground again.

Out of Rescue Group partners who were willing to try this route, Geoff and I made a third attempt by ourselves. Armed with our best pitons, we reached the horn and tried to place them in the overhanging crack. Our largest piton was a half-inch-wide army angle, but the crack was two to three inches wide. Stacking several angles together, we got one rickety placement in the crack. It was not secure, but I clipped my stirrup to it anyway, then gingerly transferred my weight onto it. I carefully moved left until I could just reach around the corner where the overhang became a slab that led up to a small notch in the edge of the sunny east face. Geoff called from below, "What's it like?"

Only twenty feet from the sun and triumph, I replied, "My hand is there! Now for the rest of my body!" Though connected, my hand and body were two different entities. I needed a second piton placement to get my body past the overhang. I fumbled with our remaining three angles, but it was no good, since I needed four to construct another placement. I also wondered if I might need a third placement beyond that. Before retreating I paused to look around, since I was suspended high above Boulder in a place that had more air than rock. I looked straight down 200 feet, not to the rock below, but to the ground. I looked down into town and spotted Boulder High. Knowing that I had another week of torment ahead, Geoff and I descended once again.

The Summit Club prepared carefully for its fourth attempt. Geoff and I laid out all our available pitons and made a detailed plan. Preparing for the possible third placement, we borrowed several more angles from Prince, who knew all about our mission. When the great day arrived, we hiked briskly to the base of the climb, then pulled our gear from the pack with much gusto. "Gimme the rope," Geoff said, "I'm ready to go."

Startled, I replied, "Huh? *You* have the rope."

Annoyed, Geoff insisted, "Quit woofin'. I'm ready to go."

I glanced around to confirm my fear. "Hey, bro. We forgot the rope!"

That got Geoff's attention. "Oh shit! We left it on the stool!" With our expanded set of pitons and other gear, the rope no longer fit in the pack, so we had set it aside. It was now sitting in our basement office. We sat glumly in the overhang's shadow to consider our options, but this time, there were none. No rope meant no climb—Northwest Passage had foiled us again. Embarrassed, we hiked back to town. Except for Prince, no one else had to know about this.

The next week, with our stubbly little jaws set square, we were back with our pitons, plan, and rope. At the horn, I launched what was supposed to be the lead of my life. I achieved the second placement, then got my head and shoulders past the overhang and up onto the slab. Once again, sun and triumph were only twenty feet away. However, my effort was not enough, as my legs were still jackknifed under the overhang. I managed to get to the anticipated third placement, but it was only

Like a full moon, you don't have to work very hard to see the light when looking at the Third Flatiron. Northwest Passage ascends the shadowed right wall, and reaches the horizontal notch in the right edge of the sunlit east face.

one foot above the overhang. The crack above this point widened, and we still did not have enough pitons. Never mind, I told myself, I would manage with what I had. I struggled at the terrifying, exposed spot for an hour but could not get my gangly legs past the pesky overhang. Finally, Geoff called, "Hey, bro, my turn."

Stymied, I called down, "You're on. Lower me." Back on the ledge, I took over the belay, and Geoff started up. When Geoff reached the desperate spot, he made an attempt to duplicate my direct move past the overhang. When he failed and lowered himself back under the overhang, I said nothing but thought, "Oh my God! Here we go again." Then Geoff made the move of his life.

Swinging under the overhang, he turned himself upside down. Wriggling like a worm, he put both feet over the lip. Then, pulling on the third placement, he bent at the waist until only his butt remained below the overhang. I just breathed, "Go, bro, go!" Squirming like a squirrel, he continued to bend his legs and crunch up onto the third placement until his butt cleared the edge. With another squirrel-like movement, he reversed himself again and stood on the third placement. At this point, all I could see were Geoff's feet, so I encouraged him with our club cry, "Summit Club, climb zees route!" A minute later he was up in the sun, tugging on the rope for me to follow. However, we were not done, since seconding this maneuver would be difficult.

I removed the pitons from the first two placements as I passed them. With retreat no longer possible but with the extra pitons now available, I hung on the third placement and placed the fourth that I had needed earlier. That did it. My butt finally sailed past the lip, and after removing the fourth placement, our passage was nearly complete. No sunrise had ever been as sweet as the moment when I climbed up the easy slab to join Geoff, where the midday sun smacked me in the eyes. The final summit pitch on the easy east face felt like a victory lap. The Summit Club rested for a long time on the Third's sanguine summit to enjoy our triumph.

Independent of the Colorado Mountain Club and even the Rescue Group, Geoff and I had struggled, made mistakes, struggled some more, then exercised teamwork at the critical moment to achieve our success. Better yet, we had the entire rock to ourselves, and we left the rock clean for others to grapple with; the test-piece was still a test-piece. Northwest Passage taught me the big "A" of my rock climbing "ABCs," *Awareness.* Beyond the obvious awareness required to remember the rope, those gymnastic moves required a body awareness that was far beyond what I had experienced on other climbs.

Taking our T-shirts off, we lay against the warm rock and felt it tickle our backs while the sun beamed on our proud chests. We did not understand at the time that we were resting in the hand of God. Shutting my eyes to let the sun massage my eye sockets, time no longer had any meaning, and I felt like I was suspended in the warm, embracing air. This was my second Transcendent Summit. Like my first on Landscape Arch, this one was also on solid rock, surrounded by air. It is appropriate that my first Transcendent Summit in Colorado occurred on Boulder's preeminent rock in the company of my best buddy, Geoff. I would climb the Third a hundred times over the years, but this was the ascent that God chose to honor. Finally, with the sun not just beaming but burning, and lest our moms proclaim us overdue, we pulled our shirts back on and descended.

The west side of the Third Flatiron. Northwest Passage ascends the shadowed face on the left.

Needle Cairns

The first week of June in Boulder is always an exceptional time in an extraordinary place. With school out for the summer of '59, I finally took time to sniff the green grass while looking for four-leaf clovers. I lolled in front of Boulder High with my classmate Gabe Lee who had recently taken up rock climbing, but we didn't chat about climbing, only about how sweet the grass smelled. We didn't find our lucky clovers, but Gabe did teach me how to hold a blade of grass between two fingers like a reed and blow a crude tune on it. The neighbors woke their lawn mowers from their winter slumber, and the city was awash with the fragrance of freshly cut grass. Noise-making playing cards were in the spokes of the kids' bicycles, laundry dried quickly on the line, the Flatirons pierced the deep blue sky, snow sparkled on the high peaks, and all things were possible.

I knew that it would also be an extraordinary time to be in the high country, but I had no way to get there. Geoff was out of commission with family duties, so I tracked down Prince in the stacks of CU's Norlin Library and asked him if he wanted to climb Longs Peak. He twinkled at the prospect, then replied in the required library whisper, "I'd sure like to. You know how much I love Longs, and the weather and snow conditions are bomber right now. But I have to study for finals. I've got one more hell week to go."

"Sounds rough, man. Do you know anyone else who might be able to go?"

"Have you checked with Stan Shepard? I think he's free."

Thinking for a moment, I replied, "Stan doesn't have a car either. Even if he's free, we still can't get there."

Prince replied, "What? You need a ride to the trailhead? You're a Squirrel! You should be able to hop up there left footed in the morning before breakfast just to get warmed up!" When I rolled my eyes, Prince continued, "Gotcha! I'm just woofing you. You still need to work on your sarcasm detector."

"So, we hop right footed?"

"I'll drive you up there. You can hitchhike back."

"Do we hitchhike with our left or right thumb?"

"Gotcha again. I'll pick you up as well. I need that much break time from my work." Then, looking around nervously for any stray librarians, Prince continued, "Hey Squirrel, have you been saying the mantra?"

"Om home, Frau Maus. Why do you ask?"

"Well, the Chinese invaded Tibet, blew up monasteries, killed monks, and drove the Dalai Lama south into India. That's a big deal for the world, Squirrel. With that kind of idiocy at work, I just think that it's extra important to get the *Om* in the air."

"*Om Mani Padme Aum.*"

With a librarian approaching, Prince quickly concluded with, "You've got it. Now get outta here, Squirrel. I've gotta study."

True to his word, Prince dropped Stan and me off at the Longs Peak trailhead two days later. There was no one else around, so Stan and I just hefted our heavy packs and started up the trail. We made it up to Chasm Meadows in our usual hour and a half, then moved into the shelter there. We were used to sharing this tiny ten-by-fourteen-foot cabin with many other climbers, and we delighted in having the sacred place to ourselves. While we spent the afternoon working on our favorite boulder problems on the rocks near the cabin, Longs' great east face loomed over our heads in a staggering sweep.

Stan and I had been here many times before, and I had already done several technical routes with him, both near Boulder and on Longs Peak. We had made our first climb on Longs a year earlier via the Keyhole Ridge Route, which we did in a blasting wind. Now all was still, and I had never seen the face so pristine. Broadway, the long ledge cutting across the middle of Longs' east face, was covered with snow. As the snow melted, it left long black streaks down the smooth granite wall below the ledge; it looked like a frozen aurora. The vertical 900-foot-high wall above Broadway, called the Diamond, hadn't been climbed in 1959, and it was the topic of near-endless conversation among climbers. In one of their less-inspired moves, the National Park Service had declared the Diamond off-limits to climbers. The Diamond knew nothing of regulations, however, and it beckoned us, while sparkling in its inaccessibility.

Stan and I were not here to climb the Diamond though, but rather the snow-filled Notch Couloir, which splits the southern portion of the upper east face. While many of our favorite rock climbs, such as Alexander's Chimney and Stettner's Ledges, were running with water, the snow couloir was in perfect condition. There had been several heavy spring snowstorms that had left the normally rocky Longs Peak quite white. With luck, we could climb all the way from Chasm Lake to the summit on snow. Embraced by Colorado's extant cirque, this place felt like our own private Alaska.

We started before 5:00 A.M. and walked across the snow apron that still covered the shaded southern edge of Chasm Lake. This saved us twenty minutes. As we crunched up the undulating snow-covered slopes leading to the base of the lower face, the sun found the vertical heights above. As we climbed, the sun descended the wall toward us until it found our feet as well. Without breaking stride, we greeted the sunrise by watching it dance and play on the snow swirls that winter winds had carved into the slope. Luckily, there was no wind today.

At the base of the great face, where the rock routes took their various paths skyward, we turned to our left and continued up the broad, snow-filled trough called Lambs Slide, named after poor Mr. Lamb who did indeed slide down it to his detriment. While Lambs Slide can be treacherous in late summer when it turns to ice, today it was in great condition for step-kicking. We took turns breaking trail and gained height quickly, with sparkling snow flying from our steps. If I kicked just right, the snow flew away from my new step and the lower steps as well. If I miskicked, the snow flew up into my face then dribbled down into the lower steps. I delighted in mastering the old mountaineering skill.

Stan and I did not need to use our rope on Lambs Slide. As we climbed, we played with the morning shadows that filled the couloir like a dull saw blade. In the shade the snow was much firmer, but when we burst back into the sun, the snow softened. When crossing the sun-shadow lines, we learned to use the snow's firmness to judge which way the shadow was moving across the slope and how many minutes it took for the softening to take place. This is what we had left Boulder's green grass for—we were learning snow craft.

The traverse across the snow-covered Broadway ledge was much more serious, and we uncoiled the rope for this scary endeavor. The term "ledge" is a misnomer, especially when Broadway is draped with heavy snow, as it was now. With no snow, Broadway is a steeply inclined area between nearly vertical rock walls. It is made up of several tiny ledges just wide enough for one boot. When dry, the climbing is easy but very exposed as you traverse above an increasing drop. Draped with snow, Broadway is nothing more than a steep snow slope that ends above the proverbial killer cliff.

Taking all our gear, I led and placed protection at intervals in the rock above the snow as we sidestepped across. We didn't stop to belay, but we always had several pieces of protection between us. When Stan reached a piece he removed it, so that when we reached the base of the Notch Couloir Stan had all the gear. So far we had been following the famous Kieners Route, or Mountaineers Route, as it is sometimes called. We had done the upper part of Kieners many times, but today we would be on new terrain above this point.

Stan and I knew this exposed spot well. An unprotected slip here would send us hurtling down to the bottom of the Notch Couloir, then into space past the water-streaked wall that we had admired the evening before. After smashing against the lower part of the frozen wall, our carcasses would end up back at the bottom of Lambs Slide. The last thing I wanted was for the Park Service, or worse the Rescue Group, to name this place "Squirrel's Slide," so I took the gear from Stan, placed an anchor that was as sure as death in the rock wall on the couloir's left side, and continued up on belay.

One of our concerns was that the snow might soften too much and avalanche, which could send us to the same demise if our anchors failed. However, today's snow was perfect. It was this hoped-for perfection that had enticed us from Boulder. With my ice ax sinking in nearly to its hilt and my size-twelve boots disappearing into deep platforms, there was little concern. Still, the vertical drop below tugged at my heels, and I placed protection in the rock then brought Stan up on belay. While I belayed Stan, I could often just lean over and suck a drink of icy water directly off the rock as it made its way down from the heights. I was no longer just looking at a painting in the Louvre—we were climbing inside the painting, indeed inside the fairyland that we had only been able to admire from below.

When the couloir twisted and narrowed above us, it also steepened, and our heavenly snow became icier. We were too poor to own crampons, so I continued by using rock holds on the side of the couloir and cutting an occasional step in the steep, icy bulges. While not yet a master, I did know the ancient art of step cutting. Above one such bulge, a chunk of ice took off from my belay stance, scuttled down, and ungraciously conked Stan on the head. We were also too poor to own helmets, so I immediately held Stan on the rope in case he was hurt. He was shaken, pissed, and made sure that I heard all about it. I felt bad about sending the volley down on him, but this was my first serious snow climb. I was just starting to learn a craft that would consume decades of my life. After Stan joined me at the belay stance, we carried on even more carefully; our climb was still full of hazards.

Higher, the couloir widened, and we made speedy progress up into the namesake notch. This notch is one of Longs Peak's distinguishing features, and it is visible from far away. An imposing, 200-foot-high wall rose above us to the south, and Longs' summit beckoned only a quarter mile away to the north. To the west, we had new views of snowy ranges far into Colorado, where we also saw that the weather was still perfect. As I gazed west from the notch, I saw Longs' upper south face, and its steepness surprised me. Gracefully curving boilerplate slabs arched up in a series of steps before bumping into Longs' steep upper cliffs. The snow was busy sparkling and melting on the ledges, sending more multicolored streaks down the slabs. I had no way of knowing that soon, this beautiful place would take on an entirely new memory for me.

Above the notch, we stayed on the ridge's exposed east side, but left the snow to climb a few rock pitches. En route, I bent forward again to kiss the rock and get a drink from the rivulets that now festooned the face. The rock pitches put us back in our element, and we were on top in a few minutes. It was only 9:00 A.M. I had never been on top of Longs so early in the day, and we settled down to enjoy the warming sun. All I said was, "Ig Snig?"

Stan replied, "Arg Snarg!" This private, coded summit communication was all we needed. It meant that there was no one else around and everything was perfect. Except for a few hundred feet of rock near the top, we had indeed climbed from Chasm Lake to the summit on snow.

While Stan snoozed, I hiked off to explore Longs' large, flat summit area. I went to the northwest corner of the summit plateau and spotted the place where Stan and I had topped out the year before after our ascent of the Keyhole Ridge. Then I went to the southwest corner, scrambled down a little, and found a perfect perch where I could rest my back on one rock and spread my legs across another like I was in a reclining lounge chair. Looking to the south, I surveyed many other peaks in Rocky Mountain National Park. Beyond, I spotted several of my familiar Indian Peaks. Settling deeper into my sunny chair, I pulled my hat off, placed it in my lap, and shut my eyes for a nap. However, before dozing I felt my body skipping from summit to summit along the Continental Divide. Keeping my eyes closed, I felt the sun find new places on my scalp, as my hair stood to salute the sun. Today, I felt a significant stirring. This was my third Transcendent Summit, and

I was starting to understand.

The Notch Couloir taught me the "C" of my "WHO CLIMBS UP" talisman for mountaineers. On Longs' sunny summit, I understood that *Conditions* make all the difference. With perfect conditions, we had zipped right up to the summit, but I knew that I would avoid the couloir when conditions were bad. It is appropriate that my first Transcendent Summit on a mountain was on Longs Peak, one of the Rocky Mountains' premier peaks. As with the Third Flatiron, I would ascend Longs dozens of times over the years, but this was my only Transcendent Summit on Longs.

Rising and walking back to Stan under the stunning June sky, I woke him with a simple, "Snig?"

Without opening his eyes, Stan replied, "Snarg!" Then he jumped up and we started down the north face, or famous Cables Route. The bottom of this face was equipped with inch-thick steel cables, and normally we would scoot down the cables in little time. However, the face was now solid snow. As we heeled down, I wondered if there was enough snow to allow us to heel past the cables, and if the snow would be stable in that steep section. There was not only enough snow, but it was still in perfect condition, since the sun had not softened this north-facing snow as much as the east facing snow we had ascended. An uncontrolled slip here would have sent us hurtling over the Diamond, but we ignored this hazard and descended like gentlemen. I have never again seen that much snow on Longs Peak. We heeled down more perfect snow in the Camel—a shortcut back to Chasm Lake—and were back at the cabin by noon. I was quickly learning snow craft and loving it.

Prince was not scheduled to pick us up until noon the next day, so with twenty-four hours to spare, we invented a contest, which was to see who could build the highest needle cairn. A needle cairn is a stack of rocks only one rock thick. That is, you start with one rock and add one rock at a time until the cairn collapses. We defined two types of needle cairn—those with and those without chinking. Chinking meant that you could place tiny rocks between the cairn's main rocks to give added support. The problem with chinking was that we did not know how to limit the size of the chink rock. With Longs soaring overhead, we worried about the great question: when did a chink rock look like a cairn rock? Igging and snarging, we finally set the question aside. Obviously, a cairn without chinking is far more difficult to build, so this quickly became our standard—and coveted—record.

Our early attempts collapsed with fewer than ten rocks. Later, more careful attempts approached the twenty-rock barrier. Soon, the twenty-five-rock barrier loomed. We had one advantage that few people have today: we had time. Prince was still twenty hours away, and the hike back to the trailhead would only take us an hour. As afternoon shadows crept across the cabin, we struggled with a thirty-rocker. It was now less of a competition between the two of us and more of a competition between us and the rest of the world. What grand, unbeatable record would we announce to the Rescue Group?

When the evening chill found our meadow, we stopped, content with our thirty-one-rock beauty, which was five feet high. While the late sun played on Twin Sisters Mountain to the east, we fired up my tiny Primus stove and prepared a small feast. We had a one-pot creation of soup mix, spiral noodles, rice, and raisins. It was enough. Then, we sat next to our needle cairn, but not too close, and watched the shadows rise up the western slopes of Twin Sisters. As the sun disappeared from our slice of paradise, we watched Longs' shadow streak out across the eastern plains to meet the rising dusk. We watched until the rising cold drove us into the cabin and our mummy sleeping bags.

In the morning, we goofed off, making shadow figures in the meadow in front of the cabin, then rocketed down to the trailhead. It was 9:00 A.M., and we still had three hours until Prince showed up, so, of course, we built another needle cairn. When Prince arrived promptly at noon, he wanted to hear all about our climb, but all we could do was point excitedly at our eight-foot pile of rocks. Rising to the occasion, Prince said, "What's that guys? Your IQ?"

I replied, "Hey man, that's a world record."

Eyeing it with his mock-professor look, Prince said, "It's beautiful, gentlemen, but what is it?"

Standing at attention, Stan replied, "It's a non-chinked needle cairn, sir."

After a careful examination, Prince replied, "And gentlemen, is it the height or number of rocks that count?"

Still rigid, Stan replied, "Number of rocks, sir."

Then, Stan and I fell silent while Prince counted, since his independent verification was important. He counted twice, then said, "Fifty-two rocks. You guys have way too much time!"

To which Stan replied, "Yes sir, and we like it that way!"

Obviously jealous of our time, Prince finally just said, "Ig Snig?"

To which Stan and I replied in chorus, "Arg Snarg!"

Stan and I had Longs Peak to ourselves for three days under those perfect early June skies. Even in the parking lot, I knew that I would never forget the pristine snow flying away from my solid steps and the beauty of my third Transcendent Summit. No new-cut grass has ever smelled as sweet. After tossing our packs in the Oldsmobile's huge trunk, Prince spun out of the gravel parking lot, leaving the impressive height of our needle cairn for others to ponder.

Grand Dreams

Life is like a chess game. In a Hollywood film, the people-pieces are moved according to a set of plot rules that pander to a limited attention span and that are designed to lead the viewer through a series of tension-building events to a unifying conclusion. There may be plenty of action along the way, and the ending may be happy or sad, but there is always a timely ending. Thank you for buying a ticket.

In real life, the game is much more complex. Sometimes the pieces don't move at all, and sometimes the pieces move randomly without any rules. Sometimes there are four colors instead of two. Sometimes, the game becomes one-dimensional, and sometimes it is three-dimensional, and sometimes it is both, with different players moving in different dimensions. The ending of the game can come at any moment, or not at all, and sometimes the board itself changes dimensions midgame. Thus, the real-life board's confused collection of humanity is far more complex than a regulation chess game. Even more devastating is the fact that sometimes the queen, the most powerful piece, just walks away from the board, and is never seen again. Just knowing that such a move is possible infuses even the pawns with anxiety that blankets all the other tension-filled moves, and the result often far surpasses Hollywood's best thriller. However, if the pawns are open to the possibility of desertion, they will be stronger. Thus, truth is stranger than fiction, and the next move in the Summit Club's mountaineering nascence was chosen for them.

▼ ▼ ▼

When Geoff's parents, Harry and Catherine, planned a family vacation to Wyoming's Tetons for June of 1959, Geoff and I immediately looked at pictures, read the Teton guidebook, and came up with the idea that we could climb the Grand Teton. While "the Grand," as we called it, looked horrendous in photographs, that just inspired us more. I reasoned that if I could climb a snowy Longs Peak in June, why not the Grand? Difficult as it appeared, the Grand was not Mount Everest, and it was only one state away. Our passion was now aimed in its direction simply because we had a northbound ride in the Wheeler Buick. Yet Geoff and I had never actually seen the Grand with our own eyes, and our first view nearly changed our minds.

At 13,770 feet, the Grand Teton is the second highest peak in northwest Wyoming and the namesake of Grand Teton National Park. Only Gannett Peak in the state's central Wind River Range is higher, but while the large Wind River Range contains about thirty peaks over 13,000 feet, the much smaller Tetons rise abruptly, thrusting just one peak over 13,000 feet—the Grand. As a measure of the Grand's greatness, it rises about a thousand feet higher than the Tetons' other high peaks. None of Colorado's high peaks—or the Wind River's, for that matter—can match such a statistic.

Early French trappers who explored the West saw three great peaks in this beautiful countryside and dubbed them Les Trois Tetons, or the three tits, and their reference to this abundant anatomy stuck. The three Teton peaks are the Grand, of course, and its neighbors to the south, Middle Teton and South Teton. When viewed from the west, the Tetons are impressive and can easily tickle fantastic fantasies. But when viewed from the east, 7,000 feet below in Jackson Hole, the Grand leaps out of time and takes its lower neighbors halfway to heaven with it.

▼ ▼ ▼

Deepening the combination of fear and awe that Geoff and I felt was the knowledge that the statistics and accolades were just that—numbers and words. We knew that the real mountain would take us far beyond mere enumerations, but we had no idea how long it would take us to get there.

Never mind our fears, Geoff's dad, Harry, had other ideas for his hard-earned family vacation, and they did not include climbing. Only after our impassioned speeches followed by incessant heckling did Harry take Geoff and me over to the ranger's cabin to see what the ranger had to say. This was our big moment, and we assumed that we would be on our way to grand heights in the morning. Geoff and I flanked his father on the porch of the ranger cabin, just so he wouldn't let us down. While we nearly burst with anticipation, Harry rapped his knuckles authoritatively on the rough-hewn log door. When the green-collared ranger opened it, Harry spread his arms wide to indicate Geoff and me, and announced in his most deleterious tone, "These boys have the idea that they can climb the Grand Teton!"

We may have known the mystic mantra, but we were still scrawny kids, and the ranger's eyes widened as they drifted down to us. After the ranger and Harry exchanged knowing glances, the ranger began in a slow drawl, "Well, you know, there's a lot of snow up there right now. I don't think that the Grand is a good idea." With the blood draining from our faces, we had to think fast.

Launching into our routine, Geoff said, "We're not beginners!"

Before the ranger could respond, I went on. "That's right! We've climbed many peaks higher than the Grand, including technical routes on the east face of Longs Peak. In fact, I just did one last week!" That got the ranger's attention, and he raised one eyebrow.

Sensing an opening, Geoff pressed on with, "Yes, and we've climbed the Maiden." Unfortunately, Geoff's voice cracked when he said "Maiden." However, before the ranger could say another word, Geoff saved the day by pulling a tattered photo of the Maiden out of his jacket pocket and holding it up toward the ranger. We had given it our best shot and now waited for our fate.

The ranger peered at the photo with interest, then gave us a new looking over. Holding our breath to puff out our chests, we endured the deciding gaze. Finally, the ranger said, "Well, that's great that you have some experience, but that doesn't change the fact that there is still a lot of snow up high. You know, the Grand is a rock climb, and it's not much fun with this much snow."

Exhaling, I practically shouted, "We can do it!"

However, the ranger had made up his mind and ignored my enthusiasm. "I tell you what. There are lots of peaks here in the Tetons. How about I check you out for a lower peak so you can get tuned up on the rock without bogging down in the snow? Then if you do OK, we'll talk some more."

Geoff blurted out, "At least give us one with a good view of the Grand!"

Before handing the photo back, the ranger looked at it one more time and said, "This rock is amazing. How hard is the standard route?"

Puffing from our partial victory, I exclaimed with pride, "It's 5.7! That's hard."

Now smiling, the ranger ended with, "Yes, I know. Stop by in the morning, and I'll set you up for a climb that you won't soon forget."

Thus at 10:00 the next morning, Geoff and I found ourselves halfway up the east ridge of Storm Point. It was only when the little indignities of family, school, and society intruded that we felt like scrawny kids—we were only small in someone else's view. When Geoff and I were on a mountain dealing only with rock, snow, and sky, we felt like masters of our destiny. Today was such a day, and knowing that the mountain didn't care whether we were five or six feet tall, we roared up the ridge of our first Teton peak, while our rope remained coiled over my shoulder. We were on the 10,040-foot summit before noon.

The ranger had chosen well, as the view from here took our eyes halfway to heaven in an attempt to catch up with the Grand. Even from our summit, the peak still receded above us by nearly 4,000 feet. Most of the mountainscape we gazed upon was the northeast snowfields of 12,922-foot Mount Owen, the Tetons' second highest peak. The ranger knew that this was the snowiest face in the range and that our view would drive home his point that there was still too much snow for an ascent of the Grand. Above and beyond Mount Owen, the top thousand feet of the Grand flew beyond our reach like a flag on the moon.

After climbing down Storm Point's north ridge, we scrambled up to the summit of the nearby 9,900-foot Ice Point to claim our second Teton peak, then descended to the valley to report our triumph to the ranger. Of course, even with sobering, snow-covered views playing behind our eyes, the Summit Club still had the idea that its members could climb the Grand Teton. Alas, family vacation activities consumed us for the next several days, but Geoff and I carefully saved the last two days of the vacation for our assault. Finally back in the ranger cabin, we had our next surprise. Continuing in his drawl as if no time had passed, the ranger said, "You boys did good on Storm and Ice Points, but there's still too much snow for the Grand. Didn't you see it?"

Now more than a little irritated at this petty bureaucrat who stood between me and my dream, I ratcheted up the pressure. "Sir, just over a week ago I climbed almost all the way from Chasm Lake to the summit of Longs Peak on snow via the east face, a well-known rock-climbing mecca. You've heard of the Notch Couloir, right?"

Disappointment
Peak reaching
for the Grand.

"All I know about Longs' east face is that the Park Service doesn't allow climbing on the Diamond."

Hurling his word toward the floor, Geoff replied, "Figures!"

Once again, we were on, or more accurately off, the ropes, so I delivered my best punch line. "Sir, we are not asking for your opinion on whether or not we can make the summit, we are only asking for permission to try. I believe that the spirit of the Constitution grants us the right to try." While I was a pretty good climber, I was not yet a very good negotiator, especially with self-important government employees, and I probably should not have made reference to the Constitution. After another hour of haggling, Geoff and I were lucky to emerge with permission for another practice climb.

Thus at 10:00 the next morning, Geoff and I found ourselves striding along halfway up Disappointment Peak. After taking one of the trail's switchbacks, I looked down at Geoff, who was approaching the turn a few strides below, and said, "Summit Club, climb zees mountain!" In obvious frustration, we ground the switchbacks under our boots while whacking at the snow with our superfluous ice axes. We were on the 11,616-foot summit before noon.

When viewed from the valley floor to the southeast, easy slopes appear to lead halfway to the top of the Grand. However, the easy slopes belong to Disappointment Peak, and a large, precipitous notch separates it from the Grand's upper difficulties, hence its name. Once again the ranger had chosen well, for he knew that we would not be able to sneak onto the Grand from our isolated summit perch. As we gazed up at the Grand from a lesser summit, the ranger's choice seemed especially sadistic, since of course he knew that we would be disappointed. From the summit of Disappointment Peak, we were only a little more than 2,000 feet below the top of the Grand, and while it looked difficult, it did not look impossible.

As the family Buick rolled away from the Tetons, Geoff and I were happy to have climbed three Teton peaks, but thanks to the ranger, we would never know if we could have made it up the Grand under those perfect June skies.

▼ ▼ ▼

In July of '59, I had my chance to climb a Colorado Fourteener with Prince. After driving from Boulder, we tossed our sleeping bags on the ground near the shore of Maroon Lake and sacked out. In the morning we admired another one of Colorado's postcard views, this time of the fabled Maroon Bells, which we just called "the Bells." The two well-named peaks rise above Maroon Lake in a colorful sweep of layered sedimentary rock. Seen from the lake, North Maroon Peak is the more prominent peak, and the higher Maroon Peak, or "South Maroon" as we called it, sits neatly behind to complete the classic composition. While beautiful to look at, the Bells are rotten to the core, and climbing them is almost like participating in another sport. I had first climbed North Maroon in the summer of 1956, and on this trip, I wanted to do the traverse over to South Maroon as well.

In those days we learned climbing routes by following someone who knew the route. When that option was not available, we just made it up as we went along. In the case of the Bells, there was a third option, since there was a ten-by-fifteen-foot photo of the Bells in the University Memorial Center's Timberline Lounge, which also held the Rescue Group office. Even before my climb in 1956, I knew the route up North Maroon from hours spent in front of this great photo tracing and debating every inch.

Prince, several other Rescue Group members, and I made good time up our much-discussed route to the top of North Maroon. Interestingly, our old route, while more circuitous, was easier than another modern standard route. Perhaps our photo-viewing sessions were more valuable than we imagined. The others wanted to descend from the top of North Maroon, so Prince and I split from the group, and launched on the traverse to South Maroon by ourselves.

On slabs of rock poised to rocket down while we stood on them, we found the traverse to be an exacting affair. In one place, after reasoning that difficulty was preferable to a longer, lower route, we belayed each other down a pitch right on the exposed ridge. The traverse took longer than anticipated, and it was midafternoon when we reached the summit of South Maroon.

As we relaxed on top, I started piling some extra rocks on the summit cairn, then Prince surprised me by saying, "What are you doing that for, Squirrel?"

Confused, I replied, "Well, to make the cairn higher, what else?"

"But, the cairn doesn't need to be any higher."

"Huh? Why not?"

Prince had obviously thought about this, so I remained quiet while he continued. "Look, Squirrel, your needle cairns were neat, but if they are a work of art, then they should be glued together and placed in a museum so people can sit in front of them. Now obviously a needle cairn is no good as a navigational aid, since the first storm will knock it over, so there is no practical application for them in the mountains. A summit cairn just indicates that a human has been here before, but it doesn't need to be big to do that. Large summit cairns are just ego cairns."

Getting interested in the subject, I asked, "OK, Frau Maus, I'll bite. What's an ego cairn?"

"Oh, you've seen 'em—they're all over the Front Range. When you see a huge tower of rocks out on the roll of a summit plateau, that's usually an ego cairn. It's not a navigational aid, nor even a summit cairn. Its only purpose is to gratify the ego of its builder. People usually place them where they can point to them from their car and impress their mother. As far as I'm concerned, ego cairns are fair game for random acts of disassembly."

"Yeah, I've seen those big piles far away from the summits, but I guess I never thought about it. OK, smarty, so what's wrong with a large navigational or summit cairn?"

"Same logic," Prince continued. "After they serve their function, they just become an eyesore—they're just visual pollution. We come to the mountains to get away from pollution, Squirrel."

"Are you telling me that we can't even have a summit cairn?"

"Oh, you can have one, but small is beautiful when it comes to cairns, Squirrel. Two rocks are sufficient to indicate that a human has been somewhere. If it's carefully placed, you can see a two-rock navigational cairn for a hundred yards. Heck, some people think that summits should be left pure with no cairn and no register at all. I don't go quite that far, but you get the idea."

"Oh, I see. Do I have to atone for my cairn-building sins by taking rocks off existing cairns from now on?"

Chuckling, Prince said, "Yes! You owe society a huge debt. Now get to work!" Prince let me rip a dozen rocks off the summit cairn before saying, "That's enough. We've gotta get off this peak before dark."

We had to make up our descent route as we went along, since neither Prince nor I had ever done this route and the Timberline Lounge photo did not show it. We spent an hour descending a maze of unsteady rocks to the south of the summit, then climbed south along a ridge looking for a suitable route back to the valley. We spent more energy looking for a route than we did climbing it. Finally spotting the weakness we needed, we descended 3,000 feet to the valley, reaching it just before dark. We rocketed down the trail and arrived back at the cars after dark, just as our rescue-ready companions were starting to look at their watches and fidget. It was a great day spent with Prince, and I was starting to feel like his peer in the mountains, although his cairn speech had me a little confused. However, like *Om Mani Padme Aum,* I figured Prince's small cairns would make more sense later.

Back in Boulder, Geoff called an emergency meeting of the Summit Club. Emergency meetings were reserved for events of life-changing importance, so I rushed to our office. Breathless from an uphill sprint, I bolted through the back door, went down the basement stairs four at a time, burst into the tiny office, skipped the preamble, and gasped, "Om belay, bro. What's up?"

Geoff, as serious as stone, announced, "The CMC is having an outing in the Tetons at the end of August!"

Tingling, I replied, "Om home! Climb ze Grand? But bro, as I'm sure you well remember, I got tossed out of the club on my fanny for being good and quick!"

"Well, we've gotta think of something. This is the chance we've been waiting for."

"Damn it! I'm only a month away from getting my driver's license. One of these days … Argh! Look, the Grand is more important than politics. If I crawl and grovel, do you think the club will have me back?"

Geoff had already been thinking about this, and he replied, "Frankly, no. Anyway, I have no intention of ever joining that club. Bro, we may have to stand on our principles with this one."

Pausing for a minute to reflect, I remembered well the CMC's painful sting. After looking at our pitons, I said, "My butt is still bruised from the crash landing I had after the club heaved me out of its lofty, energy-uniting window. You're right, club membership is not an option. Now what would Frau Maus have us do?"

"I've been thinking about that. We should go for a double victory."

"Brilliant! I assume that you mean sneak into the outing without being club members, then do the climb while we thumb our noses. But how?"

Geoff continued, "I've done some snooping, and I think there is a way. The outing needs two camp boys to help with all the kitchen chores at basecamp. I don't think we have to be club members to be measly camp boys."

"So that solves the transportation problem and gets us to Jackson Hole, but what about the climb? How are we going to climb if we're working?"

Resolute, Geoff continued, "We'll think of something, bro. It's one thing to grovel for membership to this castrating club, but it's another to just grovel for a chance to climb. We're used to doing that, especially in the Tetons. Worst case, if the basecamp is close to the trailhead, perhaps we can sneak the climb. We're used to doing that too."

After opening our energy-uniting basement window a crack, I said, "This could work, bro. It's August, so the ranger's beloved snow will be gone, and using the club as a shield, we won't have to deal with the ranger anyway. Let's slide in under the radar as camp boys, work hard, kiss ass, scope the scene, then when we see our chance, Grand ho!"

Conversation over, Geoff offered our Summit Club contract with, "Climb zees mountain, camp boy?"

I confirmed with, "Grand heave camp boy ho! Climb zees mountain!"

A Summit Club plan and contract was a good foundation, but we were nearly stopped before we could begin, since the CMC did in fact require us to be club members in order to be measly camp boys. With the Colorado Mountain Club standing squarely between the mountain and us, Prince stepped to our aid. Prince was a well-liked member of the CMC, and he was versed in our membership morass. If anything, Prince was more disgusted by the club's denial than we were, and he quickly made his move by resigning from the club. After a midnight meeting that Prince would never discuss with us, the club decided that Geoff and I could be camp boys without being members. Prince's reverse logic was not lost on us, however. Knowing that a direct appeal would fail, Prince resigned, then solved the problem as a nonmember.

Thus Geoff and I found ourselves once more looking up at the Grand, this time from halfway up Symmetry Spire two days before the beginning of the outing. We had hitched the first ride north, and of course accepted the opportunity to do a warm-up climb with our car-pool companions. While still not the Grand, 10,546-foot Symmetry Spire was a bonus peak, which gave us a chance to compare notes from our June climb of nearby Storm Point. Indeed, except for the permanent snowfields on the northeast side of Mount Owen, June's ranger-hopping, Grand-stopping snows were long gone, since a heat wave had hovered over the Tetons for the last six weeks. Nevertheless, the still-stellar view of the Grand from the top of Symmetry Spire made us feel like we were greeting an old friend. We hoped that our grand friend would not become a fiend.

With our fourth Teton peak tucked into our now well-notched belts, Geoff and I arrived at the CMC Teton outing basecamp at Colter Bay on the shores of Jackson Lake on August 14. Mighty Mount Moran dominated the view across the lake, but farther to the south the Grand still gleamed high above its neighbors. Turning away from the inspiring vista, Geoff and I had to park our reverie right after we met Ted Lee, our new boss and the cook for this extravagant outing. Ted had to feed sixty people for two weeks by cooking on a wood fire, and there was a mountain of work to be done to help Ted accomplish this monumental task. Our camp boy chores quickly consumed us as we unpacked, sorted, and stored supplies; pitched several large tents; cleaned and prepared the fire pit; fetched water; hauled, split, and stacked firewood; placed tables and chairs; and raised the flag. The first night's dinner was a huge success, and everybody praised Ted's cooking, but we knew that he could not have done it without the Summit Club. Ted was also well aware of this fact and treated us like sons while he heaped the chores upon us. Our camp boy pay was that we got to eat Ted's good camp cooking. After dinner, we discovered our next chore, dishwashing.

Geoff and I loved our new job and the view that came with it, so we bent to the tasks with an untiring enthusiasm. However, as the days rolled by and the climbers left basecamp for their climbs then returned with stories of glory, we realized that we were expected to stay in camp helping Ted for the duration of the outing. Another problem was that Colter Bay is many miles from Jenny Lake and the trailhead for the Grand, thus a sneak ascent was not realistic, at least not right in the middle of the outing. Because of our substandard status, we had no chance to officially join a climbing party. But after well-phrased inquiries to the best-placed people, we learned that we might be tolerated as tagalongs if Ted would give us permission to leave basecamp for a couple of days. Slowly, we were becoming better negotiators. Thus, we turned to Ted with our impassioned speeches and enthusiasm. Ted, who was sympathetic to our cause, considered our plea for a day then offered that we could leave one at a time on different climbs, so that he would always have at least one helper. All we had to do was convince Ted that either one of us could do the work of two. This arrangement meant that Geoff and I would not be able to climb the Grand together, but at least we could make the climb. This was the best arrangement that we were likely to get, and we quickly redoubled our efforts to convince Ted that we were both capable of heroic camp boy chores and also serious about climbing.

We each had only one thirty-six-hour window to climb the peak of our dreams. In a spirit of total fairness, Geoff and I always flipped a coin at the bottom of a climb to see who got the first lead, and now we flipped for the first shot at the almighty Grand. This time I won, and feeling like I was headed for Everest, I quickly prepared my pack. I would hike up into Garnet Canyon by myself in the afternoon, meet my climbing partners at their high camp, and climb with them the next morning. At long last, I was actually on my way to the Grand!

When my great day arrived, my all-important ride dropped me off at the Lupine Meadows trailhead in the afternoon, just as the first fat raindrops fell. Assuming that it was just a passing thunderstorm, I sped up the seemingly endless switchbacks leading to the Garnett Canyon campsite. As my wool pants took on water and my boots started to squish, I knew that this was not just a shower—the weather had changed. After months of scheming and dreaming, I was not yet deterred, since it was tomorrow's weather that counted. However, when I reached the campsite in a dank downpour, I felt doubt fingering my resolve.

My arrangement had been that half a tent would be empty and waiting for me. This was important, especially with the rain, since I had no tent of my own. After checking every tent, I learned to my dismay that there was no room for me in the entire camp! It was now dark, I had no dinner, and my Grand clock was ticking. Feeling that there was more to it, I made a second lap. Watching the raindrops bounce off the nylon, I announced my presence and intentions in loud, assertive tones. The voices from inside the cloth sanctuaries made it clear a second time that I, the bottom feeder, was not allowed in. As I prepared for a third lap, a faint female voice in the last tent asked, "Have you checked the tent down by the creek? I think there is room there." In the dark, I had missed it.

Why had it taken two laps to learn this, and why was this other tent so far from the others? Never mind; my sleeping space was there. Slogging along in a now ferocious downpour, I finally discovered the errant tent. Feeling like my negotiating skills were at an all-time low, I nevertheless tried again to be polite. "Hello! This is Gerry from the CMC basecamp. I understand that you have room for me in your tent. Can I come in?"

I heard a rustling inside and knew that the tent was occupied, but with no response, I tried again. After my third attempt, I fought off an impulse to shake the tent. Instead, I said, "Hello! I know you're in there. I guess I'll just come in and see for myself if there is room!"

At last, I heard a voice, "Oh no! Don't do that! This tent is full anyway!"

"Who is in there with you?"

"On no, the tent is full!"

"But you're alone in there right?"

Silence.

"What do you expect me to do all night? Sleep in the creek?"

Silence.

This was my second encounter with a moronic member of the Colorado Mountain Club. "Sir, the other tents are all full. If you are alone in there, then I need to come in out of the rain. I'm starting to shiver."

At least this try elicited a response. "Sorry, kid, this tent is full."

At this point, I knew that I had to switch gears. I was convinced that my space was in there and that this comfortable turkey just didn't want to deal with me. Thinking for a moment, I realized that my direct tactic was no good. This was the club that had abandoned me on a summit and thrown me out for doing the right thing. Thinking that perhaps a dose of Prince's perverse reverse logic would help, I said, "Sir, I'm starting to shiver uncontrollably now. I'm going to run down while I still can and report you to the authorities. I'm pretty sure that I can get you thrown out of the club!"

That did it. "OK, OK, OK. You can come in, but you have to let me get set up first."

While I stood at the tent's now sagging entrance for another twenty minutes, listening to my bucolic benefactor rustling around protecting his stuff from my wet entrance, I did indeed start to shiver badly. When my moment of salvation came, I crawled into the tent to face the turkey, only to learn that he was prissily paranoid about any moisture touching him or his things. I watched him trace a line with his finger down the center of the tent, then listened to him give detailed instructions about not touching his sacred space, letting him direct my every move for another ten minutes. When I could stand no more, I put my flashlight under my chin to create monster light, sucked in my cheeks, went crazy-man wild eyed, and said, "Oh sultry sir, you are under tent arrest for reintarnated idiocy!" Then I flicked my light off and on three times for effect, grabbed a candy bar, wriggled into my sleeping bag, rolled away from him, and munched my miserable dinner in the privacy of my bag. When the churl started complaining again, I just pulled my flashlight out of my bag, pointed it at him, and flicked it on and off three times.

Just as I was falling asleep, desperate for the last word, he went at it again. "You silly boy, it's reincarnated, not reintarnated."

I had spent much of my youth being late with a catchy comeback, but this time I was ready with a response. "Sir, in your case, reintarnated is quite correct, since it's obvious that you will come back as a hillbilly. Now, in language that I'm sure you can understand, shut the fuck up!" Before he could reply, I was asleep.

My approach to the Grand had been anything but gracious, and as the rain drummed on the tent all night, my Grand dreams were anything but grand. At first light I quickly stuffed my bag, collected my meager things, and bolted from the tent before the tentmonger could stir. Once outside, and feeling like a hobo, I made my escape with bundles of stuff under my arms. I didn't mean to, but in the dark I tripped over one of the tent guylines, which sent a shower onto the turkey's sovereign territory. Smirking, I hoped that it had delivered the last word. Over at the main campsite, I met the others who were milling about outside their tents. The woman who had spoken up last night greeted me with, "Good morning. Did that sad sack let you into his tent last night or did you have to bivouac?" After I sketched my story for her, she continued, "Figures! No one here can get along with him either. His tent is way down there by the creek since he can't stand voices. Anyway, he'll head down later this morning, and we won't have to deal with him again. I'm sorry that things were so confused last night."

I pressed ahead with, "Thanks. So, what about climbing the Grand today? The weather doesn't look very good."

"No, the weather is shot, but we're going to head up South Teton, which is easy. You're welcome to join us for that."

I was pleased that there were some sane folks here and that I was included in a climb, but I was bitterly disappointed that it was not the Grand. However, as the growing dawn revealed the drops still flying from low-lying clouds, I knew that I would not climb the Grand today. Nature had delivered a most untimely storm. Thus it was that I found myself on top of the South Teton peering north into the heavy, rain-filled clouds looking for any sign of the elusive Grand Teton. That day I couldn't even see my goal.

The 12,505-foot South Teton is the fifth highest peak in the Tetons, and it was also my fifth and highest Teton ascent. The fact that I had climbed one of Les Trois Tetons was small compensation; I felt that my creep toward the Grand was stiflingly slow. Squishing back down the trail that afternoon, I knew that I would be back, but with the logistical barriers that waited for me in the valley, I had no idea when that might be. Time was running out, and the Grand Teton remained heavily guarded by a seemingly impregnable ring of practice peaks.

Back in basecamp, I related my soggy story to Geoff, who could do nothing but be sympathetic. Back at my wood-splitting duties the next day, I found new energy in each stoke of the ax. The next day Geoff left for his attempt, and the Summit Club was asunder again. As Geoff's summit day rolled by, I kept looking up from my wood splitting to scan the sky. The now pesky peak floated on the horizon mocking me. The weather was good again, and sure enough, Geoff returned with a tale of triumph. He had climbed the upper Exum Ridge and reached the summit of the Grand Teton! As we huddled in our tent, he told me all about his climb and the route, which did not sound that hard. I dreamed of rounding the famous corner at the end of Wall Street and greeting the sun on the crest of the Exum Ridge with nothing but solid Teton rock between me and the summit. However, the outing was just about over, and Ted needed extra help to prepare the last dinner, which would have almost everybody in attendance. After that, we had to clean up, break everything down, and pack it away. Time was running out.

I called an emergency midnight Summit Club meeting in our tiny tent. While Geoff listened attentively, I vented my frustrations. "Look, bro, we've had a good time here splitting wood, but it seems like this cult club needs a new name and a new charter. Instead of the CMC, this is the STOP, which stands for Separate The Obviously Productive. The new club charter should read, 'We are organized to separate already well-united climbers and strive to keep these bottom feeders off of the peaks!' Gadzooks, man, we would have been up the Grand months ago if it had just been you and me against the mountain."

Geoff propped up on his elbow and said, "Hey, bro, we are the Summit Club. We are pointedly not members of the CMC or the STOP. We stopped doing that last year, remember? Now, if we lay down with the dogs, we will wake up with fleas, so it's time to be true to *our* charter. For the rest of the outing, our Summit Club job is simply to climb the mountain any way we can; even split up, we are still a team. Now here is what I propose. I'm a better negotiator than you are, so let me go to Ted and convince him that I can turn triple flips to help him get ready for the grand victory dinner at the end of the outing. There are lots of cars heading from here to Lupine Meadows right now, since people are coming down for the last time. If you work with me all day tomorrow, we can get ahead on a bunch of chores. Then, you split in the late afternoon with one of the cars going to the trailhead to pick people up. Blast up the trail, do the climb in the morning, and boogie back here for the victory dinner. You and I can help Ted through the dinner then clean up afterwards. That way, we'll both be here the next day to pack up the camp."

Smacking my lips, I replied, "That sounds like a good plan, but I still need some climbing partners. I don't think I can solo this one."

"Yeah, I'd vote against soloing it. Never mind the political fallout, there are a couple of pitches up there where you are going to want a belay. You'll also need two long ropes for the rappel, and that is more than you want to carry by yourself. Look, there are still two days left in the outing, and I think that there is a father-son team still up in Garnett Canyon that wants to get up the Grand. Their name is Shoumatoff, and being from New York, they are not in the greatest shape, but they really want to do the climb."

"So, if I can get a message sent up to the Shoumatoffs in the morning that I will be up late in the day, then hopefully, they will wait for one more attempt."

Thinking ahead, Geoff continued, "There is always someone heading up that trail, so we can get a message up to Garnett Canyon. Oh, there are two sons, so you will have three Shoumatoffs to deal with."

"That's a load, but it sounds like my last shot at the Grand this year. Jeesh, school starts next week."

"Stay focused on the Grand—the Summit Club is only halfway there. Climb zees mountain, bro! Now, let's get some sleep—we're going to need it."

After turning toward sleep and pondering for a few minutes, I said, "Bro? One more question."

"Om belay."

"It's great that the Shoumatoffs are inspired, but there must be a reason why they haven't made it up the Grand yet. Can they climb?"

"I was afraid you would ask that. The word on the trail is that their skills are rather rudimentary. After listening to the camp chat, I gather that the father just turns around, and when he turns, he takes his sons with him. Seems like he just has mental meltdowns. Forget about the kids, the old man is the one you have to convince."

"Well, I'm used to doing that!"

"You can handle the climb just fine, but the politics are going to be tough, bro."

"I'll prepare an 'Oh, Mommy, take me home' speech."

"Better prepare several, and reduce them to mantras."

"OK. Oh, Mommy, hear my tome!"

"*Aum!*"

While loading my pack late the next afternoon, Ted walked up to me and said, "Gerry, you know that I'm on your side, and I really want you to make this climb. I can't do these climbs myself, but I do admire you kids for being so persistent. Listen, Geoff made me a deputy member of the Summit Club for your climb." Then Ted held a large bag toward me and said, "Here, take this. It's my contribution, and after watching you chow down for the last two weeks, I know that you will like it! Now get on up there, be safe, and then get back here for dinner tomorrow night. It's going to be the best meal of the outing!"

Taking the bag and looking Ted in the eyes, I said, "Thanks, Ted. I am going to need some help up there. Welcome to the Summit Club team!" As I walked toward my ride, Geoff and I flashed upward thumbs at each other.

That evening I met Nicholas Sr., Nicholas Jr., and Alexander Shoumatoff in Garnett Canyon after supper. As we exchanged pleasantries, I saw that they were obviously excited to try for the Grand one more time. I quickly went over our equipment and strategy, gave them a pep talk, and announced a 3:00 A.M. departure time. At fifteen, I was the youngest member of the team, but I didn't tell them that. Before falling asleep, I carefully worked on my speeches, then peeked into Ted's package, sniffed, and smiled.

True to plan, we marched out of camp at 3:00 A.M. toward the most elusive goal of my climbing career. I set a steady pace, and we moved up under the stars in silence. After a half hour, Nick Sr. announced, "Ah, I don't feel so good, so I'm heading back to camp."

Before he could say another word, I zoomed down to face him as the boys flanked us. This was a crux moment, since my Grand was gone if the father turned. "Do you mind if I call you Doctor, sir? Listen, Doctor, of course you don't feel perfect. It's the middle of the night and your body is all confused since you are walking up this hill instead of sleeping. Worse, the candy bar that you ate earlier is just churning around in your stomach. Now you're not doubled over with appendicitis or anything like that, so here's what I want you to do. Let's walk up until sunrise, then let's stop for a decent bite to eat. I've got something from Ted that you will enjoy. Trust me, Doctor, I've done this a hundred times—you will feel better when the sun comes up."

"OK, let's keep going for now, but if I don't feel better, me and the boys are heading down!"

With speech one delivered, I thought that I had the procession under control, but on the steep slope below the Lower Saddle, the doctor tried again. "Oh, really, this is too much. Look, it's not just my stomach, I just don't feel right about this. I'm going down."

I thought that we would at least be able to reach the Lower Saddle before I needed speech two, but poised on the steep slope, I had to let 'er rip. "Oh, Doctor! Come on! I saw you walking that log next to camp—your balance is really good by the way—and I know that you could literally climb this slope before breakfast just to get warmed up. I'm not talking about the Grand Teton, I'm just talking about the next few hundred yards up to the saddle. I've got a care package from Ted in my pack, but we can't eat it right here. By the time we get to the saddle, we will be in the sun and we can chow down. Ted would be crushed if you turned around before even eating his breakfast. Let's go!"

This time I even got some help from Alex, the younger of the two boys, when he said, "Yeah, Dad, let's go!"

Rising above Disappointment Peak, the sun did indeed find us in the Lower Saddle at 11,644 feet. I was a few feet higher than the summit of Disappointment Peak here, and I looked down on my third practice peak thinking that this had to be my day. I quickly retrieved Ted's bag and passed out several thick pieces of Ted's breakfast quiche. The boys dove into it, and one bite told me that it was magnificent. The thick, well-baked crust was slathered with a veggies-and-cheese poof thing that held ten fragrant flavors, and it was topped with tiny bits of bacon. The doctor looked at it and said, "Oh. I can't eat this. I'm a vegetarian."

Diving back into my bag, I quickly dodged another bullet, since Ted the master had anticipated this as well. "No problem, Doctor! I've got a second veggie quiche that is all for you!" Seated to face the sun, the munching became our mantra. With their mouths full, I figured that my charges couldn't complain, so I continued my spiel. "OK, team, listen up. We're only 2,000 feet from the top, and we can get about halfway there before we even need to think about the rope. The weather looks OK, so I propose that we head on up. The critical point of no return on this route is where we do the step-across at the end of Wall Street. We can scamper from here to there, but once we do the step-across, we're on the Upper Exum Ridge. Let's go to the end of Wall Street, then make our final decision about the rest of the climb. We'll uncork this baby one step at a time. For now, gentlemen, up we go!"

Swallowing the last of the quiche, the doctor replied, "Bravo. Looking up at that peak, I was thinking no way can I climb it, and I was thinking about going down, but your one-step-at-a-time logic makes sense."

I set a steady pace to keep the team together, and we reached the beginning of Wall Street without incident. Like Longs' Broadway, Wall Street is a vital ledge across an otherwise featureless cliff. It connects the easier terrain above the Lower Saddle with Upper Exum Ridge, which is the south ridge of the Grand. Unlike Longs' Broadway, Wall Street is a well-defined ledge, but there is a catch. Wall Street narrows as it approaches the Exum, and there is an exposed step-across right at the end of the ledge. This was our next decision point. I watched the team carefully as we moved along the ledge, which traverses above an increasing drop. This was the first big air that we had encountered, and our success depended on everyone maintaining a stable mental state. Everything was fine until we reached the step-across.

Alex and Nick Jr. looked at it with a combination of fear and awe that I recognized, however the doctor took one look at the exposure and proclaimed, "Oh no! I'm not going there! No way! Look at all the air!" It was time for another speech.

Acting nonchalant, I said, "Oh, Doctor, that air won't hurt you, and the moves won't be that hard. Now, we're going to rope up here, and that will make all the difference. You will be belayed from both sides, and *I will tie your knots my very own self.*"

"But I thought that we were going to discuss going down!"

"Oh no, Doc, we've got to continue. Listen to me for a minute. This is the Grand Teton, not a walk around Central Park. Of course there is some air up here. What did you expect, a banister-bedecked staircase? Remember the inspiration that you felt back in camp to do this climb? If you turn around here, you'll regret it for a long time, since this is indeed the Grand Teton. Doc, inspiration is just the first step, but now it's time for action. This is precisely the moment when we must steel ourselves and focus all our powers on the moves at hand. Look at those moves! They are not that hard. Really, the air won't hurt you. If you can just get a handle on it, your mind won't hurt you either. The meaning of all this will come later."

Turning toward the security of the nearby cliff, Doc said, "Well, you may have the power to overcome, but I am sadly lacking. I'm going down."

For the umpteenth time, my Grand was on the line. Pausing for a moment, I considered my response carefully. Finally, I said, "OK, Doc, let's take a break. I'll see what else is in Ted's care package. I don't know about you, but I'm hungry."

"Me too. I'm starving!"

Digging into my pack, I said, "Om city! Look at this!" After passing out Ted's sumptuous sandwiches, the four of us sat munching again. Still munching, I rose, walked to the edge, and talked to the boys about the step-across. When it was clear that they wanted to continue, I set an anchor, roped up, and Alex belayed me across while I tried to make it look as easy as possible. Nevertheless, the air still snuck up my pants. Sensing that this was their moment as well, the boys took over the management of their father's fear, and soon we all stood on the Exum Ridge looking up at the remaining route. My pep talk was now much shorter. "See, that

Gerry heading for the heights on the Upper Exum Ridge.

wasn't so bad after all, and look, the next stretch looks fine as well." After organizing our ropes, we headed for the heights.

Our action on the ridge quickly displaced unfounded fears. Soon, our communication was reduced to a few terse climbing signals as the pitches moved steadily below us. When a thunderstorm approached, we took another break to don clothing and polish off Ted's sandwiches. With lightning striking nearby, I wondered if, after all my struggles, nature would have the final word—and just what that word might be. We hunkered on a ledge in silence while a terrible tempest toured the summit. When the storm moved on, we did too, and we soon approached the gleaming summit that the storm had decorated for us. After all these months, I had no trouble taking the last strides up to the sparkling high point.

With time ticking toward Ted's dinner and clouds billowing toward us, our summit stay was short, but it was enough. I took pleasure in doing a quick 360 to look down—way down—on all my practice peaks, then I shook hands with the Shoumatoffs. I will never forget the look of joy on the Shoumatoffs' faces, especially Doc's, and it was sufficient reward for my efforts.

Ropes in hand, we hustled down to the top of the rappel, and a few hours later we arrived back at the Garnet Canyon camp. It was late and I still had to make it back to the big dinner, so I quickly packed my things for my descent to civilization. I had assumed that the Shoumatoffs would descend with me, but Doc came up and said, "Gerry, I'm exhausted, so we are going to stay here and come down in the morning."

"But you'll miss the dinner!"

Looking back up, Doc replied, "That's OK. I have climbed the Grand Teton."

"You'll remember this day for the rest of your life, Doc, and so will I."

"Thanks, Gerry. The boys thank you too."

Rummaging in my pack, I said, "Doc? There's one more thing."

"Yes, Gerry?"

Holding out a bag, I continued, "Ted figured that this might happen, so he left you this. Go on, take it!" As I hefted my pack, Doc peeked into Ted's bag, sniffed, and smiled. Waving, I strode out of camp and barreled down the trail.

A month later, back in the Summit Club's basement office, Geoff and I reviewed the Summit Club's split conquest with both bewilderment and amusement. The summer had been grand, and our plan had worked—sort of. We had not been on the summit together, and this bothered us, but we still had to acknowledge our team effort in the face of adversity. The Summit Club may not have looked like much to outsiders, but those people were never in attendance at the basement meetings. Geoff and I had founded the Summit Club on the high ideals of truth, honor, fairness, and teamwork, and felt that when applied in the mountains, these traits would be at their best. This trip had tested us both physically and politically, but inspite of the craziness, we felt that we had been true to our ideals.

However, we were not ego free, so when we got our hands on the post-outing issue of *Trail and Timberline*, we looked to see if our names were mentioned. To my amazement, my name did not appear in the list of people who had climbed the Grand. Geoff's was there, along with all three Shoumatoffs, plus several others. I carefully scanned the list a second time to be sure, but my name was not there. It was probably just a typo, but at the time I felt like the CMC had gone out of its way to sting me again. With the stroke of a pen, they had swept my entire effort away!

Geoff grabbed the magazine, studied the list, then looked at me with suspicion. "Bro! How do I know that you made it?"

Feeling the frustration roaring back, I defended with, "Bro, the CMC is still trying to separate us. We're home now, and we need to revisit our principals. First of all, how do you think the Shoumatoffs got up there? Second of all, if I say I made the summit, then I made the summit, because I am a man of honor, right? We agreed on that years ago."

Geoff pitched the pitiful publication into the trash and said, "You're right. What was I thinking? It's the Summit Club that is forever. Now let's get back to work."

"OK, bro, here's a piece of new business."

"Om belay."

Extending a small card toward Geoff, I exclaimed, "Check this out!" It was my brand-new driver's license, and it represented freedom. With my new license, I resolved to climb on without the CMC. Decades later, quite possibly because of that choice, they often invited me to speak to them about my adventures.

The Grand Teton was my fourth Transcendent Summit, and my most complicated one so far. God's nod rarely comes with an explanation, but I assumed that this summit was transcendent not because I was inspired or even that I had worked hard, failed, and tried again. The summit was not expansive, full of visionary thoughts, or perfect. I would make many future Teton ascents to laze in the sun and dream, but in my quest to reach the summit of the Grand in 1959, I had indeed gone beyond the normal barriers. I believe that this summit got God's nod because I learned and executed *Leadership*, and this trait became the "L" of my "WHO CLIMBS UP" acronym for mountaineers. The CMC had given me a perfect example of poor leadership, but in the end, at the age of fifteen, I gave them a grand example of how to unite mountaineers with good leadership. Unfortunately for the club, they never noticed my climb or my example, however the Shoumatoffs did, and once again, that was enough. Without knowing it, the Shoumatoffs had helped me give voice to my "I AM" acronym, which stands for *Inspiration, Action,* then *Meaning.*

T 2

In the late '50s, Boulder's climbing community included many talented rock climbers, and the quest for first ascents was in full swing. However, even though Geoff and I had been actively climbing for three years, we paid little attention to a route's status. We hiked around in the Flatirons looking for fetching routes that we thought we could climb. In the process we did make first ascents of many routes, but that was never our focus. Sometimes we made new ascents by accident. For example, when Geoff and I decided to climb the south face of the Maiden, we knew that the face had been climbed, but we assumed that it was a free climb, when in fact it had only been climbed with direct aid. We reached the hard part where our predecessors had resorted to hauling themselves up on their pitons. Looking at the direct-aid crack, we concluded that it was too hard for us to free climb. We looked around the corner for a better way and found one. That day, the Summit Club made the first free ascent of the Maiden's south face without even knowing it.

Room 140 in the CU Chemistry building, or Chem 140 as we called it, was the usual gathering place for shows about climbing and a host of other subjects. Everybody knew everybody in those days, and the gatherings were very social. After one show in October, Layton Kor sidled up to me and said, "Want to go climbing tomorrow, Gerry?" It was such an important question that he could not look me in the eye. We stood side by side looking out at the room together with all eyes upon us.

I had climbed with Kor on numerous occasions and replied, "Sure, Layton. What's up?"

"Just a route in Eldorado. I'll pick you up at 4:00 A.M."

"Four! Must be some route." When the other climbers in the room all dropped their eyes—a sure sign of impending doom—I realized that they knew something I didn't. I feigned enthusiasm but was secretly terrified.

Kor was Boulder's best climber in 1959, and he was actively pursuing new routes all over the area. In particular, Eldorado Canyon, which is only eight miles south of town, was the land of hard, serious routes. When climbing on high-angle rock, I vacillated between a passion that drove me to brilliant heights and a deep-seated terror that was always just a step behind. Even on my best days, the terror was always a close second. On bad days, when the terror won, I retreated to the ground, sure that I would never climb again.

Layton Kor was well on his way to becoming an international climbing hero and legend, but all we knew in 1959 was that Layton was better than we were; no matter how much passion we brought to the bottom of a cliff, Layton brought more. Layton the master had tapped me for his secret project, and of course I would say yes, but my personal struggle with terror quickly moved into a new arena.

At 4:25 A.M. the next day Layton's rickety bucket-of-bolts Chevy sped toward Eldorado Canyon at ninety-three miles per hour. Recently, after borrowing the family Nash Rambler in the middle of the night, I had taken these curves at seventy and had nearly rolled the Rambler. My dad's car was forever after called "the Bathtub," because if I had turned the car upside down, it would have looked just like a bathtub. I vowed to never test that possibility again, since the Bathtub was a marvel of terrible engineering.

Our current speed was far beyond that late-night Bathtub experience, so all I could do was grip the door handle, steal glances at the speedometer, and stare ahead to the next curve, calculating the probability of my impending death. Cars were an extension of our personalities in 1959, and the logic at work here was that if we were going to risk our lives on the rocks, then we might as well do it on the highway as well, just to get warmed up. But rickety as it was, Layton's Chevy was superior to the Bathtub, and more important, Layton had done this crazed drive many times.

Spitting dust, the Chevy roared into Eldorado with Layton sputtering, "Damn, it's still dark!" Pretending that everything was perfectly normal, I said, "Whatcha expect, Layton? It's the middle of the night!" We sat fidgeting in the car for a while, then started toward the wall at the first hint of dawn.

As Layton started up the rock, I protested, "Layton, this is Redguard."

"Just wait—you'll see," was all Layton would offer. The Redguard Route had first been climbed three years earlier, and it was now the standard route up the center of Eldorado's main 800-foot-high south-facing wall. I had climbed Redguard and was confused, since I thought that we were going to do a new route.

Layton's need for speed was intense, and I climbed as fast as possible with no chance for observation, analysis, or conversation. In the dawn's half-light, I recognized the moves on Redguard's first two pitches. On the third pitch, Layton moved left, and I was on rock that I had not climbed before. This pitch took us to the Upper Meadow, a sloping garden partway up the steepest part of the wall. Finally in the light of day, we started the fourth pitch above the meadow, and now even Layton was on virgin rock.

As Layton moved up, lichens tinkled down well away from the yellow rock. In spite of my preclimb fear, I was now strangely calm, as was often the case when climbing with Layton. He was so focused on the climb that there was no time or room for fear. With sun on my face, I hollered up, "Whatcha calling this route, Layton?"

Layton stole a second from his concentration to reply simply, "T2." This was an acronym for "Tower Two," which was one of the summits of Redguard Wall. While the name was simple, our climb was not, and higher up, Layton got into trouble. I had followed him many times but had never seen him so gripped. He did some incredible leg-splitting stems that I knew I could not duplicate, since Layton was six-foot-five and I was only six-two. When my turn came and I reached the stem, Layton announced, "If you can't make it up in thirty seconds, I'll start hauling! This route has gotta go."

"Thirty seconds? Jesus!"

I looked frantically for a hold, found one, pulled up, and had just about worked out the critical combination when Layton hollered, "Time's up!"

"Wait, Layton, I'm making it!"

My cry was too late. With a great, "This route's gotta go!" Layton hauled on the rope. I came up sputtering and protesting, but Layton could only think about the fifth pitch. He tiptoed across a difficult, airy traverse, then nailed a steep crack. As I followed, I knew that I had never been on rock so steep, difficult, and exposed, and I felt my fear return. Understanding, Layton employed another tactic—he launched into an incredible patter: "Atta boy—just keep inching along—grab that knob—great move—hang on—just keep inching along—atta boy!" Soon I was only thinking about inching along, and my fear dissipated. Near the end of the pitch, I felt a surge of joy that I could actually make these moves. Feeling poised, I no longer needed Layton's patter. Without articulating it directly, Layton was teaching me mind control on the rock.

At the top of the fifth pitch, our rack of carabiners and pitons jammed behind a large flake. Immediately furious, Layton yanked so hard that the entire ledge we were on shook. As I pondered our anchors, the shaken rope slithered down the wall like a portent and jammed fifty feet below. Now it was my turn to calm Layton. "Slow down, for Pete's sake! You'll knock us both off. We can recover the gear if we reach behind the flake and work it together. Then I'll lower you to the jam." After carefully extracting our equipment, I lowered Layton. He released the rope and free climbed back up the steep crack on finger jams, an impressive display of Layton's climbing prowess.

On the sixth pitch, Layton climbed eighty feet up a ramp without placing a single piton for protection. Only when I protested did he place one. When I reached it, I plucked it out with my fingers, which meant that it was worthless. I hollered up to Layton, "Hey! This pin is just sitting here!"

"Yeah, well I didn't want you to get too worried, since you might report me to your mom!"

On the seventh pitch, we had our last great struggle at the overhanging exit off the ramp. Layton used an aid pin then made a long move from high in his stirrup. I could either make the move or retrieve the pin, but not both. We were so broke in those days that I had to get the pin. Layton held me on tension while I removed it, but the stretch in the rope left me hanging free in a horrible position. After a great thrash, Layton lowered me back to the ramp. We tried again, but it was just a replay of the first time. On my third attempt, I had to replace the piton, use it, then leave it behind.

At the top of the pitch, Layton berated me with, "Since you couldn't get it, you buy the new one!"

Frazzled and fried, I replied, "Oh shut up. This route was your idea in the first place. You know damn well that I'm the only sucker you could get to come up here with you."

As Layton turned to the eighth and final pitch, he said, "Slow down, Roach. I was just woofin' ya. Anyway, I found that pin last week." Layton was much calmer now that he knew we could make it. As we shook hands on top, it dawned on me what we had just done. T2 was no longer just a dream of Layton's, it was a route and a life-changing experience.

Climbing with Kor had a huge impact on my abilities and psyche. He taught me how to forget fear, push myself, then survive a desperate situation. In spite of his brusque manner, Kor cared as much about his partners as he did the rock. T2 taught me the big "C" of rock climbing: *Centering*. Only now, after climbing for over three years, had I learned the ABCs of rock climbing: *Awareness*, *Breath*, and *Centering*. I was still far behind Hillary and Tenzing and still a long way from Everest, but at least I had graduated from the beginner's spelling class and knew what to do with the "two-men-as-one" rope.

Over the years, this climb up T2 has become one of my best memories, and T2 is still one of the best routes in Eldorado Canyon. T2 was my fifth Transcendent Summit and my hardest climb yet. When Kor and I shook hands on top of the climb, we were not actually on a mountain summit, we were on the summit of a dream, a route, and a climb, and that was enough. Pure rock climbs are often just routes that do not reach a summit, and it is appropriate that such a metasummit found its way onto my rapidly growing list of Transcendent Summits.

While Kor was the star, there were other more reclusive climbers who operated on their own outside of the normal social circle that congregated in Chem 140. After my experience with the CMC, I identified with these quiet, self-reliant climbers. One such solo climber was Karl Pfiffner who, though less charismatic than Kor, was just as driven. I spent many hours huddled in Karl's tiny, cheap room sharing schemes and dreams. Kor was busy showing the climbing community how to convert dreams into reality, but Karl's dreams went beyond individual routes. He wanted to link many routes and create long traverses. Karl's idea of what to do with a mountain range was to traverse it while climbing its best and highest peaks. Karl thought out of the box, and he had me thinking beyond the rocks.

Climbing in the '50s was a counter-culture activity. The "normal" world, for the most part, did not even know about the sport. When they did give it a thought, most people believed climbers were stupid, wasting time and needlessly endangering not only themselves but also potential rescuers.

I was young, but I knew better. Climbers were certainly not stupid. Most of my climbing companions were university students studying math, physics, and a host of other solid subjects. Climbing was dangerous, but not excessively so. I quickly understood that my smart climber friends did risk assessment, while my friends in other arenas made hurried choices only to stumble into a bad outcome. I knew that if they had studied the probable scenarios more carefully and made a more informed choice, their pitfalls would have been avoidable. After a little thought, I realized that on a rock or mountain the consequences of a mistake were usually immediate and grave, but in the everyday world the consequences of a mistake were often delayed and usually just meant less gain, not death. Climbing taught me how to do risk assessment, and I felt that others had a lot to learn from mountaineers. As for the potential rescuers, they were climbers doing their own risk assessment. In the end, the creation of joy justified the risks, and I knew intrinsically that without joy, we would quickly devolve. I found joy in many other areas, but climbing provided the greatest return on investment.

Climbing was my deepest interest, but it was not my only passion. Another was being on Boulder High's cross-country team in the fall and the track team in the spring. My track career had started years earlier at Baseline Junior High in the seventh grade when I made the mistake of going out for football. After getting pushed around on the line, I moved to end, but immediately became mired in an open-field tackling drill. My goal was to tackle Jerry Burns, the school tough guy. After watching my repeated misses, the frustrated coach announced a stiff penalty for missing a tackle: run a lap. Again and again I sprinted around the field with my knees up lest I be accused of loafing, and I quickly realized that I was happier running laps than trying to tackle the sidestepping, stiff-arming Burns. After my sixth penalty lap, one of the assistant coaches called me over and said, "Roach, I want you to take another lap, but this time go as fast as you can go."

"Why?" I squawked.

"'Cause I'm going to time ya. Run around the edge of the field. Ready ... Steady ... Go!"

Sensing that I had to run fast or face a fate worse than tackling Jerry Burns, I sprinted around in a heart-pounding, leg-pumping, neck-bending effort. Nosing forward as I passed the coach, I heard the stopwatch click. As I rested with hands on knees thirty yards beyond the finish line, the coach called me back.

Walking back on wobbly legs, I saw him staring at the stopwatch. "Did I do OK, coach?" I asked.

Lifting his eyes from the watch, he replied, "Forty-five flat. That's good. Say, Roach?"

Here it came. "What?"

He then offered the best advice that I ever received from a coach. "Roach, go out for track." I quit football on the spot, broke the Baseline record in the quarter mile for the next three years, and passed Jerry Burns in the hall with my head held high.

Now in my junior year at Boulder High, I was running the mile with one of my teammates, Mike McCoy, who brought as much passion to the starting line of a race as Kor brought to the base of a climb. After Coach Swinsco patted his sides and said, "Coke will cut your wind, boys," Mike immediately vowed to consume no more pop. When Coach went on to explain that staying out past midnight was bad for a runner's time, Mike vowed to never go on a date. Throughout high school Mike's social skills languished, but he won all his races. Even though Mike and I were fast friends, I still thought that I should be able to beat him. After numerous second places, I considered that I would have my victory if I could beat him just once at any distance. Perhaps because of my occasional coke dates, this turned out to be a tougher challenge than Northwest Passage.

That fall, at the start of the big cross-country meets, our team lined up five deep with the fastest runner, Mike, in front. Mike was so excited that we had to hang on to him to keep him from disqualifying the whole team by sprinting off before the gun. I hollered at him, "You gotta hold it in, Mike!" At the state meet, we almost ripped his shorts off trying to keep him on the line, and we ran very well that day.

Willpower

Thanksgiving break has always been a tough one for Colorado climbers. The wings of summer are gone, there is not yet enough snow for good skiing, the days are dismally short, and the high country feels like it is already gripped by winter. Worse, even if you do make a heroic ascent, it can't count as an official winter ascent. Nevertheless, we always attempted something heroic, simply because we had four days off. On this holiday weekend in 1959, I took off to climb the Ellingwood Arête on Crestone Needle with Warren Bleser and Jim Greig. The Needle, as we called it, was the last of Colorado's fabled Fourteeners to be climbed, and the Ellingwood Arête is its historically tough, technical route. My lesson for this outing would be: don't try climbs when they are dismally out of condition.

After backpacking in to the South Colony Lakes below the Needle, we pitched our tent and settled in to endure a tremendous storm. While winds whipped the peak and snow piled higher around our tent's walls, we still talked of doing the climb. However, every time we peered out of the tent, all we could see was a blinding white whirlwind. After twenty-four hours there was a tiny break in the storm, and we rushed out to behold Crestone Needle; not surprisingly, the normally dark, rocky crag was almost completely white. It was beautiful in its stark snowy loneliness, but in no condition for climbing, even for heroes.

Back in Westcliff's café, we schemed a new plan to make use of our remaining day. We were learning to make every hour count, especially if it was an hour of vacation. Thus we headed for 14,336-foot La Plata Peak, which is easier but higher than Crestone Needle. La Plata would still be formidable, especially since we would be approaching it from the north and the storm had dumped considerable new snow. We planned a one-day assault.

The next morning we stuffed the soggy tent and Primus stove in the trunk, parked Warren's car on the highway, crossed a bridge over the nearly frozen Lake Creek, and started up La Plata's northwest ridge. The storm had also left La Plata covered with fluffy powder snow, and after several hours we were not as high as we needed to be. Taking turns leading, we snowshoed into the white world. This was a storm that the ski areas had been waiting for, and also the storm that ensured there would be no further ascents this year in anything resembling summer conditions. Even though the day was sunny, this effort was the opposite of the effort Stan and I had made on Longs when the snow flew away in graceful arcs from my perfect steps, but this was also snow climbing.

There were at least two feet of new snow on the ridge, and in places the wind had piled it into five-foot drifts. I snowshoed upward creating a trough and trying to dodge the drifts while the precious daylight hours sped by. My well-worn leather boots were barely adequate for this task, and cold nibbled at my toes. My best option for keeping warm was to keep moving. At 13,000 feet the wind had blasted much of the snow off the ridge, and I finally found better footing. Without looking back, I charged toward the summit, assuming that the others were close behind as they had been all day.

When I did look back, I was astonished to see Warren and Jim far below but still moving slowly up. Should I retreat to them? That might mean giving up the summit, which was now tantalizingly close. Was something wrong? I suspected that they were just tired and cold, and I felt that these minor problems could wait a few more minutes, so I sped ahead toward the summit.

When I arrived at the summit, the sun was setting through cold-cracking skies. I had never been on top of a Fourteener so late in the day, especially in such cold conditions. Nevertheless, I quickly spun 'round to enjoy an incredible sunset over Colorado's highest peaks. The sun's last kisses sent long shadows from the peaks like they were pulling a winter quilt up to my chin and turning out the light. The sky struggled against the shadows, then it, too, let its light go. Just then, my companions arrived on the summit.

With the sun gone and the cold now stabbing at my toes, there was not a moment to lose, so we sped down. Warren wanted to argue with and berate me, but without breaking stride, I charged into the gathering gloom hollering, "Follow me!" I descended the slope to the east toward La Plata Basin, reasoning that we could lose elevation more quickly this way and follow the basin out after dark. This was one of my less-inspired mountaineering choices.

We reached the basin quickly enough, then dug our headlamps from the bowels of our packs for the long trudge back to the highway. Near treeline the snow depth increased dramatically, and once we were in the trees, it was even deeper. I had no way of knowing that, like Longs' south face, this place would soon send me a new, harsher memory.

Our immediate salvation from frostbite lay in continued motion. If we stopped for the night, our toes would surely freeze. This option was unthinkable and I was strong, so I dug deep into my track training and plowed into the night while the others followed doggedly. When mere track training was not enough, I found new strength and quickly spent it in my deep trough. Lower down, just as we hoped the terrain would relent, it got worse.

We were committed to the very bottom of the gully, which now fell away in a series of ramparts and small cliffs. Hanging from branches and even making some irreversible drops from them, we thrashed along. I mused that the climbers from other states who sometimes belittled Colorado climbing as too easy for their distinguished tastes had never been here. After hours of silence, I hollered into the night, "Bring the bums on and let them lead for a while!"

Warren stammered from the rear of the procession, "Whazat? You're doing a great job, man!" That was all the encouragement I needed. Finding a deeper determination than I had ever felt before, I plowed my trough on toward the car with its precious heater. This was the first time that I had felt my will take over both my brain and my feet. With my will in command, the rest of me was just along for the ride. What if I could summon this strength any time I needed it? That would allow me to tackle even greater challenges. What if I could bottle and store this energy for a future trial, or a track meet? I wasn't sure how to do that, but I wanted to try. What if I could store some of this energy for my old age? At 1:00 A.M., the car interrupted my musing. After blasting the heater on our tingling toes, we rumbled off down the deserted, icy road toward our 8:00 A.M. classes.

Neither the Needle nor La Plata provided me with a Transcendent Summit, but the weekend did underline the "C" in *Conditions* from my "WHO CLIMBS UP" acronym for mountaineers, and it also added my first good lesson in the "W," which stands for *Weather*.

Eruption Express

The famous and brilliant warrior Popocatépetl fell in love with the emperor's daughter Iztaccíhuatl, who was a prosperous and beautiful young woman. As fierce Aztec warriors often did, Popo went off to a faraway war. While Popo was returning victorious to claim his beloved, a jealous rival sent a false message to Izta that Popo had been killed in battle. Expecting that Izta would now turn her affections to him, the sadly mistaken rival was shocked when Izta fell into a deathlike swoon. Popo returned to learn of the tragedy, but wasn't sure if Izta was dead or just sleeping. Deep in his own grief, Popo carried his sleeping lover high up onto the mountain, gently laid her down with her lovely face up toward the heavens, and covered her with a white shroud. Then Popo moved to her feet and sat patiently waiting for her to awake. When she did not rise, Popo stood up to hold her funeral torch for all time. Izta still sleeps today, and Popo's torch still burns.

▼ ▼ ▼

My eyes bugged out as I read an ad for an upcoming climbing trip to Mexico that would take place over the '59 Christmas break. The ad announced that the team would attempt not one, but three Mexican volcanoes with enticing, unpronounceable names. These peaks' altitudes were all considerably higher than Colorado's highest peak, Mount Elbert, which at 14,433 feet was the highest peak that I had climbed so far. The ad went on to proclaim these peaks to be the seventh, fifth, and third highest in North America. Without reading further, I was hooked and completely committed to going on the trip. I signed on with a group of seven CU students, including some of my Rescue Group buddies. Sadly, due to family commitments for the holidays, Geoff would not be able to join us for this adventure.

The team's major priority was to secure transportation, so we bought a milk truck. The old bucket of bolts was not much to look at, but the engine seemed in good shape, and it was cheap. We spent two months preparing our "Volcanic Chariot" or "Eruption Express," as I preferred to call it. The Express received two new tires, much engine work, a large storage compartment, bunk beds for all eight of us, and, most important, a navigator's chair. We planned to drive straight through to Mexico City, and our rule was that six of us could sleep, but the navigator had to remain awake with the driver. Since we were on a tight budget, we borrowed a chair from the math building on the CU campus, Hellems Hall, for the navigator's seat. We reasoned that the chair would not be needed during the holidays and planned on returning it at the end of the trip. The classroom chair was perfect for our task since it had a rounded surface that was just big enough to hold a map of Mexico. We bolted our copilot's seat to the floor of the Express, just to the right of the driver's seat.

The ministers and their machine. Gerry is standing, second from left.

Loaded down with packs, maps, stoves, a table, food, water, fuel, and endless enthusiasm, we launched into the night after Friday's classes, but we had a flat before we got out of town. Undeterred, we fixed the flat, bought yet another tire, and drove south into the wee hours. Expecting bad roads in Mexico, we decided that we should stay on the U.S. side of the border as long as possible, so we chose to drive to Laredo, Texas, and cross into Mexico there. This was a dismal choice, since the Mexican roads south of Laredo were not just bad, they wound through mountainous terrain for hundreds of miles.

With a bit of perverse reverse logic, the group decided that since I was an inexperienced driver, I would have to wait until we were in Mexico before I could drive the Express. After all, I was a Squirrel, therefore I should be able to drive like a champ, however, other than my clandestine speed trials, I had little experience in cross-country driving. My first hour of driving into the Mexican night nearly proved that, while Squirrels could climb, they could not drive into the Mexican night. With nobody sleeping, I received a barrage of advice while I dodged donkeys, carts, and drunks on the road's shoulder, as well as potholes that looked like lunar craters, all the while carefully avoiding oncoming trucks whose drivers kept their lights off until the last moment. One by one the others all had their chance to taste this driving challenge.

In addition to road hazards, downshifting in the milk truck required double clutching, one clutching for the move to neutral and another for the move to the lower gear. The vital shift stick rose out of the engine compartment, which was under a hump between the driver's chair and the navigator's chair. After eighty-four hours of double clutching, we arrived in Mexico City, slept for a few hours, had a meal, marveled at all the new sights and sounds, then looked for the volcanoes.

We couldn't see the peaks from the city, but we did know the colorful Aztec legend of Popo and Izta. The multisummited, 17,343-foot Iztaccíhuatl looks like the profile of a sleeping woman, and the more symmetric, cone-shaped, 17,887-foot Popocatépetl emits a near-constant volcanic cloud of smelly sulfur smoke and sometimes ash—

the funeral torch. The two great peaks stand ten miles apart, and they are only forty miles southeast of Mexico City.

We planned to climb Izta first, then Popo. By spending three days climbing Izta, we hoped to acclimate to the high altitude, but we almost outsmarted ourselves. By driving from the Cuidad to the end of the road at 13,100 feet then immediately packing up to a high hut at 15,500 feet below Izta's knees, we just guaranteed that we would spend a miserable night. My head pounded as if the entire percussion section of the Seattle Symphony was inside. Walking around outside the hut in the morning, I felt a little better, so I joined the others for a ragtag trek to the top— Izta's breast. Two days later I felt much stronger while climbing the higher Popo. Thus I had my first lessons in high-altitude mountaineering: driving is more dangerous than climbing, and acclimating to high altitude takes more time than you think. On these climbs, I also had my first experience using crampons.

We spent Christmas Eve at a plaza in Puebla, where the Mariachi bands belted out their best until someone hired them and whisked them away to their own private party. However, there was plenty of music and laughter left for the plaza patrons. After Christmas we drove our now well-clutched milk truck east for our final peak, 18,701-foot Citlaltépetl, also known as the Star Mountain. Pico de Orizaba, as it is commonly called, is Mexico's highest peak and the monarch of a vast region. To find a higher peak in North America one has to travel north to Mount Logan in the Canadian Yukon or to Mount McKinley in Alaska. I knew that there were higher peaks in the far north and remembered a slide show I had seen of a McKinley climb and Uncle Laurie talking about Alaska's summer snows, but for now Orizaba seemed like the highest peak in the world to me.

Another cone-shaped volcano, Orizaba, is more shapely than Popo. While Popo's sides are classic and straight, Orizaba's slopes, when seen from a distance, curve gently inward. A child tasked to draw a volcano would more likely draw Orizaba's shape than Popo's.

After making arrangements to park the milk truck in a private courtyard in the town of Cuidad Serdan, we started walking from the town plaza toward our distant goal, which was more than 10,000 feet above us. As we hiked out of town, we poofed along in ankle-deep dust while engaged in nonstop negotiations with children-merchants who tried to sell us everything from stones to stuff they had stolen from the previous expedition. Seeing no vehicles, we wondered at the intermittent tire tracks that we saw, until we figured out that the Mexicans made their sandals out of old tires. Finally above the dust and niños, we spent the night in the Cueva del Muerto at 12,500 feet, but I hardly slept. This time it was not the altitude that bothered me or even the cave's name, but my nonstop enthusiasm for the morrow.

We crept from the Cave of the Dead at 4:00 A.M. with our headlights dancing eerily on the surrounding cliffs and started toward the still-distant summit more than 6,000 feet above us. Our initial trek was up easy-angled pumice, and we quickly learned that we could turn our lights off and navigate by starlight. This gave us a chance to fully observe and appreciate the dawn. Orizaba is visible from the Gulf of Mexico, and we hoped to snatch a glimpse of the water before the coastal clouds rose with the day's heat to block the view. Alas, the clouds climbed quicker than we could, but we did enjoy watching the tops of the roiling clouds. The rising sun shot through them with the opposite effect of the engulfing, cracking cold that I had recently watched from the top of La Plata. With each passing minute, the sun peeled my quilt back and opened the curtain.

Full sunlight found us on the steeper pumice slopes leading up to Orizaba's fabled snows. The pumice beneath my boots seemed destined for the depths with each upward step, so I used my conditioning and surged forward to more quickly reach the snow. The snow was easier, and I walked up in a series of large sun cups, or *penitentes* as the locals call them. I carried my ice ax like a cane, but never even bothered to put on my newly purchased crampons.

There was no need to rope up, so as I was now in full stride, I pulled steadily ahead of the others and became completely immersed in the task of climbing this huge slope. Steps became dozens of steps until the slope that had been immediately in front of me was below. These hundred-foot slopes multiplied into thousand-foot slopes. One thousand had already become two. At the snow line, two became three. In the *penitentes*, three became three and a half, and it was here that I learned that I loved the upward labor of a high, large mountain. Three and a half became four, then, almost an hour later, four and a half. I was now at 16,500 feet, but still a long way from the summit.

In addition to the labor of love, there were ever-expanding views, and I paused to ponder. The lower world fell away until it was no longer recognizable as a place of cities, cars, churches, bases, bombs, bands, boats, pets, plazas, paintings, or other people-made things. The human world diminished, and the land took over. What I looked down on was simply Earth—the land of sunrise, sunset, sky, air, rocks, roots, rain, soil, snow, clouds, couloirs, trees, lightning, thunder, volcanoes, mountains, shores, slabs, tides, water, sand, ice, storms, rivers, washes, avalanches, fog, forests, animals, people, and all things God made. We are part of the Earth, but just one small part. Since I was alone at the moment, I felt like I was the only human on the planet. With each upward step, this feeling increased.

During my march, I concentrated on a boulder that was perched high above me on the crater rim, since I knew that when I reached that boulder, I would be close to the summit. The boulder was certainly not going to come to me, so I had to go to the boulder. Four and half became five. The boulder seemed no closer. Five became five and a half. Now, the boulder looked a little nearer. By the time I reached 17,500 feet, I knew that I was addicted to high-altitude mountaineering, since, in addition to my other growing feelings, the higher I climbed, the better I felt. Five and a half became six. The boulder was noticeably closer now, and ten minutes later I reached out and touched the rock. My mom was right—touching certain rocks is like touching Mother Earth. The higher you climb, the easier that is to do. A few minutes later, I was on Mexico's highest point.

This was my sixth Transcendent Summit and my first outside of the United States. It was appropriate that it occurred on the highest peak that I had climbed so far. Gazing into Orizaba's deep crater, I was more excited by my feelings and by how good I felt than the accomplishment of the climb. If I could feel and do this, what else could I climb, and what feelings could be unleashed there? Doing slow turns, I gazed far beyond the horizon in all directions for several hours. In 1959 the Star Mountain gave me my first good lesson in *Perseverance*, which is the "P" in my "WHO CLIMBS UP" acronym. Feeling better and better as I broke my altitude record, I also learned about true *Strength*, which is the "S" from the acronym. Also, part of what touched me on this Transcendent Summit was the knowledge that I wanted more.

Back at the milk truck, we felt like masters of our mountains and ministers of our machine. I had been completely charmed by Mexico's unpretentious society and marvelous mountains. Double clutching through the night, we chose a better route and pushed the Express back to Boulder in a mere sixty-four hours. We quickly sold the truck for a hefty profit; after all, it had bunks and a navigator's chair. My total cost for the two-week trip was $40, which was the best return on investment for an international trip that I would ever have. The navigator's chair never made it back to Hellems Hall.

Om Mani Padme Aum

In March 1960 I was heavily involved with my class work at Boulder High and the track team. The math classes were easy and I enjoyed them, but my real passion was outside the classroom. On the track, my mile time was just as important as my next climb. I was tired of finishing second to Mike McCoy, so I doubled my efforts to beat him. After sticking to Mike like a shadow for the first three laps of the mile, my fourth-lap strategy was always the same. I would simply stay with Mike down the back straight no matter what, fly around him coming off the last curve, then sprint down the finishing straight to nip him at the line. Race after race we flew down the straight to start the bell lap with everybody screaming at me, "This is it, Roach! Stay with him!" I put my mental tractor beam on Mike's skinny legs and motivated myself with the thought that those ugly legs could not beat me. As the last lap progressed, light appeared between us, Mike's scrawny legs slowly pulled away, and I ended up second again. I had no way of knowing that I would someday rely on Mike's passion for another project at a much higher altitude.

I was also struggling to better understand girls. Like my initial climbs, my serious dates were classified. In desperate times, Prince loaned me his Oldsmobile for dates, which I executed with all the stealth of my early climbs. I quickly learned that, even with a car, stealth dating was not as easy as classified climbing. In the

The Summit Club
preparing for a run
in spring 1960.

midst of all this activity, the news of Karl Pfiffner's death on March 19 caught me completely off guard.

An avalanche killed Karl at treeline in La Plata Basin on the north side of La Plata Peak while he was descending from the Ellingwood Ridge. This is where I had chosen to descend with Warren and Jim just four months earlier. The shock was deepened by the fact that I knew exactly where Karl had died and could not get the image of the place out of my head. Why him and not me? For a month after Karl's death, I struggled to understand what happened and why. Then Geoff and I received news that Prince was missing on Longs Peak.

On Tuesday April 19, Prince, Dave Jones, Jane Bendixen, and Jim Greig started an ascent on Longs' east face. The four university students were on their spring break, and Prince started by taking a trip to the Utah desert. Returning from the desert with two days to spare, Prince met the others and decided on short notice to attempt the Kieners Route. This was the route that Stan and I had followed to the base of the Notch Couloir, but Kieners has a more straightforward upper section. Geoff and I did not even know they were doing the climb, so with Karl's death, this news came as a double shock. We had climbed with Jane, a newcomer to the Rescue Group, and Jane and I had shared several fear-filled ascents. Geoff and I had much in common with Jane since she was only two years older than we were and was a newcomer to the Rescue Group struggling to prove herself.

Sensing something during the climb, Jim turned around at the base of the face and returned to camp, but Prince, Jane, and Dave continued up. By Tuesday evening, the three climbers were near Longs' summit, but unfortunately so was an unexpected spring storm. After traversing over the summit and starting down the mountain's south side, darkness and swirling snow trapped them. They carved a crude snow cave and huddled together for warmth through the night. Jim reported the three missing on Wednesday. When Geoff and I first heard the news Wednesday afternoon, we were shocked but assumed that they would be all right. We had been late many times ourselves, and a report of someone being overdue was not cause for more than alarm. Down in sunny Boulder, we could not fathom the desperate struggle that they were engaged in high on Longs.

Perhaps lulled by thoughts of the desert he had just left, Prince had not brought good mittens on this climb. The storm intensified, and by Wednesday morning their position was beyond desperate. Prince had deep frostbite on his hands, and even his face was blistered. Knowing that he could not continue, Prince told Jane and Dave to leave him in order to save themselves. When they protested, he ordered them to go. There was no time for tearful good-byes; if Jane and Dave were going to live, they had to descend. Jane last saw Prince sitting in their miserable half-cave looking at his frozen hands.

Jane and Dave descended to the top of a long slab where they needed to use their rope, and Dave offered to belay Jane down the pitch. With no anchor available, Jane told Dave to get in a good position, since she was likely to fall. We were all used to belaying with a secure, braced body position in those days. Halfway down the pitch, Jane looked up and saw Dave belaying her, but standing right on the outside edge of the ledge—he was not secure. She couldn't wave him to a better stance, since she needed both hands to hang on, and the wind swallowed her shout. She last saw Dave looking up for Prince. Then she fell down the slabs that I had admired from the Notch just ten months earlier.

Jane was unconscious for an hour. When she came to, she collected herself and looked for Dave, but could not find him. She traced along the rope but found the other end empty. Apparently, Dave had not tied into the rope. She called for an hour, but there was no answer. Finally, in despair and desperation, Jane started down by herself. She struggled down into Wild Basin, then post-holed through the deep spring snow for hours before reaching safety late Wednesday night.

Her report spurred the Rescue Group into action, but it was too late. By the time searchers reached the accident site, all they found were Dave and Prince's mangled bodies. Both had massive injuries from long falls. When Jane fell, she pulled Dave off, and he fell more than 600 feet. Apparently, Prince made a last, desperate attempt to save himself, but with his frozen hands, he fell.

On Friday afternoon I was stretching on the infield grass getting ready to start track practice. Geoff came out of the field house, where he had just heard the news on the radio, walked up to me, and announced solemnly, "Frau Maus is no more." I slumped onto the infield grass and cursed everything I could get my mind on. I cursed the weather, Longs Peak, and the Rescue Group for not calling the Summit Club to help them get up there sooner. As soon as we were allowed, Geoff and I visited Jane in Wardenburg, the CU student health center. Seeing Jane in a hospital bed with her hands bandaged was the biggest shock of our young lives. We talked in low tones as Jane related bits of the story, but it was not a time for intense analysis. Jane had frostbite on her hands and feet and would recover, but none of us could fathom Prince's death. It felt like a cannonball had plowed through my chest and removed my insides. How could our mentor be dead? Prince was the climber who had taught us how to be safe! The preacher had fallen from the pulpit.

Only after considerable reflection did I realize that the Rescue Group had done the best it could under the circumstances. Both Prince and Dave were likely already dead when Geoff and I first heard that they were missing on Wednesday afternoon, so even the Summit Club's best efforts would have made no difference. Further reflection made me realize that Prince had made a grievous mistake in not taking proper mittens. He had not practiced what he preached, and indeed, a momentary negligence had killed him. Far surpassing previous events, Prince's death, with its searing lesson, lodged deep within my mangled insides. My age of innocence was over.

chapter three

life spiral

Love among the Giants

when the summer of '60 came, I was especially sad that Prince
was not there to climb couloirs, master mantras, discuss needle cairns, or even just
revel in the newly cut grass. As my insides settled, I resolved to carry on in his
name. Prince had transmitted the best reason I knew of for climbing—I climbed
to create joy. I could certainly carry that joy forward, since I was living it. Prince's
other drumbeat had been safety. He left me with the best example that I would ever
have about why it is important to be safe, not just in climbing but, since climbing
was emerging as a metaphor for my life, in all endeavors. Prince had lost his opportunity for personal joy, but perhaps if I lived long enough, I could somehow create
more than my share and give it to others. I would not only do climbs that Prince
would have loved, I would try to add his spirit to mine and carry it forward. As a
first step, I added the "O" to my growing acronym for mountaineers, "WHO
CLIMBS UP." The O stands for *Om* and serves as a simple blessing in the midst of
all the other climbing principles. For me, the *Om* in my acronym represents Prince
and all that he stood for.

Karl, too, was gone. One of the projects that Karl had talked about doing was
traversing the Continental Divide between the Arapaho Peaks and Longs, and he
was making plans to do this traverse in the summer of '60. I resolved that I would
someday do the traverse in his memory. Indeed, decades later, an extended version
of this traverse still carries Karl's name, and the next generations would do well to
remember the namesake of this route. However, my chance to do Karl's traverse
would have to wait.

I could not consider the Pfiffner Traverse or any other Colorado climbing projects
in the summer of '60, since I was locked into going on a family vacation to Norway.
My sister Charlotte had married a wild, brilliant Norwegian named Georg Vedeler,

who had just finished his degree in civil engineering at CU. Charlotte and Georg had moved to Oslo and Georg's family was there, hence it was high time for a family visit.

I had visited Norway briefly in June of 1951 during the family's summer tour of northern Europe. My dad was half Norwegian, and he had planned that visit to look up relatives whom he had never met. After a family visit in Larvik, my dad had driven us from Oslo to Bergen and I had seen some of the mountains in south-central Norway. In June they were still draped with winter snow, and we had driven through recently plowed canyons on the highway where the snow towered over our car. Our 1960 visit would extend into August, and this time I hoped to find my way to Norway's heights. I knew nothing about Norway's mountains, but I carefully packed my boots, ice ax, the Summit Club rope, and other gear.

In Oslo Georg's mom, Sofie, whom we just called Grandmother, or the Norwegian *Bestemor*, hosted us with Old World graciousness. The only time she complained was when I threatened to break her banister by doing record-setting jumps down her stairs. "Ja, my Gerry! You really are part Norwegian, but you need to climb real mountains, not my stairs!"

Seeing this as an opening, I said, "Tell me about Norway's mountains, Bestemor."

"Ja, Gerry. You should go to Jotunheimen. They will slow you down."

"Who will slow me down? Not the mountains!"

Twinkling, Bestemor continued, "The giants will slow you down, Gerry."

"What giants? Are they trolls?"

"Nei, the trolls are not giants. Jotunheimen is the Home of the Giants. You go there, you see."

"How do I get there?"

"There is a shop in town that knows. You can find it."

"I'll go there this afternoon!"

"Nei. Let the snow melt. This afternoon we go to Blåskjell."

Encouraged that there was at least a possibility of getting to the mountains later, I traveled with the family to Bestemor's beloved Blåskjell, which was a small house on the rocky east shore of the Oslo Fjord, about fifty miles south of Oslo. Here, we luxuriated in a feast of time without obligations. I learned that I loved goat cheese but was not so sure about the *fiskeboller*, boiled fish balls. I also learned that the highest dive from the rocks to the fjord's icy waters needed to be timed with the tide and the surge. Bestemor graciously gave us her heart and the best of Blåskjell.

I often found Georg at the rocky point surveying the ocean. "What's out there?" I asked.

"Freedom. If only the wind would blow!" Georg, a full-blooded Norwegian, was as nuts about sailing as I was about climbing. His big dream was to repeat the Vikings' journeys from Norway to America and back, but first he had to practice. Georg had a twelve-foot skiff anchored in Oslo's sailboat harbor, and once back in Oslo, Georg immediately wanted to return to Blåskjell, but this time by sailboat. I immediately signed on as the first and only mate for the journey.

At dawn on the appointed day, we loaded ourselves and little else into the skiff while a vicious wind whipped spray into our faces. I hollered against the tempest, "You've got your wind now! I don't think we can even get out of the harbor!"

"Sit down, mate. I'm the captain!" Casting off, Georg sailed expertly out of the harbor, dodging the many larger boats that bobbed at us in salute. Those boats were anchored while their owners hunkered inside, but we were one with our craft as we sailed past. With the big wind, we made half the distance to Blåskjell in a few hours. Seeking some shelter, we sailed into a narrow channel between an island and the mainland. The wind dropped to a whisper of its former strength once we were on the inside passage, but it was still strong enough for us to make way. After tacking for several hours, we realized that while we were moving nicely through the water, we were making no headway with respect to the land because the changing tide was now rushing up the channel against us.

We made landfall on the island while singing our sailing ditty, "Yo ho ho, the wind blows free, but not on our sails where it should be!" After pulling the boat up six feet onto the shore and tying it to a tree, we lay on the crusty ground to catch a few winks. With naps complete and tide turned, we sailed on through the evening and into the night. Time of day didn't matter, only the tide. At the southern end of our channel, we spied an approaching town with its attendant bridge. Sailing up close, it was obvious that our tiny mast would easily fit under the bridge, but my captain docked the boat. "Why are we stopping?" I asked.

"I have to check in with the bridge meister," Georg replied.

"Why? We can sail under it."

"It's the way we do it here in the Old Country. It's a courtesy, not a requirement."

"Won't you be waking him up? It's 4:00 A.M."

"That's his price to pay. Time of day doesn't matter—remember the tide problem? Stay with the boat, I'll be right back." In a few minutes Georg hurried back down the ramp and said, "Shove off, mate. It's all set! He's going to raise the drawbridge."

"Raise the drawbridge? For this bitty boat?"

"It's a tradition. Sit down and enjoy the ride. This is gonna be fun!" Tacking out into the center of the channel, Georg lined up for a run at the center of the bridge, whose huge motors were already blaring their intent. As we slid slowly toward the big bridge, it parted in the middle, rising like two embracing arms.

"I assume that halfway up is sufficient for us?" I queried.

"Nei. All the way!"

As the arms became vertical in a grand gesture for any ship, our tiny, silent craft passed in review. I looked up and saw the bridge meister in a glassed room, working the bridge's controls. Grinning profusely, he was enjoying the show as much as we were. We gave him our best salute, but he just pointed at the bridge and waved back. The bridge had delivered his salute. We reached Blåskjell a few hours later. Ravenous, we dove into the goat cheese and *fiskeboller*, which tasted

Georg looking for the
wind at Blåskjell.

much better now. My Norwegian roots were growing.

Back in Oslo, I finally had my chance to hunt for the shop that knew about the Jotunheimen. With my experience from prowling the streets of Paris, I quickly tracked down Oslo's climbing shop and entered to find the smell of leather, the sight of ropes, and the clank of pitons. This was just what I needed, and I left loaded with maps, guidebooks, a plan, and a dent in my wallet. I didn't have enough money left over to buy crampons, which the knowledgeable staff said I would need for the more technical routes, but I was glad that I did have my pack, boots, ice ax, and, most important, my rope. For the next several days, I poured over my new maps as my giant plan took shape.

The Jotunheimen is a nonlinear range of rugged peaks located 160 miles northwest of Oslo and 100 miles inland from Norway's serrated west coast. Evidence of the range's glaciated past, several of Norway's longest fjords snake inland from the coast toward the Jotunheimen. In particular the famous Sogne Fjorden reaches inland to within twenty-four miles of Norway's highest peak. Inspired by Karl, I reasoned that if I couldn't do his Continental Divide traverse in Colorado's Front Range, I would at least traverse the entire Jotunheimen range and climb Norway's three highest peaks en route. Like many of Karl's climbs, mine would be a solo journey.

I loaded ten days' food and the rest of my precious gear into my pack and hopped aboard a northbound bus headed for the eastern edge of the Home of the Giants. North of the village of Gjendesheim, I moved to the front of the bus, propped the map on my knees, and told the driver where I wanted to get off. His eyes twinkled with amusement, since passengers rarely got off there. With a volley of rapid Norwegian, he told the whole bus what I was doing. Suddenly my departure was an event to behold. After the bus rolled to a graceful stop at the appointed place, the driver opened the door wide like the drawbridge. Shouldering my pack, I waved to the other passengers and marched out into the rain.

After the bus with its grinning, waving passengers rumbled off, I turned to face the Jotunheimen, but I saw absolutely nothing. Gray, rain-filled clouds covered the mountains, caressed the tundra, and kissed my nose with dew. I knew that I was now well north of Bergen and at sixty-one degrees north latitude, which put me even with Anchorage, Alaska. This was farther north than I had ever been. As I looked around, I realized that I was completely alone. There was no building here, no sign board, and no trail. However, in the distance, I did see something, and knew that I was OK. Whispering to myself, "Well, Karl, here we go" and feeling like a crafty captain, I hefted my pack and strode into the rain toward the first cairn.

There was no formal trail here, just a route marked with cairns. These were not fragile needle cairns, but robust pyramids that were as tall as I was. They were spaced so that hikers could follow them in the fog, just as I was doing now. Since I couldn't see the mountains during my march, I marveled at the spectacle under my feet. My chosen entry point into the east side of the range had so little traffic that the tundra I walked on was intact. The tundra plants loved the rain, and this was their time of summer glory.

Since it would just barely get dark near midnight, I was in no particular hurry today, so I plopped down to fetch a chunk of goat cheese from my pack and take a closer look at the ground cover. The tiny plants were close to the ground so they could better avoid the subarctic winds. Bending closer, I saw how intricate this universe was. There were many plants bunched close together, interspersed with minute flowers that radiated a unique beauty due to their size, the low light, and their transient time here in the short northern summer. I swept my hand across their surface and watched droplets of water fly from the cusps. No matter, more water was coming. The plants' roughness raked my hand like the smallest saw, and I marveled that life so beautiful could be so tough. Bending closer still, I nuzzled my nose into one patch seeking its fragrance, but all I experienced was its toughness. Then I realized that the subtle fragrance was everywhere. My goat cheese had masked my ability to smell it, so rising, I stowed the smelly cheese and marched on toward the next cairn sniffing the air. A mile later, after gaining some elevation, I was walking on rocks with no tundra in sight, and I realized that the tundra was not just transient in time, but in space as well.

The first objective of my Norwegian triple crown was 8,140-foot Glittertinden, which in 1960, held Norway's highest point. In a strange topographical twist, Norwegians considered 8,100-foot Galdhöpiggen, eight miles to the west, as Norway's highest peak. Their logic was that Galdhöpiggen's summit was rock, but Glittertinden's summit was covered by a 100-foot-thick ice cap. Should Glittertinden's ice cap melt, then Galdhöpiggen would be higher. I was amused by this logic since it implied that rock was more important than snow, but I kept an open mind and resolved to climb both peaks just to make sure that I had climbed the highest peak in Norway.

Leaving my pack in the Glitterheim hut, which I had shared with one other hiker, I started my summit trek to Glittertinden the next morning. I had 3,600 feet to gain, which would be a modest day on a Colorado Fourteener, but at these lower altitudes I gained elevation more quickly than I expected. The weather had not improved, so I followed more monster cairns up into the fog and misting rain. These cairns were even larger than yesterday's and more closely spaced, so I had no trouble staying on track.

Some of the cairns were eight feet high, and I estimated that they held as many as 1,000 rocks apiece. Many were moss and lichen covered and appeared to be very old. I wondered what the Norwegian record would be for a needle cairn. Marveling

Gerry on top of Glittertinden. "Ja elskede Norge!"

at their existing engineering extravaganzas, I guessed that they could smash the 100-rock barrier. I also wondered what the Norwegians would say to Prince's cairn philosophy that small is beautiful. Caught between the extremes, I resolved to neither add nor remove any rocks from these Norwegian works of art.

Suddenly the summit ice cap was under my feet, and I had to think about where I was going. I had been so absorbed in my silly thoughts that the summit was mine! Leaving the cairns, I crunched up onto the snow looking for the highest point, which I found a few hundred yards farther along. The fog here was very thick, and I had to be careful not to stumble off the near-vertical north face of the ice cap. The highest point was near the edge, but there was no cornice. When I was sure that I had found the highest point, I trenched an x across it with the heel of my boot, jumped into its center like a Viking, and hollered into the fog, "Ja elskede Norge!" Until the snow melted, I was on the highest point in Norway and loving it.

I was disappointed that I could not see Galdhöpiggen from this privileged position, so I hustled off to see it up close and personal. That evening, as I strode into the Spiterstulen hut system at the base of Galdhöpiggen, I entered a new slice of paradise. This place was full of Norwegians, and they were all flush with their midsummer party madness. It seemed like half of Oslo was here. I had known since my first trip to Norway in 1951 that Norwegian youths go nuts on midsummer nights, but I had never been part of the action. Since the weather was still bad, I was happy to take shelter in the huts with the teenagers. What I had not expected was that half of them would be beautiful women.

Certain liberties are commonplace, even expected, under Norway's summer sun. They even have a name for it, which roughly translates to "summer love." It comes and it goes—nothing more than that. However, as beautiful women sidled up to me and rubbed strategic body parts against me, my intellectual understanding of their summer love program offered little protection to my heart. My measly stealth dating at Boulder High had done nothing to prepare me for this, and I was ripe for a big fall. But just as it was supposed to do, my rope saved me.

In my dorm room, I pulled the sacred Summit Club rope out of my pack. When one of the Norwegian climbers saw it, he said instantly, "You have a rope? Oh great! That changes everything."

"What do you mean? It's just a rope."

"None of us have a rope. We need a rope if we are going to do the glacier route on Galdhöpiggen. Would you please come with us?"

"Ja sure! When do we start?"

"It's supposed to be fine tomorrow. We'll start early." So it was that I did not immediately move to Oslo and start a family, since I had a climb to do first.

We were on top of Galdhöpiggen by midmorning and lounged there for hours on one of the summer's finest days. This was Norway's official high point, providing a good view back to Glittertinden, which reminded me of whence I came. So far, the mountains provided enough summer love for me, since I was not ready to settle down and start a family. Heading down the hard way, the glacier lived up to its reputation as a place where we would need a rope, and it did indeed cool us off. My rope was most useful as I skittered along without any crampons, and at the end of the climb I put it back in my pack expecting that I would need it again, as I still had a long way to go.

The next day I put my head down for the twenty-mile trek to my third peak. By the end of the day it was raining again, hard this time, and my near marathon trek turned into a soggy affair, which ended in the remote Lusahg hut. In the morning, with sun dappling the storm's lingering dewdrops, I talked to a maiden with round, pleading eyes perched above breasts that would have kept the Titanic from sinking. Her father's look told me that I was no longer in Spiterstulen, but a more proper, longer-term invitation was definitely there. Once again on the trail, I marched west with the morning sun on my legs and pack, wondering about these Old World courtesies. At a 4,500-foot pass, the view of my third peak shook me back to my other reality. Rising in all its glory was the north side of 7,890-foot Store Skagastölstind. Even the Norwegians choked on this name, and they called it Storen for short. There was no question about Storen being the third highest peak in Norway, and it was obviously much harder to climb than either Glittertinden or Galdhöpiggen. Storen was Norway's technical monarch, and it was the real reason that I had brought the sacred Summit Club rope all this way.

The day was fine, and I was finally alone after my many lovely distractions, so I pulled everything out of my pack to dry it and prepare a proper feast. Eyeing the peak and now understanding that the weather here was mostly bad, I realized that I would have to descend all the way to Turtagrø on the western highway to get more food, as I would likely have to sit in the hut on Storen's south side waiting for good weather. Cupping my hands and studying the peak, it looked like I was going to need a partner. My rope was useless without a belayer. Just then I heard a noise and looked around to see the two most beautiful women in the world.

Eyeing me with enthusiasm, they dropped their packs near mine then pranced over to me with a bountiful bounce and a burst of expectant Norwegian. I had learned some of the language on this trip, but not enough to converse. The only things I could say with authority were "Thanks for the food," "My grandmother was born in Larvik," and, thanks to my dad, "I love you." None seemed like a good opening line.

When I didn't respond, the scantily clad maidens tried again, but by now I was just staring. Independent of their queries, I finally stammered, "Oh my good gracious God. How did you create these beautiful women? These bodies would *raise* the Titanic." Like most Norwegians, they spoke good English, and they tittered at my unabashed opening line. After this, my sirens moved quickly. They surveyed my gear and pointed at Storen. To my surprise, when I nodded they had a heated argument—in Norwegian, of course. No matter, I just loved to listen to them talk. By some unknown process, they made a decision, then one of them put on her pack and disappeared down the trail. The other came to me with a slow step, sat next to me, rubbed her legs against mine, hooked my arm in hers, and said in breathy, heavily accented English, "Now tell me about your mountain, ja?"

As I tried to explain my traverse and Storen, it was obvious that she was not interested in Storen, or any mountain for that matter. My sacred rope was thirty feet away, and it could not save me now anyway. Her arm tugged gently at mine for me to lay back.

Perhaps I should raise a flock of Norwegian kids after all. That life would not be so bad—I could sail, ski, and climb a little.

Her tugging was more insistent now. With plenty to look at, I couldn't help noticing her tanned, smooth skin. Small, finely tuned muscles spoke her every movement. This girl had indeed been outside and gone for many a hike.

I could travel to America to visit my relatives. When they asked about my lovely Norwegian wife, I would laugh and recount how we started our family before we knew each other's names. What's wrong with that?

With a well-practiced move, she whipped off her top, stroked my arm, and gently caressed my chest to the ground.

To hell with Storen and your silly mountains. To hell with your damn sacred rope. To hell with Boulder High and its frigid, inaccessible girls. Forget college. Forget grad school. Forget everything. It's all right here!

She looked at me with eyes that rivaled the full moon, pressed her chest closer, and breathed into my ear, "Gi meg det, ja?" The words were irrelevant; I knew what she wanted.

Of course, the kids would have Norwegian names. The first son would be Sven, the first daughter would be Sonja, and the second son would be Storen. Storen!

In a major life choice that has always tormented me, I lurched up, hurriedly crammed my gear into my pack, looked back for one last view, stammered "Ja elskede, bare nei," then bolted down the trail. I never did know her name. Nevertheless, I was especially tormented that night in Turtagrø. I had my extra food, I had my Storen plan, I had everything a lad my age could ask for, but I did not have my nameless Norwegian lass with her honeymoon eyes and near-naked body.

In the morning I took some small comfort from the familiar act of hefting my pack and striding up the trail toward my peak. I tried to focus on the tundra, the rocks, the lake I was passing, the rising grade of the path, the hard climb ahead, the desperate moves that I would have to make solo, but nothing could purge the memory of my last view of my lass. There she stood, arms outstretched toward me, breasts quivering, ready for all the life I could give her, and there she would stand for all time in my memory.

When I got to the hut at the pass south of Storen, I dropped my pack and immediately checked out the route ahead, but I saw nothing. While I had languished over my Norwegian beauty, the clouds had retaken control of the heights. As it was not raining, I hoped that the clouds would be gone in the morning, so I hustled back to the hut to prepare for my solo ascent. Alas, in the morning it was raining hard, and the clouds commanded me to remain in the hut all day with my memories.

With nothing else to do, my fantasies grew. What if I could find a lass like that who would climb with me? What if she didn't mind sitting in a tiny hut, hoping for a break in the weather just so she could climb with me toward a distant rocky summit? What if she felt the pull of the summit and the granite as I did? What if Storen's summit pitch were a perfect granite edge and, alone in the world, the two of us belayed each other up the sacred edge while we felt each lichen, each hold, and each dimple in the rock? What if, with puffy summer clouds languishing overhead, we made love on the summit? Just then, I heard a loud knock on the door. Was it my maiden, coming to rescue me from my torment?

I opened the door and my fantasy fled, as it was four rain-soaked guys who quickly pushed into the hut. In a moment, the eight-by-ten-foot hut filled with dripping ponchos, steamy socks, stoves, food, ropes, pitons, and laughter. I thought to myself, "Well, at least I have some partners now." My new friends were from Denmark, and they, like me, had traveled here to climb the fabled Store Skagastölstind. They had planned carefully and were well equipped, and they, like me, were hoping for a break in the weather. Used to crowded hut scenes from my stays at the climber's cabin below Longs' Chasm Lake, I enjoyed the company, and they certainly took my mind off what's-her-name.

The next day was rainy as well, but with my extra food I could wait two more days, and I felt smart to have brought it. This was exactly the scenario that I had planned for. The five of us spent the day in the hut trading travel stories and climbing tales. My Danish friends spoke good English, and we rambled on between blasts from the Primus stove while I carved thick slices from my brick of goat cheese.

On our third day of waiting, the conversation turned, as it always does, from climbing to women. I asked the hut's assembled wisdom, "So, what about these Norwegian girls?" Jerking their heads back, three of the Danes laughed, but one tilted forward with a twinkle in his eye and said, "Oh! They are definitely beautiful, and they will definitely take your heart!"

"So? What's wrong with that?"

"Well, Gerry, they won't give it back."

"So? Aren't we supposed to fall in love and live happily ever after?"

"Ah, Gerry, you don't understand. You do not get the girl, you just lose your heart. It's called, how do you say, summer love?"

While I pondered this, a second Dane leaned forward and said, "There is an English word for it—I think it's inveoggled."

Laughing harder, the third Dane leaned forward and corrected, "Nei, it's invaginated! You will invaginate them!"

Roaring, the fourth Dane set us all straight. "Nei, Nei, Nei. The word is *inveigle*. They will inveigle you! I have been inveigled three times now, and each time has been better than the last. I say, if the ship is going to go down, let there be love along the way!"

With my head turning from Dane to Dane, the first continued, "You call that love, Hans? Yes, we have heard all about your steamy conquests—too many times in fact. Now shut up and pass the cheese! We have a mountain to climb—a tough one at that." Thus our banter floated into the clouds surrounding Storen. If only the peaks could talk, oh the stories they would tell!

On our fourth day of waiting, the conversation turned, as it always does, from women to food. With the insistent rain still filling the air outside our tiny sanctuary, our climb was starting to look improbable. Examining my now much smaller brick of goat cheese, I cut a very thin slice. If I rationed my food, I could wait one more day, but if the weather was still bad in the morning, I would descend. The Danes concurred, since their vacation was fleeting and there were better ways to spend such precious time. Stiff from sitting around, we turned in early.

Stiff from lying down, we got up early, looked out the hut door, and immediately started packing. This was the day—to go down. With raindrops dripping off the front of my parka hood past my eyes, I marched down the path toward Turtagrø and food. I would worry about inveiglement later. Wishing them luck with their quests for food, love, and summits, I shook hands with the Danes at Turtagrø, then hopped aboard a southbound bus. When the bus stopped at an all-you-can-eat smorgasbord, I gorged myself, then sat on the front steps rocking and holding my stomach. When the bus driver saw me, he pointed inquisitively into the clouds toward Storen. When I nodded, that yes, I had been climbing, he twinkled with understanding, swung his door open wide, revved his engine, and waved me in out of the rain. My giant traverse was over.

Rolling along through the mist, I gazed out the window at the green country-side and pondered my lessons. There were many, but I summarized them by adding the "B" to my "WHO CLIMBS UP" acronym. The "B" stood for *Balance*. Obviously, physical balance is an important trait for a mountaineer to have, but I also considered that balance taught an understanding between success and failure. Used to making all my summits, my failure on Storen weighed on me. However, if I had proceeded blindly toward success on this climb without considering the obstacles, it would have been a loss of balance. Further, with my lass still bouncing in my brain, I intended that my "B" would remind me to better balance my mountaineering quests with life's other pleasures. My acronym was nearly complete, but I still had a lot to learn, and it would be years before I could fill in the missing "U" and "H."

Back in Bestemor's Oslo kitchen, I watched expectantly as she layered gjetost cheese on a thick slice of pumpernickel. Holding out her offering, she asked, "So my Norwegian Gerry, how was Jotunheimen?"

Before biting into the open-faced sandwich, I said, "I traversed the Home of the Giants, and no matter how you count, I have been to the highest point in Norway! It was great!"

Nodding approval, Bestemor perched on the edge of her stiff kitchen chair and continued, "That's all good news, but didn't you have another peak in your plan? Skagastölstind?"

"Ja, Storen."

"So how was the Storen?"

Unable to dodge the question, I dropped my eyes and continued, "Well, I was all set and stayed at the high hut for five days while it rained. Finally, I ran out of food and had to come down. So no Storen summit."

"So, the giants did slow you down! Gerry, in the long time, that is good. Someday you will have your Storen in the summer sun, but for now you must pon-der the lessons you have learned. You will come back to Norway, and you know that as long as I am alive, you are welcome here. My Blåskjell is your Blåskjell."

"Ja, Bestemor, I know. Takk, I will be back!"

"Vær sa god! So, how was the summer love?"

Trying to dodge the question, I kept my eyes down. "Summer love? What do you mean?"

"My Gerry, you know what I mean. I am your Bestemor! Was your summer love good? You know, sometimes it does work out beyond summer. Will I be expecting great-grandchildren?"

Trapped, I had to tell my story. "Ah, my Bestemor, yes, I learned about summer love. It was most exciting and most confusing. But there are no great-grandchildren on the way, and right now, I am feeling very inveigled."

"What is inveigled? I never hear this word."

"Bestemor, you know perfectly well what I mean. You have lived all these years. You know."

Now it was Bestemor's turn to pause and look down, then after peering out the small, steamed window, she held my gaze. Studying her furrowed face, I saw past the years for the first time. "Ja, I know," was all she said.

The Fist

Combative and competitive as always, Dave Roberts and I hurled insults at each other as we quickly gained height. Up to this point our climb had been a jocular scamper, but now, as raindrops pelted us, the rock unexpectedly rose up in a final steep sweep. As Dave eyed the summit pitch, I glanced at the darkening, lowering clouds. The weather did not look good, but to observe the fact that a storm was upon us would show weakness. By the time I turned my attention to the task of climbing the slippery crack above, Dave was halfway up it. He was strangely quiet.

The crack looked hard enough for a belay even on a sunny day. With no rope and thickening drops, prudence called for a retreat. However, in the fall of 1960 we were seventeen and prudence was not in our vocabulary. The crack's rounded edges provided little purchase, and Dave showed off his good technique as he struggled up the crack until retreat was not an option. Craning my neck back to watch him, the rain drilled into my eye sockets. Dave was suspended between heaven and earth on the kind of edge that climbers sometimes revere. One slip and he would die. No slip and he would be on the summit without me and would have one-upped me again. Dave also knew that rain or shine, I would attempt to follow him. Perhaps, just perhaps, I would fall, leaving him on the summit and me dead. I was always wary, since Dave usually urged me to try dangerous climbs unroped, and the urging seemed to be part of a nefarious hidden agenda.

After I drained my eyes and looked back up, Dave was gone. Had he fallen? I had heard nothing. Suddenly, his war whoop from the summit told me that he was alive. My emotions swirled. The rain was now in full drench, the crack had become a drain, and the expression "stone cold" had new meaning. Dave's single cry was all I would get. Like a chess game, it was now my move, and the clock was ticking. There were many options. I could climb the crack, join Dave on the summit, and descend with him as a team. Ha! Knowing Dave, teamwork was not an option, and, in any case, we had no rope to unify us. I could climb the crack only to discover that Dave had already descended another desperate route that I would not be able to follow, leaving me stranded on the summit. This was just the sort of perverse reverse one-upmanship that Dave liked. As I eyed the crack-*cum*-drainpipe, I knew that it was more likely that I would fall off the crack and end up stone cold. Yet another lose-lose situation had trapped me. Of course, I could quit—another losing proposition. This overall lose-lose-lose scenario left me even more tormented. Dave was winning. Again! Cursing and spitting, I started up toward the crack.

Three powerful urges motivated me. First, I wanted to succeed—to reach the summit. Second, I wanted to match Dave. The understood third motivator was that I wanted to live. The combination of the three plus the reality of the drainpipe crack was anything but simple for my seventeen years. So much instinct and passion drove me on a climb that, where my feet went, my brain often struggled to follow. I crammed my soaked shoes into the crack as my hands felt its smooth sides. There was one good hold just above me, then nothing positive for ten more feet.

You need positive holds to make it up this crack in the rain.

Whoops! That was my brain speaking, but I had no time for it now, so to hell with it. I lurched up and grabbed my one good hold. Climbing close to the rock, rainwater poured down my T-shirt and into my pants. Damn! My belt was too loose and my pants sagged down around my bony hips. Soon my clothing had trapped many extra pounds of water weight next to my skinny limbs. I looked at the next ten feet then pulled up as high as I could on my hold. I could progress no higher. For once, the rock had stopped my feet and, as if late for the dance, my brain rushed in.

Roach, you are left with option three. Retreat! You will die if you pursue the up options. Go down now lest you lose your strength and die in the pursuit of the now necessary retreat.

Panting hard, I still looked up.

Go down now, you idiot. Down!

Sliding back, I did not know if I was obeying a command or simply running out of strength, but it didn't matter, since I had only one direction to go.

Use your remaining strength to stay alive!

Slithering too fast now, my brain cautioned, *Easy does it! You're not dead yet.*

Three, two, one! As my feet touched the ledge below, my emotions surged back. I was alive, but a failure. If I were dead, then at least I would not be tormented so. With my emotions urging me to wallow in misery, my brain reappeared.

Calm down, Roach. You're not out of this yet. You are still high on a rock in a raging storm. At a minimum, you need to find a way off this rock.

"You idiot! That ledge to the right will clearly get me to the ground. Can't you see that?"

Idiot? Slow down, boy; I'm your brain. OK, wet pants, check out the ledge. Hey, have you heard from Dave lately? Has it occurred to you that he may actually be stuck on the summit? In your self-centered wallowing has it occurred to you that he may actually need your help?

"Oh great, just what I need—another scenario. That makes four doesn't it?"

Yes. Then there's five, six, and seven. Someday I'll explain eighteen, nineteen, and twenty. Now get that water out of your pants!

"Shut up! I'm concentrating on down-climbing to the ground!" By the time I touched down, my pants, while still soaked, were not carrying further excess.

Gotcha!

"I said shut up!"

Now we were getting somewhere. I was safe, but where was Dave? Breaking our silence, I hollered, "Hey, Dave! Are you still on top?"

"Yes! I tried the west side. It's no good. I'm coming back down the east crack!"

"It's too wet! Hang on a minute and lemmie see if there's another option."

"Hurry! I'm freezing!"

See, you sot? He really does need your help.

"Sot? Without me, you're nothing! I'm in control now. Be silent!"

I was now standing under the rock's small but overhanging north face, and Dave was pacing forty feet above me. The north face had a large cavity that extended to within ten feet of the top. If I could wiggle up the cavity then overcome the last ten feet, there was a chance. At least the overhanging cavity was not running with water. Before starting, I eyed the top of the pitch carefully. There was a narrowing crack capped by a bowling ball–sized chockstone. If I could belly past the chockstone and get my foot on it, I would be up.

"Dave! Hold on! I'll see if the north face goes!" In seconds I was up under the final crack, eyeing the remaining feet to the chockstone. Wedging my hips into a slot, I leaned out for a better view. The rain found my face anew as my fumbling hands scraped sand off the overhung edges. Both rain and sand fell into my eyes then on toward my pants, but this time I had cinched my belt tighter.

OK, smarty pants, climb it this time!

Thrusting up in a move that surprised me, I grabbed the bowling ball and kept going. Half grinning, I urged myself on with the thought, "Dally not, die not." After a less-than-gracious move, I had my knee on the bowling ball, then my foot. I pulled onto the summit to see an astonished Dave peering at me.

"How did you manage that? It looks much harder than the east crack."

"It is. So I just had a little chat with myself."

Flinging water from his fingertips, Dave grumbled, "You idiot!"

Striding off, I replied, "No, I am a nobody, and nobody is perfect; therefore I am perfect."

"Hey! Where are you going?"

"I'm going to touch the highest point! You know, the summit that we're always obsessing about. I didn't come up here just to rescue you!"

"Whadaya mean rescue me? We're both stuck now, you perfect idiot! If you had stayed below, at least we would have had other options."

Ha! Didn't think that through, did you?

"Shut up! For once, I have a plan. Let me enjoy my moment."

Ignoring Dave and the voices in my brain, I did a quick 360 on the highest point to survey our surroundings. We were high above Boulder on a Flatiron appropriately called the Fist. Higher than most Flatiron summits, the Fist socked it to the sky as it perched on Green Mountain's southeast ridge. The rock's final steep sweep gives the Fist its distinctive appearance. I had not been to this summit before and had hoped to enjoy it in a more relaxed moment. The view today was dismal as clouds swirled lower and rain continued to drum on my uncovered head. It smelled like snow was imminent.

Dave and I were seniors at Boulder High and climbed together simply because we were both crazy enough to accommodate each other's passions. We had conquered every math class Boulder High had to offer prior to our senior year, and by special permission we were now taking calculus at the University of Colorado. Coincidentally, our 8:00 A.M. calculus class was in Hellems Hall in the very room that had supplied the navigator's chair for the Eruption Express milk truck. The chair had not yet been replaced, and I wondered if its disappearance had even been noticed. Our studious class only needed half the remaining chairs, so I reasoned that, noticed or not, the chair had moved on to serve a higher purpose. I delighted in sitting in the chair next to the void our theft had left, and it became my calculitic navigational talisman.

We had an almost two-hour break between the end of our calculus class and our required appearance at Boulder High. During this interlude, we usually argued about everything from football scores to differential equations. Sometimes we went climbing, and we always did our speedy exploits unroped to save precious time. Our clandestine two-hour climbs had become increasingly ambitious, and today we had outdone ourselves. Never mind our lack of time, our main objective now was simply to get off this rock alive. After pondering my plan for another moment, I turned to Dave and said, "OK, Dave, listen up. We do have one piece of equipment."

"Whadaya mean? We got nothing!"

"Wrong, you sot. We have my belt."

"Oh great! I knew you were nuts. Your belt is three feet long and it's forty feet to the ground. Math isn't your strong suit, is it?"

Eyeing Dave sharply, I replied, "Dave, you can pound your soggy shoe on this rock and predict my demise ala Khrushchev, or you can follow me, or you can kick your shoe up your ass and freeze. It's your choice." Hitching up my sodden pants, I removed my leather belt, clenched it in my teeth, and slithered down until my feet were on the bowling ball.

I don't know what you're up to, but whatever it is, you're committed now! Just don't drop the belt!

Ripping the belt from my teeth and almost dropping it, I sputtered, "You think I didn't think of that?"

Confused, Dave replied, "Think of what?"

"Nothing, nothing. Just let me set this up."

"Hurry, I'm freezing!"

"You think I don't know that?" Carefully crouching as only a skinny kid can do, I passed my belt around the bowling ball and punched the pin through a new hole at the tightest spot. The remaining belt hung down two feet below the bowling ball.

Ha! A two-foot rope! Brilliant! Why didn't I think of that?

"You sot. Get with the program!"

Smooth as a squirrel, I got my left knee on the chockstone and lowered my right leg into space. Lowering farther, I embraced the ball as my nose rubbed down along my belt. In spite of the rain, it smelled of leather, sweat, and fear, but it was comforting, as it was my sweat and fear, not Dave's. I was in charge. My grip changed from ball to belt until I hung suspended on my two-foot belt-rope. This was it. I swung into the cavity and crammed my hips into the slot that I had used on the way up. My hip-jam saved me from falling thirty feet to the ground, as well as saving my pants from falling off. I saw no humor in the prospect of finishing this maneuver in my tighty whities. Slithering lower to another secure wedge, I hollered back to Dave, "Your move!"

As he approached the rock ball, I just heard him stammer, "What the … ?"

"If I did it, you can do it! If the belt held me, it will hold you. As you're fond of reminding me, I outweigh you. Now get a move on, you lightweight! I'm freezing!"

With my sarcastic encouragement, Dave repeated my maneuver into the hip jam. Together we quickly stemmed down the cavity to the security of the ground. Standing in the rain, we looked back up at my belt, which looked dismal hanging into the hole. There was no way we could retrieve it now. As we turned to descend, my brain broke its silence.

Hey, Roach! That was brilliant! You made the summit, did not die, and rescued Dave all with one scenario.

"Which scenario was it? Twenty-two?"

"Something like that."

"Well, you see, my scientific brain, it's not all about linear thought. You have to synthesize."

"Synthesize what?"

"Body, mind, and spirit. You helped me up there, and I might have died without you, but the final result was beyond your simple logic."

Touche, my friend, but consider that there cannot be synthesis without antithesis.

"Touche to you. Stick around—I suspect we'll need each other again."

"Stick around?" Dave rumbled. "Roach, what are you mumbling about now? Let's get out of here!"

"Ah, nuthin'. I was just enjoying the moment and arguing with myself again."

"Great, Roach. Let's argue while we run. Hey, why would you want to argue with yourself when you can argue with me?"

"Because your cynicism is predictable, Dave. When I argue with myself, I learn things."

"OK, argue with yourself then, but consider what happens if you lose the argument. Let's go, Roach!"

Trotting and laughing, I shook the rain out of my crew cut and sputtered, "Hey,

I live in my own little world, but it's OK, everyone in there knows me!" I clenched my pants while we accelerated toward Boulder High just as the slowing rain turned to big soggy snowflakes. My teachers were used to me coming into class dirty and late, but I had no idea how I would explain the loss of my belt to my classmates.

The Rock with Wings

With a wingspan over a mile wide, God's mythical bird swooped down from the Netherland to the north, a beginning for all people. The Indians riding on its back were looking for a home, and it was Tse Bitai's job to find it for them. Wherever the great bird landed would be their home. For miles and miles, Tse Bitai saw only white-tipped peaks, but the land finally relented into open desert, so Tse Bitai descended for a better look. Sun glinted from a large river just to the north, which would provide unfailing water and shelter in its canyons, and there was enough flat land here for all. Tired from its long flight, Tse Bitai circled thrice and landed. After folding its huge wings, the bird's elbows stuck up into the air for a third of a mile. It nodded its great head once, and the ancestors climbed down and fanned out across the land, but all was not at peace.

Rising from the underworld, Cliff Monster, a man-eating dragon, climbed upon Tse Bitai and made its nest in the space between the folded wings. Seeing this, the enraged Indians sent their own Monster Slayer to kill Cliff Monster, and a great struggle ensued. During the fury, Tse Bitai was scratched and gashed many times until the great bird's blood ran down through its own furrows, making them even deeper. Infuriated, Monster Slayer ripped Cliff Monster's head off and flung it far to the east, while Cliff Monster's coagulating blood radiated across the land. Cliff Monster was dead, but sadly, so was Tse Bitai. Before descending, Monster slayer honored the life-giving bird by turning it to stone for all to see for all time. Thus, the Rock with Wings was born.

In mythical times, the ancients often climbed the Rock with Wings to visit and pay their respects. Ascending the bowl that once held Cliff Monster's nest, they climbed above it into the notch between the still-folded wings, then climbed onto the elbows' highest points. They sat on the wing tips for long periods, surveying their homeland, then descended to perfectly describe the distinctive block that perched on the Rock with Wings' highest, northern summit. Legend preserved this uncanny description through the ages.

▼ ▼ ▼

"Gerry, wake up!"

"Ummph?"

Stan Shepard's insistent voice continued, "Wake up, roll over, and look at Ship Rock!"

Expecting to whoop and roar, I rolled over in my mummy bag onto the sand and had my first look at the Rock with Wings. Instead of roaring, I was silent for a full minute. Finally I said in a low tone, "Big time Ig Snig land! It's a lot more than we expected, isn't it?"

Already munching his granola, Stan replied, "She's a beauty all right."

Propping up onto my elbows and squinting through the morning sun, I studied the rock for another minute, then said, "Good grief! How high is this thing? I can't tell if it's a few hundred feet tall or a thousand."

"It's almost 2,000 feet above us! I think 1,700 to be exact."

After another studious look, I continued, "Wow. That means that crack there is not a chimney that we could climb, but a gully thirty feet wide!"

"If that's true, then that dark streak is not a piton crack but a chimney, and that chunk of black basalt rock must be several hundred feet high."

Brushing the sand off my bag and stuffing it, I replied, "Well, let's go climb it and find out."

"Whadaya mean, climb it? There's a huge blank wall above it. That's not a route! Anyway, were supposed to ferry loads up to the cave for the summit climb tomorrow."

While lighting my Primus for oatmeal, I replied, "It's not a summit route for today, but it definitely has a purpose. Let's see how high we can get! I need to do more than just tap this baby. I want to get up on it and understand the different kinds of rock. We'll climb up for six hours then hustle back down, carry double, and get our loads up to the cave by dinnertime. Ig Snig?"

Filling his quart water bottle from one of our gallon jugs, Stan clinched our climber's contract with, "This is your mom's touch-the-rock thing isn't it? Well, this time I feel it too. OK, Squirrel! Arg bloody Snarg!"

An hour later Stan and I uncoiled his new rope at the bottom of the mysterious basalt tower that jutted up into Ship Rock's vertiginous, unclimbed southeast wall. We had one pack for the two of us that contained some water and a second rope for our rappels on the way down. The second climber would carry the pack while the leader carried the pitons and a hammer. Already moving toward the wall, Stan called back, "The first pitch looks easy. That's my lead! Then it's all yours, Squirrel!"

"Arg Snarg! On belay, bird man!"

After quickly seconding Stan's first pitch, handing the pack to Stan, collecting the pitons, and taking over the lead, I continued up the steepening black rock for a second pitch. The climbing difficulty was moderate, but the rock was broken and angular blocks often shifted in precarious positions. When the magma that made Ship Rock forced its way upward from far below the Earth's surface, it brought with it chunks of the crust. Hence Ship Rock's friable inner core is festooned with harder remnants of basalt as well as remnants of other sedimentary rocks. I was climbing one of the basalt remnants, and well aware that no one had ever climbed this way before, I exercised great caution lest one of the blocks take me for a fatal ride. Expecting to reach the top of the tower, I led a third long pitch, which was even harder, but I was still far below the tower's summit. Only at the top of the fourth pitch did I reach our objective. After Stan joined me, I said, "Well, old man, it looks to me like we are a good 600 feet off the deck here. Ship Rock is way bigger than I thought."

"Gerry! Wake up, roll over, and look at Ship Rock!"

All Stan said was, "Nice leading, man! That was harder than I expected—felt like 5.7."

"Seven's heaven. Look up!" The wall soaring above us for more than a thousand feet was no longer basalt but the lighter-colored tuff-breccia that formed Ship Rock's main massif. Ship Rock's summit was made of this rock, and I wouldn't feel like I had touched the Wings until I had climbed on this rock.

"Hey! Where are you going? I thought we were heading down from here."

"I've got half an hour of up time left, so I'm heading up to touch Ship Rock's soul."

"Are you nuts, Roach? That's a blank wall. You're going to end up in the middle of nowhere with no way to get down!"

"That's the whole idea, Stan. I'm heading up to touch the blank space on the map, so tie into that anchor and get me on belay! Clock's tickin'."

"Ay yai yai, that wall looks wicked hard. So *this* is your Arg Snargin Squirrel land! OK, you're on a capital BELAY. Be careful, man!"

"CLIMBING!"

I descended slightly then crossed a small saddle where the basalt diminished and the tuff-breccia took over. For a few precious feet, they were both there, interlaced. A few feet above, I was on near-vertical soul rock. Moving better than ever before, I made steady progress up a series of knobs that diminished in size. After fifty feet of freedom, I looked up to consider my future. There were few options for piton placements, and I did have to think about how I was going to get down. Fifty feet higher, I spied a crack and above that, a small indentation.

Stan hollered from below, "Hey! You've got your sacred-soul rock touch. Look, there are no placements above you. Now come on down while you still can!"

"It's OK. I've got the Summit Club Chicken-Out Kit with me. I'm heading up!"

"Chicken-Out Kit?"

"Watch me, man!"

Fifty feet later I reached my hoped-for piton crack. To my dismay, it was just a shallow slot, not really a crack. It was no good. As I searched the rock ahead, Stan hollered, "Twenty feet for God's sake! Twenty-five if I really work it."

That meant I had twenty feet of rope left. Bobbing my head from side to side to better see the small indentation above, I finally saw what I wanted and continued up.

"Ten feet!"

I climbed with my toes on small rounded edges while pressing my hands sideways on shallow scoops, making hard moves that I knew I could not downclimb. I reached my indentation just as Stan hollered, "NO MORE ROPE!" This was as far as I could go, and the rope hung slack and unprotected between Stan and me. I was on my own up here, but that was just the position that I wanted right now.

After peering into my indentation, I paused to survey my position. I was 700 feet above the desert floor and far enough into the vertical section of the wall to feel its power. My world here consisted of a near-infinite desert floor stretching beyond the southern horizon, air, and a vast vertical wall made of rock from the Earth's interior. No one had ever been here before, and since this was not a good summit route, it was likely that no one would ever come here again. This was the perfect place that I had been looking for.

Stan hollered up, "What now, master Squirrel? How ya gonna get down? I don't see a damn thing up there!"

Hooking my fingers into the indentation, I called down to assuage my nervous partner, "I've got it! Just let me set this up."

Then I reached down for the Chicken-Out Kit that Geoff and I had put together for moments like this. It held rappel rings, extra cord, wire, and even a homemade hook. Geoff could not join me for this climb, but before I left, we had added a very special item to the kit. Holding on to the indentation with my left index finger, I opened the kit with my right hand, reached in, rummaged past the other items, and pulled out Prince's piton. He had given it to Geoff and me as a token of his friendship. Being oh-so-careful not to drop it, I moved the pin toward my indentation, which was actually a hole that was just the right size for the piton. I pushed the precious piece halfway into the hole, reached down for my hammer, bent my knees slightly, and balanced against the wall with my nose. Braced, I raised my hammer and drove Prince's memory home. The piton went in perfectly, emitting a musical tone that rose in pitch with each stroke: bing, Bing, BING! This was the best music for a climber, since it meant that the piton was solid. When it was all the way in to the eye, I struck it three more times just to release the resonate tones. BING, PING, PLING! One tone was for the desert and its endless horizon. One was for the air and all that would come its way. The last was for the rock and Mother Earth. Piton in place, I clipped a well-used Summit Club carabiner through the piton's eye and clipped my rope to the biner. Now I was safe.

I called to Stan, "I'm secure! Get the second rope out of the pack."

Understanding our next maneuver, he just said, "You got it, man!"

After Stan tied the second rope to his end of the first and reset his belay to the second rope, he called up, "Ready to lower!"

As I prepared to leave, I patted the pin and said, "*Om Mani Padme Aum*—enjoy the view, buddy!" After Stan tightened the rope, I leaned back against it and started down. After five feet, I paused, looked back up at my little memorial, and added, "*Donna Nobis Pacem*, Prince." Then, Stan quickly lowered me back to the basalt. After I untied, Stan reversed his direction and pulled my now loose end of the rope up toward the biner. After the end of the rope kissed the biner in a final salute, it popped free, leaving the pin and biner in their lofty place. Then the rope fell into the small saddle with an accelerating *whoosh*.

Preparing the ropes for the next rappel, Stan said, "Wow. That was really something, Squirrel! Just one pin for the whole pitch. How did you manage that?"

"Hey, Stan."

"Yeah?"

"That's Prince's piton up there."

"Oh. I had no idea, Gerry."

Stan had known Prince well, and I wanted to share this special moment with him. Together we looked back up at my memorial. Even at this close distance, we could barely see it; from below, it would be invisible. However, no matter what the distance, we knew that the minuscule memorial was up there on that vast blank wall, and that would make all the difference. A part of Prince would enjoy a grand vista for as long as the Rock with Wings remained. Three long rappels and an hour later, we were back on the desert floor, striding toward the car and our loads for the morrow. We did not look back.

By the time Stan and I reached the cave under Ship Rock's northwest face with our double packs, the party preparing for the summit climb the next morning was in full swing. For our Thanksgiving break we had driven from Boulder with six other buddies including Tom Quinn and Jim Greig, the climber who had turned around at the base of Longs' east face before Prince's fateful day. Jim had even brought his girlfriend, Shirley, which was an unusual event for one of these male-dominated climbing trips. Shirley would not do the climb, however; she was just along for the ride. When I counted noses in the cave and discovered that there were twenty-one souls here instead of our expected nine, I pulled Tom aside and asked him, "Tom? Who are all these people?"

"It's a group of twelve from the University of Wyoming in Laramie. They're just as keen on this climb as we are. Look, they already led the first pitch above the cave and fixed a rope."

"Well, with twenty people on the climb, we're going to need a lot more fixed ropes."

"They can rig 'em. They must have fifteen ropes, and they plan to start up at three in the morning! So where were you and Stan all day?"

Just then Shirley, who was the only woman in camp, walked up, extended her hand straight at me, and introduced herself with, "Hello! I'm Shirley Claire. You must be Gerry—I've heard a lot about you."

Chuckling, I took her hand and replied, "Depending on whom you've talked to, that could be good or bad!"

Squeezing back, Shirley responded, "Prince talked a lot about you to Jim."

"I didn't know you knew Prince," I replied.

Turning to Tom, Shirley continued, "Stan and Gerry spent the day climbing halfway up the other side of the rock. I watched them."

Chuckling, Tom said, "I figured you two were up to something. Say, Gerry, Jim wants to climb with Stan. Can I climb with you tomorrow?"

Used to climbing with Tom, I said, "Sure! What time do we start?"

"We'll never get ahead of this Wyoming team, so we'll start up about 4:00 A.M. after they get off the first ropes." Then Tom hustled off to tend to dinner, leaving Shirley and me alone.

While I emptied my pack, Shirley asked, "What were you doing up there today, Gerry?"

"Just getting used to the rock; and we were only about a third of the way up, not halfway."

"Never mind those details. You left something for Prince up there, didn't you?"

Jerking up, I looked more closely at Shirley before responding. She had a classic oval-shaped face, high cheekbones that supported round, twinkling eyes, and auburn hair pulled back tightly into a French braid that disappeared inside her jacket. Her expression was at once mysterious, questioning, and all knowing. "How could you possibly know that?" I asked.

"I thought so. That was a very nice thing to do. I enjoyed watching, and I'm glad you shared it with me!"

"But how could you know?" I stammered.

"Oh my young Gerry! For me, when the world is clear, it's crystal clear. Sometimes, I just know things. You will do fine on the wing tips tomorrow, and I'll talk to you some more later." With that, Shirley strode toward the fire in the cave. Halfway there, she paused and turned back to face me. With the crackling fire behind her, I could not see her features, just her shape and the outline of her braid. In a voice that was more singing than speaking, she said, "Gerry! I heard the tones!" Then, as she turned back to the fire, I watched in astonishment as she pulled her braid from under her jacket and let it swish toward her knees.

Later, in my sleeping bag, I pondered that I knew a little about Transcendent Summits. I knew a little about danger and death. If only for a few seconds, I had touched summer love. During this night in the cave, I learned a little about my night mind. Winged rocks, inspired climbing, Prince's piton, perfect holes in the perfect place on a thousand-foot wall, a firelit cave, and to top it all, a beautiful, celestial woman with an amazing braid who just knew things. It had been a big day, but tomorrow loomed just as big. My mind tried desperately to sort it all out and made very little progress. Finally, breathing deeply and thinking only of the morrow's moves, I fell into a deep sleep.

"Gerry! It's time! The others are already well above the cave." It was Tom shaking me. Instantly awake, I felt amazingly good. If I believed Shirley, then I already knew the outcome, so what did I have to worry about? Today I would just enjoy the ride. Pulling on my boots, I said to Tom, "Put that breakfast food in the pack. We'll catch up to the gang lickety-split and eat in the sun while we wait for them." Within minutes I was tied in and started prussiking up the rope that hung free across the cave's overhang. Other than my breathing and occasional voices floating down from above, it was strangely quiet.

After I belayed Tom up the prussik pitch, we moved out. Following my headlight's beam, I led several easy pitches up the Basalt Gully into the much-discussed Black Bowl, which is an extensive basalt feature reaching halfway up Ship Rock's west face. Here I saw the lights of the gang ahead. I knew that the first hard pitch was at the top of the bowl, and with only the first streak of dawn showing, I knew that we were in good shape timewise. Finally, it occurred to me that I should offer the lead to Tom, since the etiquette among peers was to swing leads.

"Ah, sorry, Tom. I've been hogging the lead. Do you want to take over for a while? Or we could swing leads?"

"Um, no, Gerry. To be honest, I don't feel so good. Could you lead all day?"

Eying the pitch above, I realized that I had offered at a ridiculous time, right before the first hard pitch. "No sweat—just let me have my sniggin' nose." That code meant that I understood that Tom did not have a physical ailment, he was just nervous; that yes, I would take the lead for the rest of the day; and that we did not need to speak of this again.

Tom replied, "Snarg, Squirrel. On belay!" That meant, "Thank you very much; I'll make it up to you somehow, and I will be extra attentive to your every rope need. Go man go!"

In the dawn's early light, I moved up onto the vertical moves. Just as I pulled around a corner and disappeared from Tom's sight, Tom, as nervous partners often did in our eclectic club, hollered, "Ig Snig?" In this context, "Ig Snig" had a different meaning from when Stan and I had used it the day before, when it offered a contract. Here the call meant, "My God, that looks hard! What's it like? Can I make it? Can you make it? Are we gonna die? Progress report, please!"

With my hand on an especially good hold, I cried down, "TG!"

Tom parroted, "TG!"

This was our special code for "I've got my hand on a Thank God hold and will not fall here. All is well for the moment!" Tom's reply meant literally, "Thank God!" A "TG" did not convey the overwhelming goodness of an "Arg Snarg," it was just a progress report and a brain ping when the rope was not enough. At the top of the pitch, I tied to the anchor that was already there, pulled up the excess rope, and called, "Arg Snarg!" That meant that I was secure, on belay, ready for Tom to climb, and that, because of Tom's earlier "Ig Snig," I would pay special attention to the belay and keep the rope tight as he climbed. The incoming rope told me that Tom was indeed climbing.

Our code might have seemed like adolescent nonsense to an outsider, but it was real communication, and it was incredibly efficient. With fewer than twenty words between us, we had climbed one of Ship Rock's crux pitches, reviewed our fears, and communicated volumes. I used a slightly different code with each partner, but since the vocabulary was so small, this was not a problem. One of the unspoken undertones to all the code was, "This is really great! The world is good, and this climb is full of joy!" If there was a serious problem, we had another vocabulary.

After this effort, Tom and I stood in the history-filled Colorado Col. We were actually quite high on Ship Rock at this point. The first modern-day climbers had tried to head directly to the summit from this point by climbing over the Fin, which is a northern subsummit. In particular, Robert Ormes, a pioneer of technical routes on many of Colorado's Fourteeners, had been here on four attempts between 1936 and 1938. While climbing above the Colorado Col on his second attempt, Ormes fell thirty feet onto a small piton that was only two and a half inches into the rock. The pin bent ninety degrees but held his fall. Ormes wrote a vivid article describing this harrowing event titled "A Piece of Bent Iron," which was published in the July 1939 *Saturday Evening Post*. After the national spotlight hit Ship Rock, the mysterious monolith was considered America's toughest climbing challenge, and it galvanized America's best climbers into electric action. By the autumn of 1939, Ship Rock had seen more than twenty unsuccessful attempts. In October 1939 a team from California, which included David Brower and Raffi Bedayan, stood in the Colorado Col and made a different choice. Instead of attacking the Fin directly, they rappelled down a narrow, block-filled gully to the northeast, traversed around the base of the Fin, and gained the honeycombed basin that had held Cliff Monster's nest. From there, they followed the mythical route up to the deep notch between the elbows and onto Ship Rock's elusive summit, which they reached on their fourth day of climbing. Ship Rock was not climbed again until 1952.

In 1960 Tom and I stood in the Colorado Col and reviewed all this colorful history in fifteen seconds. Looking up at the steep wall leading to the Fin, I just pointed at it and said, "Snargin hard!" Tom nodded and we turned to the rappel ropes in the gully, which the others had already rigged. It was here in the Colorado Col that we left the basalt and moved onto the lighter-colored tuff-breccia. The transition was more confused here, but I enjoyed it just as I had yesterday. Hooking into the ropes, Tom and I quickly slid down into the morning sun.

On the soul rock in the basin below, we caught up with the gang, and as promised paused in the sun to eat our breakfast. Expecting a jam-up long before this, I was pleased that our large group was moving so well. This terrain had elicited electric ambition in the 1930s, and our visit was no less exciting. There may have been a lot of us on the rock, but we had split into many semi-independent teams, and each team was moving efficiently. This was especially important during November's short days. We were like an army that had somehow managed to all step forward at the same time.

Joyous to be in the sun and on easy terrain where I could unrope for the moment, I left the others and scrambled north to get a better view of the route ahead. Stretching and munching, I looked back at the fabled traverse around the base of the Fin. Seen head-on, it looked impossible, but as I watched Stan make the moves, I knew it would go as well for me. We planned to leave a fixed rope across this traverse to protect our retreat, and I saw that the Wyoming climbers had already placed it. Beyond the traverse, I could just see the edges of the great honey-combed basin high on the rock's east face, which was the key to reaching the notch between the twin summits. We still had a long way to go, but the day was young.

I looked down a terrifying drop where the effluent from the honeycombed basin had carved large, vertical gullies which probably only looked like piton cracks from two miles away on the desert floor. From here, however, the folds in Tse Bitai's body were readily apparent. If it were reasonable for climbers to do so, they would climb directly up into the honeycombed basin from the desert floor to avoid the long, difficult, circuitous route that we had just taken. Knowing that the view from above was very different from the foreshortened, neck-bending view from below, I peered down, looking for a route.

The mythical climbers had supposedly reached the honeycombed basin. But how? The route we had just taken required long ropes and the ability to ascend a vertical rope, which we would do with prussik knots on the way back up the gully. This seemed like an improbable scenario for prehistoric climbers, who may have been very good free climbers, but who would not likely have had multiple long ropes and the means to ascend them. However, I also felt that most myths and leg-ends had some basis in fact. While the details were often obscured by many retellings, there was usually a truth hidden in the story somewhere. Also, I noted that their legend did not specify *how* the Indians had reached the honeycombed basin—they just appeared there. Was their route easy? Did a giant bird drop them off? Was the story fiction? I did not know, but I peered intently at the modern-day Ship Rock looking for any clues. While beautiful to look at, the convoluted folds, gullies, and grooves below the honeycombed basin all looked vertical, dangerous, and ridicu-lous for climbing, even with modern methods and equipment. Ship Rock had been climbed more than fifty times by now, and indeed, no modern climber had ever reached the honeycombed basin from below.

Finding no clues, I scrambled back to the beginning of the traverse, as it was my turn to climb. I tied back in, nodded to Tom, and took off across the slab. Since he could see most of this pitch, there was no need for any verbal communication here. With only occasional steep spots, the ascending traverse was on rock that reminded me of climbing on the Flatirons above Boulder. Having climbed many miles using these kinds of moves, I scooted up quickly, even though I moved more directly above the terrible terrain below. Looking down between my legs, the gullies looked even more terrifying than they had from my breakfast perch.

Beyond the traverse, we made good time up into a cave below the dreaded double overhang. Almost all of the earlier climbers had overcome this barrier with a long direct-aid pitch. This time-consuming effort was one of the main reasons that early climbs took many days. A free-climbing alternative had only been found a little over a year earlier, and our key to a one-day ascent lay not just in continued efficiency but also in bypassing the double overhang by free climbing around its left end. The main reason that the pioneers had not found this passage was that it ascended an improbable, highly exposed, terrifying place. As I tiptoed away from the security of the ledge under the double overhang, my world changed dramatically in a few feet. Suddenly I was poised on a slab far steeper than any on my favorite Flatirons, the minute holds were friable, and the exposure was tremendous. Below me was the direct route to the desert floor that the basin above had used as a garbage chute for thousands of years.

Using Kor's mind-control training, I ignored the exposure, pushed fear aside, and paused briefly to appreciate my position. I was under Cave Monster's nest site where the great mythical battle had occurred, and to me, this was the climb's critical moment. This was the secret passage leading to the easier basin above; below me was the impossible direct route. Already feeling the embrace of the stone-frozen wings, I felt the power of this tragic place. During the battle, Tse Bitai's blood ran freely here, and according to the legend this surge of blood created the great gully below me. Even to nonbelievers, this was still a powerful place, fueled by a force from beyond the rock.

Refocusing on my climb, I finished the pitch, reveling in each move. The angle and steepness eased toward the top. Unable to see Tom from this belay stance, I tugged hard on the rope and offered him extra encouragement with a well-spaced cry of "Arg—Bloody—Snarg—Man!"

Without a reply, Tom expertly followed the famous pitch. While our code spoke volumes, Tom and I had not spoken beyond these basics for several hours, and I wondered what Tom was really thinking and feeling about our position. When he reached me, I asked, "Man! Wasn't that something? Did you check out that expo-sure? What a gully!" Once again, I had chosen a miserable time to try and talk with my companion.

Plopping down next to me, Tom replied, "Roach, I'm having the day of my life, but I'm scared shitless, and no, I did not check out your beloved exposure! I don't need to, 'cause even when I'm looking up, it's pulling on my heels like a ball and chain. Look, I really appreciate you getting me up this thing, but I don't want to talk about it right now, OK?"

Trying to encourage him, I said, "Oh, sorry, man! Look, Tom, you're moving really well, and you are definitely going to get up and down this mighty rock just fine."

"How the hell do you know that?"

"'Cause Shirley told me."

"Oh! *That*."

"Come on, it's easy for a while now."

Looking up, Tom replied, "Yeah, but then we have the Horn Pitch, and that's the most exposed of all."

"Hey! How about some mind control, man? What did Kor teach us? One pitch at a time, remember? Anyway, these Wyoming cats are moving well, Stan is ahead of us, and by the time we get there, they will have a top rope set up on the Horn Pitch." Then I reached down toward Tom's ankle.

"Hey! What are you doing?"

I snapped my arms together like a large chain cutter then hefted an imaginary weight and pitched it into the abyss. "There! I just got rid of your beloved ball and chain. Ig upward snig?"

Tom didn't have any choice, since I was already heading up, so he hollered after me, "Arg upward Squirrel snarg!"

Our trek up along the right side of the honeycomb basin was a climb through a fairyland that no Disneyland fantasy designer could ever re-create. The multicolored pockets on the steep wall above us to our right varied in size from piton-sized holes to large caves, while to our left rolled a heaving sea of rock waves, each tormented differently from the last. It looked like, well, like there had been a great struggle here. Beyond the basin leered the impossible-looking cliffs of the southern summit, so I knew that we were getting significantly closer. In some areas it was so easy that we coiled the rope and moved along together. Then I led a proper, Flatiron-like pitch up a ramp. Tom was relieved to be on this easier terrain, and our more rapid motion calmed him as the abyss faded into the shadows far below. At one point he joked, "It's much easier now without that ball and chain!"

At the famous notch between the two summits, we caught up to another gang jam, but that gave us a chance to sit down and eat some lunch. When I peeked over to the south side of the notch, I immediately decided to say nothing to Tom, but instead kept his eyes focused on the view to the north.

As predicted, there was a top rope waiting for us with Stan already on top of the Horn Pitch working the belay, and after my sneak preview, I accepted the top rope without comment. All Stan said was, "Never mind that Snarg stuff, Roach. You really will like this pitch. Come on up!" In 1960 when a climber used the word "like" you knew it was going to be desperate and tremendous at the same time. The fact that the Horn Pitch was well known as the route's hardest and most exposed pitch added to the dread and anticipation as did the fact that it was first free climbed just a year ago. Nevertheless, up I went. I climbed a few difficult feet up a near-vertical crack system on the north side of the ridge, took a deep breath, then stepped around a corner to the south side. This was the famous spot, and of course, I checked out the exposure. I had heard for years that the air wouldn't kill you, only the fall, but at this moment I doubted that the author of that sentiment had ever been here.

We had circled two-thirds of the way around the rock and now looked down the sheer southeast wall that Stan and I had played on yesterday. Even with my hardened tolerance for exposure acquired in places as airy as Landscape Arch and T2, the view startled me, and I felt a swirl of detachment, as if I were flying. I had been doing technical climbing for many years now, and this was the most dramatic spot that I had ever been. Somewhere, a thousand feet below, was Prince's piton, and I could see the specks that were our cars 700 feet below that. When I looked up, I saw Stan perched on top of the namesake horn, grinning from north to south. Gleefully he said, "I knew that you would like it! Now get on up here—clock's tickin'!"

Back in climb mode, I moved up the remaining thirty feet to Stan and the horn, which jutted out over both sides of the ridge. I greeted Stan with, "Wow. I'll remember that as long as I live."

Stan added, "Yup. These are the days we remember, Squirrel. Now let's get Tom up here—we gotta keep moving."

Taking over the belay from Stan, I dispensed with the snigsnarg and called down to Tom, "Hey, my man! I saw that second ball and chain around your other ankle. Get rid of it and come on up here!"

Trying to laugh, Tom replied, "I already tossed it off the south side and almost hit the cars! Hey! I'm gonna *like* this, right?"

"No! You will hate it. Now get a move on—this route's gotta go!" As he had done all day, Tom followed the moves easily. His issues were in his head, not in his movement, but in any case, I said no more.

With the Horn Pitch below us, the rush was on to reach the summit. The Wyoming climbers were already descending and setting up the rappel back down the Horn Pitch. One of them hollered to me, "We'll leave all these ropes, but the last man down has to bring them, right?"

Since the Wyoming climbers didn't speak snigsnarg, I confirmed this new contract with, "You got it, man!"

With Stan ahead of us again, Tom and I hustled ahead on easy terrain that was on the ridge's north, or less exposed side. After one short, difficult, vertical step, we moved up on more moderate terrain until I stopped, pointed, and said, "Holy cow! There it is!"

"There what is?" Tom queried.

"The summit block! We're there, man!"

Less than a minute later, Tom and I took turns walking up on the piano-size block that lay on top of a stumpy supporting leg that, without the block, would have been Ship Rock's highest point. The block, which was tilted up at an easy angle that invited a last pensive step, was just the Wing's last skyward kiss.

We didn't have a lot of time, but we didn't need a lot of time, as one look at this view would embed it in our memories forever. We spent ten minutes there and emblazoned the memory for several future lives as well. Seemingly, there was nothing but air, and far beyond, a receding horizon. Even with my boots firmly on the summit block, the bottoms of my feet tingled as if I were dangling barefoot in midair.

During a sandstorm, wild horses urge the Rock with Wings to merge with the sky.

This feeling was not the fear-inspiring tug at my heels that I had felt so many times before. On Ship Rock's highest point, my seventh Transcendent Summit, there was no fear, only elation.

"Hey, Tom?"

"Yeah, man?"

"I left one of Prince's pitons at my high point on the wall yesterday."

Tom let this sink in for a moment, looked south into the void, then said, "So that's what you were doing. That's pretty cool, man. Prince's spirit will get to enjoy this view forever. Thanks for getting me up here, and thanks for telling me about the piton."

"Snarg Pacem, Tom. Now let's move out!"

Tom and I were the last to leave the summit. On the descent, we made good use of the Wyoming ropes, retrieved them, then carried them with us. At dusk, last man down, I rappelled into the cave looking like the Michelin man with ten coiled ropes crisscrossed over my aching shoulders.

That night we all scattered into the desert for our own private reveries. Too tired to make a proper camp, I just wandered off, plopped my bag directly onto the sand, and fell sound asleep instantly. Somewhere in the depths of the darkness, I woke to the sound of silence. Rolling onto my back and squinching into the sand, I surveyed the shadows sliding across Ship Rock's still silhouette. Propping up on one elbow to see better, I watched while, slow as a desert tortoise, Ship Rock's night shadow crawled across the sage. I thought about getting up to go shadow bagging, but with my Transcendent Summit ringing in all my senses like a solar symphony, I had no need for a nocturnal tour. Having been above, I now knew what lay in the folded shadows, but what of the rock? Hosting climbers' electric excitement and light touch by day, the Rock with Wings quietly calmed the desert by night. It was all the same to the rock. Laying back and closing my eyes in the embrace, I let the Rock calm me as well. Shading my soul, the Wings lulled me back to my sublime slumber.

Return to Paradise

Back in Boulder, my life accelerated. My university calculus class was now testing me, and I had a serious final coming up in January. Minischolar that I was, I should have utilized the upcoming two-week Christmas break to study. However Mike Stone, who had been on the Eruption Express with us a year earlier, had just bought another milk truck. Well, this truck was a lamp mobile, but it looked a lot like last year's milk truck. Mike was actively recruiting climbers to fill his ten-bunk bus, so of course, I signed up for the second Mexico trip. I reasoned that I would take my calculus book along and use the excess hours to study.

This time Geoff joined the team, and we looked forward to strutting our Summit Club stuff on the heights. Another neighborhood friend, Bruce Munroe, also joined us. Since Bruce lived two doors away from me, we had gotten into plenty of trouble together, both on and off the rocks. Mike, our organizer, reasoned that if we crammed ten bodies into the truck instead of eight, the trip would be even cheaper than last year's. That was one of Mike's less-inspired mountaineering choices.

More efficient at double clutching, the ministers of the lamp mobile arrive in record time.

Since Mike and I were the only returning members from the Eruption Express expedition and Mike was busy with organizing the expedition, he appointed me climbing leader. I took my new duties seriously, planned a detailed climbing itinerary, and borrowed one of my dad's French berets to be my captain's cap. Another navigator's chair appeared from a CU classroom, I carefully packed my calculus book separate from my crampons, and once again, we rumbled off into the night.

Smarter about the route and more efficient at double clutching, we rolled along nicely. I now had a well-worn driver's license and relished my turns behind the wheel, but it wasn't just the lure of the white line that drew me to the hot seat. One reason I relished a chance to drive was that the driver's seat was the least crowded spot in the truck. With ten guys in the bunks, asses and elbows prevailed and some tempers flared. The second best place to be was in the navigator's chair, but I quickly discovered that the desk's small rounded platform was barely big enough for a map of Mexico or a calculus book, but not both. As we always needed a map at the ready, my book stayed packed. Thankfully we rolled into Cuidad de Mexico after only sixty-two hours, shaving two hours off last year's return record.

My first act as climbing leader was to pack away my beret, as it looked ridiculous in Mexico. My second act was to spend more time acclimating to Izta's altitude, so that we would not suffer so through the first night. We spent thirty-six additional hours approaching the Iglu Hut at 15,500 feet, and this helped tremendously. We were still ascending to altitude too fast, but I was learning.

Geoff and I wanted to climb all of Izta's summits, so we woke ahead of the others, stepped out of the hut into a bitter wind, cinched up our packs with frozen fingers, pulled on our mittens, and started up into a dusky dawn. Our first goal was Las Rodillas, Izta's knees, which were not too far above the hut. Since this minor summit was right on the route, we dispatched it without breaking stride and continued on the beautiful La Arista del Sol Route along Izta's long, convoluted south ridge.

Daylight did not deter the bitter temperatures, since the sun hid behind eastern clouds and the wind did not diminish as we quickly climbed to a higher, colder place. Beyond Las Rodillas, we stopped briefly to put on our crampons, since the snow was iron hard and showed no signs of softening. Cramming our near-frozen fingers back into our mittens, we crossed a small rise, which we unofficially dubbed Izta's mons, and marched across La Barriga, Izta's long, flat belly. When the wind permitted, we joked that Izta had been in good shape when she swooned. Beyond the belly, we fell in one behind the other to climb the route's namesake Arista del Sol, or Ridge of the Sun. This was the only significant ridge on the route, and for the first time we used our ice axes for more than just walking sticks. Continuing without breaking stride to stay warm, we marched up onto El Pecho, or Izta's broad breast. Ignoring the fact that Izta only had one breast, we found the highest point at the summit plateau's northernmost end.

It was 8:00 A.M., and the still-bitter wind kept us under our parka hoods. Our plan was to keep traversing north to climb La Cabeza, Izta's head, then return back over the main summit. As we descended to the north, the slope steepened rapidly then fell away into an unexpected gulf. When I had a full view of the steep terrain ahead, I stopped and waved Geoff forward. Our crampon points squeaked on the still–iron hard snow. We saw that La Cabeza was a long way away and that the connecting saddle was far below us. With the wind tearing at us, we realized that our plan, while grand, was beyond today's effort. Unable to speak in the wind, I just drew my mitten across the front of my throat. Geoff nodded in agreement and we turned around, but not before I took another look at La Cabeza, resolving to return someday to climb this mysterious peak. After all, this was not just Izta's head, it was her face, and I wanted to at least touch it.

Dinner inside Izta's Iglu Hut. We were still ascending to altitude too fast, but I was learning.

We hustled back across the main summit and, wishing them well, descended past our companions, who were still on their way up. After collecting our gear at the Iglu Hut, we continued down to Portillo, which is the 14,400-foot saddle between Los Pies, Izta's feet, and the rest of her body. The wind was gone, and the sun at this lower elevation warmed us. Unable to touch Izta's face, we sought consolation at her feet. Leaving our packs in Portillo with a note for the others explaining our intentions, Geoff and I started up the steep, rocky north face of Los Pies. Our quick ascent soon turned into more of a rock climb than we had anticipated, and to our dismay, we realized that our sacred rope was back in my pack. We had forgotten the rope again, however this time we pressed on without it. Committed to the climb and assuming that we could find an easier way down, we continued up over moves that we really should have belayed. At one point an overhang threatened to stop us, but the shame of defeat loomed larger than the danger, so we climbed the overhang. With the sun now fully in command, we pulled up onto the 15,420-foot summit of Los Pies with the afternoon to spare.

We were suspended between Izta and Popo here, and we finally paused to soak up the view from our unique position. From here, we looked at Izta end on, and I just saw a beautiful mountain, not a woman. I mused that this was the view that Popo had, and that he had not chosen a very good viewpoint from which to watch over his sleeping lover. This part of the legend did not make modern sense, and I wondered what the hidden truth might be in this case. If Popo had wanted to admire his beautiful love, he would have positioned himself to see her in profile. However, he was not just gazing at her, he was guarding her—and willing her to rise. Perhaps Popo had reasoned that it was better for the rest of the world to see her beauty, and perhaps thus flattered, she would wake. Also, it was customary for guards to stand next to a doorway looking out, not to stand in the doorway itself, ogling the jewels.

Resolving to go see what Popo had to say as soon as possible, Geoff and I hustled down to the west and found an easier way back to our packs. Down at the

Izta cradles Popo
between her knees.

lamp mobile, we still had an hour of daylight left, so we hiked back up to a sub-summit on the west ridge of Los Pies, which we dubbed the Toenail. Without real-izing it, like Popo, I had fallen in love with the beautiful Iztaccíhuatl.

Two days later, Geoff and I paused briefly at 15,300 feet on Popo's north slope above a maze of crosses called simply Las Cruces. With our crampons secure, we marched nonstop to Popo's summit, which we reached three hours and eleven min-utes after leaving the truck. We were in top shape from our recent cross-country season at Boulder High and relished this workout. Today's cross-country event had a summit for a finish line.

With hours to spend on top, we pondered Popo's 1,500-foot-deep crater, which emitted his belching funeral torch, now a little too close for comfort. Indeed, bil-lows of sulfurous smoke brought tears to my eyes. Perhaps I was just crying with Popo, since neither Popo nor I were one with Izta. I gazed north to Izta's sleeping shape, trying to understand. I had just been there on Izta, and now I wondered why I had dashed over here to be with the man when the girl was over there. No wonder I couldn't get a decent date.

That evening Geoff and I mentioned our Popo ascent time to the Mexican pro-prietor of the Popo hut, which nestled between the two great peaks. He gazed toward Izta for a long moment, then replied, "Si, that is as fast as the mountain has been climbed." Then he went back to his own meditation in front of the large stone fireplace that graced the old hut's main room. Perhaps our ascents had honored both peaks in some small way. I knew that I would be back to this enchanted place, however I had no idea that my next visit would be with my own Izta, who would definitely have two breasts.

After another Christmas extravaganza in Puebla, we headed for Cuidad Serdan and my second ascent of Orizaba, or the star summit as many locals called it. Remembering my Transcendent Summit the year before, I was eager to get back up there and look beyond the horizon once more. The Aztec legend surrounding Orizaba may not be as popular or as colorful as that of Popo and Izta, but it is perhaps even more potent. Citlaltépetl, as the Aztecs called the great peak, contains the spirit of Quetzalcoatl, who was a feathered serpent. During the serpent's ascension to the summit, the peak's divine fire immolated Quetzalcoatl. Since the fire was divine, the serpent's spirit remained in the peak and became Venus. Perhaps Citlaltépetl is keeping watch on both Izta and Popo, all of central Mexico, and half of the Gulf of Mexico.

We repeated our approach trek to the Cueva del Muerto. Once again I didn't sleep the night before the climb since Bruce, who had no watch, woke me up every few minutes to ask me what time it was. Geoff was strangely quiet, but I knew he wasn't sleeping either. After Bruce's tenth interruption, I took my watch off, handed it to him, and said, "Here, you figure it out!" Our alarm went off five minutes later, and Bruce was so eager that he was almost dysfunctional. We didn't creep from the Cave of the Dead, we rocketed from the cavity and roared up the hill into the dead of night.

The lower slopes flew by in a blur of stumbles, bumbles, flashing lights, and silly attempts to pass each other. At dawn I looked down and realized that Geoff was no longer behind me, then I finally spotted him some distance below moving up very slowly. When I stopped to wait, Bruce caught up to me and said, "Geoff's sick. Montezuma's revenge got him." Bruce and I watched Geoff for several minutes until he slowed to a stop, looked up at us, drew his mitten across his throat, and started back down.

All I could say was, "Wow. He must be hurting!"

Bruce replied, "Yeah. He was going at both ends. I'm amazed he made it this far."

I was disappointed that the Summit Club would not reach the highest point in Mexico together, but there was nothing I could do about it, and I had no way of knowing that a far higher summit awaited Geoff and me. Turning back to Orizaba's heights, I said to Bruce, "It looks like it's you and me today, buddy. Now let's get a sane pace going here. Trust me, it's much farther up there than it appears."

Bruce replied, "You got it! I'm right behind you." When I took one more look down at Geoff, who was descending quickly now, Bruce added, "Let's go! Time's a-wasting!"

Three hours later, as I pulled steadily ahead of Bruce in our quest for the crater rim boulder, I hollered down, "Hey, Bruce! Let's go! Time's a-wasting!" Bruce held his mitten in the air with the back of his hand toward me, and I knew that inside the mitten, he had one finger extended.

The summit purged our silliness, and after handshakes all around, Bruce and I, along with several of our other lamp mobile companions, enjoyed the sentry summit. I saw Popo and Izta holding their own vigil far to the west, and to the east, I caught glimpses of the Gulf of Mexico between curious clouds. I hiked north in hopes of getting a glimpse down Orizaba's north face, but all I saw was part of the crater rim and a great gulf of air. Orizaba's crater was smaller in circumference than Popo's, but it was still steep sided and deep. Peering as far into the crater as I could manage, I looked for any sign of activity, but saw none. Quetzalcoatl's spirit did not need to smoke, and I hoped that Popo's spirit would ultimately find the Venus peace that this star summit held.

Orizaba's summit was grand, but it was no longer transcendent for me. Transcendent Summits were out of my control, so I could neither plan for nor create one. All I could do was graciously accept them when they arrived. I suspected, but had no way of knowing for sure, that a summit could not be transcendent on two successive ascents. For now, I knew that I had to keep moving in new directions, since I was not looking for Transcendent Summits, they were finding me.

Satiated for now, we ministers descended to our machine, double clutched back to Boulder in a record fifty-eight hours, and sold the last of the milk trucks. Mike's ten-man plan did not work, as this trip cost us $60 each, but it was still the second-cheapest international trip that I would ever take. Once more, the navigator's chair was never seen again, but more important, even though my calculus book never left its bag, I managed to do well in my final.

Mythic Domains

I survived my calculus final, but I did not get an A in the class. This bothered me until I realized that I had received an A in every math class at Boulder High, and more important, an A in climbing Mexico's volcanoes, an A in climbing Ship Rock, and As on hosts of other difficult climbs. I had to choose my energy expenditures carefully, and I had chosen Ship Rock and Mexico over an A in calculus. It was an excellent trade.

As my second semester of university calculus continued in the spring of 1961 and my last term at Boulder High proved to be as boring as the others, I made another choice. I abandoned my stupid stealth-dating program. It had consumed too much of my time and energy and had been spectacularly unrewarding. I had not even made a decent female friend, much less achieved a relationship. On the physical front, I had settled for a half-dozen goodnight pecks on the check before my date fled from the porch to disappear behind closed doors.

Heavy winter clothing thwarted my few spastic attempts at something more, and the iron will of my dates proved impregnable. Ten seconds with my nameless Norwegian lass had been more exciting than all my other dates combined, and I thought of her often. If I had been able to hop in the Bathtub and drive to Oslo to find her, I would have done so.

Shirley intrigued me, but after some inquiries, I knew that she was not a candidate for a girlfriend. She was ten years older than me, and for a high school student, that canyon was uncrossable. More important, she was Jim's girlfriend; being a man of honor, I could not even consider stepping on Jim's toes.

On Thursday evenings I rehearsed with the Festival Chorus, which was a choir composed of both university students and town people. My dad took me to the choir rehearsals when I was in junior high and sat next to me pointing at the passing notes until I figured them out. Since he was a bass, I became a bass. I immediately loved the grand performances and had been a steady choir member since. Shirley was also in the choir, so I had a weekly opportunity to chat with her. I had assumed that she was lofty and unapproachable, but I soon discovered that this was not the case. She was always effusive, wise, and warm, and she encouraged me to drop by her apartment on occasion so that we could continue our discussions. By good luck, her apartment was on my walking route between the house and Boulder High.

Whenever the mood hit me, I would ring Shirley's doorbell. When she was there, she always invited me in, dropped what she was doing, and sat down for a talk. Shirley was a schoolteacher, and when we understood each other's schedules better, our visits became more frequent. I usually stopped by on my walk home from track practice to ramble on about my track meets, my classes, my climbs, and my nonexistent dates. Shirley always listened patiently then offered her opinion about what was really going on. When Shirley talked, she favored grander themes, and I soon enjoyed her insights more than my own ramblings. I learned to listen carefully to what she had to say and to muse on it until our next visit. Thus, we built a repertoire of ongoing discussion topics that often spanned months. By March we were fast friends, but I still rejected all thoughts of a romance with Shirley. Her friendship was far more than I had found so far with any other girl, and that was sufficient for now, since I had little time for more than that anyway.

One of our discussions centered on domains—not the math domains that I had learned about in class, but Earth's domains. After one poor attempt at sorting out my ideas, I thought about it for several days then tried to explain my thoughts to Shirley on our next visit.

Shirley started with, "Any progress on your domains?"

"Yeah, I've thought about it. First, there are Earth's three elements: earth, air, and water."

Settling in to her chair and crossing her legs under her long dress, Shirley said, "We're not talking about outer space, fire, or spiritual spaces here, just the physical Earth, right?"

"Right. Damn gravity keeps me on the Earth. So, derived from the three elements, there are eight earthly domains that humans can interact with. In water, you can be on the surface of the water or you can be submerged, so water gives us two domains. With air, you can only be in the air, so that adds one more. With the Earth itself, you can be above or below the surface. Below Earth's surface is one domain, and if you are on the surface, you can be in mountains, desert, jungle, or plains, so Earth gives five more for a total of eight."

Shirley responded, "I'm with you. So out of all this grandeur, why did you pick mountains? You could also be sailing, scuba diving, flying, caving, hiking in the jungle, canyoneering, or farming. Why mountains?"

"I knew that you were going to ask that, so I thought about it in advance. I have a two-part answer. First, all sports can be divided into two categories: gravity sports and antigravity sports. Skydiving is the ultimate gravity sport, since you just take one step, and everything happens. Climbing is the ultimate antigravity sport. If you don't take a step, nothing happens. The defining feature of gravity sports isn't just gravity. If you are not the primary motive force, but are working with a greater force, then it's a gravity sport."

"Like sailing?"

"Yes! Sailing is a good example of a gravity sport that doesn't depend directly on gravity, but on another force: wind. Anyway, I consider that antigravity sports generate more Karmic Points."

"Ah! Now we are getting into it. I understand your Karmic Points, but why are we awarded more points for climbing up a hill, rather than, say, sliding down it on skis?"

"OK, distill sliding to its purest form, just sliding on your butt down a snow slope, for example. A dead person could achieve that—no points there! To the extent that an active downhill skier is exerting, he does get some points, but clearly not as many as an active uphill skier."

"So your up-down distinction has only to do with the amount of exertion— something that could be measured in a lab? What if a superactive downhill skier exerts more than a lazy uphill hiker? Does the downhill skier get more points?"

"Well, yes, any exertion counts, but that's not the whole story. An uphill activity gets bonus points from the Karmic Kiss."

"That sounds exciting! What's a Karmic Kiss? Is it something that you and I could do?"

"At a surface level, no, but at a deeper level, yes. But, slow down, you're getting me confused."

"Sorry—you're blushing! You're cute when you blush, but you're right, I shouldn't do that. Go on, Ger."

Shirley always called me "Ger," and I liked the small intimacy that it provided. Trying to keep the conversation serious, I continued, "A dead skier could tumble down a slope for 5,000 feet, with his limbs moving and muscles contracting, creating a grim form of exertion, but there is no Karmic Kiss there. The Karmic Kiss comes from beyond and is awarded to life. For example, Himalayan ascents require an iron will and tremendous exertion. They require a huge life force, and that force triggers the Karmic Kiss. Now is the difference clearer?"

During these discussions, I spent my time looking at Shirley's face. I had not seen her braid down since that first night in the cave. Just knowing that it was so long was exciting, but today I noticed something else. Her braid, as usual, was rolled neatly and stacked just behind the top of her head, but it looked like her life force was coming up out of the top of her head, emulating the spire of a cathedral. That was an even more exciting feeling, and I almost said something, but as usual I held back.

Shirley shook me from my reverie, prompting me to continue with my discussion of domains.

"OK. Well, I think we are just about there for part one. Never mind the occasional, fringe examples. In general, antigravity activities get more points from their increased exertion and also from the Karmic Kiss. Now, the part-one punch line is that mountaineering provides the biggest bang for the antigravity buck."

"Why does mountaineering get more points than say, running a marathon uphill?"

"Good question. Because the mountaineer faces greater difficulty and danger than the runner."

"The details of that sound like a good subject for another visit."

"I hope so. Say, where are you going?"

"To make some tea. At this rate, you're going to need it! Ger, you know that I agree with your part-one conclusions. Of course Himalayan mountaineering gets more points than sliding down a hill on a cardboard box. Since you will be doing Himalayan expeditions, I just want to make sure that you have thought it through, and that you don't fall into a loophole someday. You know that I do care about you! Now, tell me about part two. I expect that it is the more interesting reason why you choose mountains over scuba diving."

"How do you know that I'll be going to the Himalayas?"

"Ger, I'll tell you more about that later. I'm working on my theories too, you know. Now, tell me about your second reason."

"OK. Switch gears."

Recrossing her legs, Shirley twinkled and said, "Should I double clutch?"

Chuckling, I continued, "This is an up shift, so one good push will do! The second reason that I choose mountains is that I get the best return in another arena. When I'm on a mountain, I'm also in the air. The steeper the mountain, the more I am one with the atmosphere as well as the Earth. Just look at Ship Rock—that was almost solid air up there!"

Holding her arm out to show me, Shirley said, "Oh my God! I've got goose bumps with that image! Go on."

"The higher the mountain, the more I am one with the atmosphere."

"Why don't you just go flying?" Shirley asked.

"'Cause I'd be stuck in a cage. When I'm climbing, I have a direct connection between the wind and the bottom of my lungs, and my feet make a direct connection with the Earth at the same time. I can also see and understand more of Earth from on high—I can't get that from an airplane. So, on my high, steep mountain I have the best of Earth and much of the air—I've got not just two of the eight domains, but two of the three elements as well, all for the price of one domain!"

"Now, I'm *tingling*! Hang on, I'll get the tea." Returning from the kitchen, Shirley said, "I've got one more question." Handing me a cup of tea in an ornate cup that looked like it came from China, Shirley continued. "You indeed have a large Karmic Opportunity by linking two of the three elements, but what about the other element—water? Can you do even better?"

"Hmm. I suppose the closest I come to touching the element of water is when I'm climbing on snow. Then I'm touching all three of the elements—a steep, high, snowy mountain is my ultimate opportunity for Karmic Gain."

"I'm with you, Ger. You know that you can do even better, don't you? In fact, you already have."

Shirley usually wore long, flowered dresses that hid her shape. She had a full bosom, but it was always modestly hidden. However, it was large enough that I couldn't help noticing, and I often wondered about her breasts. I somehow just knew that, if revealed, they would raise the dead.

"Ger? You're blushing again!"

Coughing, I stammered, "Ah, sorry Shirley. My mind wandered."

"That's OK. Mine goes sometimes too. Let it go Ger—that's the only way we make progress."

"Where are we going?"

Eyeing me evenly, Shirley responded, "You tell me when you're ready."

"Ahem, where were we?"

"You were going to tell me how you touch four domains simultaneously."

Then we sat in silence looking at each other for three minutes. During our Karmic Rest, as we called them, I shifted my position seven times, and three times Shirley recrossed her legs under her long dress while our gaze remained locked on each other's eyes. When Shirley smiled effusively, I continued with, "It's the volcano, right?"

"Yes! Go on, my love!" She had never used the term "love" before, and it sent a shiver straight through to my soul.

"I know now. When I'm climbing a volcano, I'm touching rock from below the Earth's surface, another one of Earth's five domains. I don't need to go caving when I can climb on the core rocks above the surface! Ship Rock was extra special, since we got to climb on rock from several different subsurface levels. So you're right, I can touch three elements and four domains at once!"

"That means that a high, steep, snowy *volcano* is your best opportunity. No wonder God gave you a Transcendent Summit on Orizaba! So, are there any volcanoes higher than Orizaba?"

"Well, not in North America, but there are several higher volcanoes in South America."

Ahead of me as always, Shirley said, "What about Kilimanjaro? How high is that?"

"I'd forgotten about Kilimanjaro. Yes, Kili is over 19,000 feet, which makes it higher than Orizaba. And it's the highest peak in Africa, which earns us another Karmic Kiss."

"And it's easy to climb?"

"Yes, it's a walk up."

"Ger, I've always wanted to see the snows of Kilimanjaro. Let's go there!"

Breathing heavily, I said, "When do we leave?"

Standing, Shirley reached up to her head, pulled some pins out, and uncoiled her braid. It was longer than she could hold out at arms' length, so she just cradled it in loops as she walked toward me. Gently swinging her hair near my face, she said in a throaty voice that I had not heard before, "My love, you tell me when you're ready!"

Reaching out, I took her braid and held it to my cheek. Dropping the end of the braid into my lap, her hand cradled mine. Now strangely calm, I said, "And this is our sacred rope?"

After a minute, Shirley said in the same husky tone, "Yes, Ger, this Karmic Kiss is sacred."

We stayed in our tremulous Karmic Rest for five minutes, then trembling, I rose to leave. Seeing me to the door, Shirley said, "Ger?"

"Yes, my love?"

"We are missing some fine routes by not being able to climb clouds."

▼ ▼ ▼

It was a week before I dared ring Shirley's bell again. When I did, she did not answer, and I assumed that she was out at a meeting or running errands. When she was not at choir practice, I assumed that she was out of town. A week later I tried again, and this time the door opened wide. Knowing that we had to make a fresh start, we took our places in facing chairs and talked about myths. I explained my thoughts about myths holding some truth and my observations of the impossible-looking, tortured gullies below Ship Rock's honeycomb basin.

Shirley, as usual, cut to the chase. "So, Ger, you're a scientist like your dad and need some rational explanation before you can invest in a belief, right?"

"Right."

"Do you believe that Indians, or anybody else, made a prehistoric ascent of Ship Rock?"

"I've thought a lot about it, and I have to either believe that there was a prehistoric ascent or explain away the legendary description of the summit block. Their description predates modern ascents, balloons, and airplanes. Also, I checked, and you can't see that block from the desert floor—you need to be up there to even see it, much less describe it. Right now I can't explain away their description, so I must believe that there was a prehistoric ascent."

"Is there *any* basis that you can accept to explain a prehistoric ascent of Ship Rock?"

"Yes. One."

Clearing my throat, I launched into my explanation. "The magma came up 50 million years ago and brought a lot of the Earth's crud with it, which was piled up around the base. Stan and I climbed one of those basalt towers leaning against the core rock."

"Yes, I watched you."

Shirley was leaning forward intently, so I continued. "Now 50 million years is an enormous amount of time by human standards—more than we need for my argument. My theory is that the original Ship Rock looked very different and that there was basalt and other rocks piled high around the core rock, almost to Ship Rock's summit. It was probably just a hike all the way to the top several million years ago. Then, erosion took away the crud from the top down. Now, what will we accept as a "prehistoric" time frame? Three thousand years would likely do it. But the ascent could have been 10,000 years ago. We have also been assuming that the Ship Rock we see today is close to what it was 10,000 years ago. The punch line is that the prehistoric climbers 10,000 years ago were able to hike, scramble, or climb up into the honeycomb basin on crud that has since eroded away."

"That's great reasoning, Ger, but they are still not on top. As you have told me, there's some hard climbing up there. Do you think that our heroes could have climbed up and down the upper pitches without modern equipment?"

"Yes, I do. We free climbed it, and I think it's presumptuous to think that prehistoric people could not achieve the same basic free climbing abilities that we have. We're not talking about 5.99; the Horn Pitch, although exposed, is only 5.7. The vertical step above the Horn pitch is tougher, but it's short—they could have stood on each other's shoulders to make it over that."

Twinkling, Shirley said, "Or used a ladder. Could they also have used a ladder on the Horn Pitch?"

"Gee, you've thought about this too, Shirley! Yes, a Horn Pitch ladder would be a long one, but it's possible. The ladder theory is just as feasible as their free climbing it, and maybe more so. After all, the free climbing ethic is ours, not theirs."

Just as I thought that everything was under control, Shirley surprised me again. She pulled her dress way up above her knees, and instead of her usual dainty leg crossing, she plopped one ankle up on her other knee. The folds of her dress fetchingly fell where they chose. Bending sideways, she cocked one elbow on her hip and continued as if everything were perfectly normal. "So they made it?"

Blushing beet red but staying calm, I sat at attention and continued as if everything were perfectly normal, which in retrospect, it was. "They had different motivations, but yes, they made it."

"Different motivations? I think that climbers' motivations are ageless. They went up there to pay respects, just like you did, my love."

"Shirley, how could you know that? Did you talk to Tom?"

"I didn't need to, Ger. I told you that sometimes it's crystal clear."

"So, why the big quiz? What do you believe?"

"Ger, I just wanted to see if we end up in the same place. You have your means of supporting this belief, but I do it a different way."

"Different how?"

"I've told you—sometimes I just know the answer. I've known for a long time that ancients climbed the Rock with Wings."

I started to say something stupid, then just fell silent for a minute. Finally, I raised my gaze from Shirley's legs back to her eyes and asked, "Crystal clear?"

Standing, her dress fell back into place, and just as I thought I might survive with my soul intact, Shirley came to me, placed her braid on my cheek, gave me a penetrating look, and said in her low voice, "Crystal clear, Ger." Then, she wrapped me in her braid and held my head to her breasts for a five minute Karmic Rest, while her heartbeat thundered in my ears.

This time, it was two weeks before I dared ring her doorbell again. When I did, there was no answer. Chirping birds and newly mown lawns signaled that it was now late May. The Festival Chorus spring performance of Mendelssohn's *Elijah* was over, so I couldn't look for Shirley at rehearsal. My calculus final loomed and I needed to study, but I couldn't get Shirley's heartbeat out of my ears. I tried her bell several more times, but the door stayed shut. I assumed that she was out of town, but on several occasions I felt sure that she was in the apartment, just choosing to not answer the bell. Then one time, just as I stepped up onto her small porch, I heard her inside. Desperately needing to see her face, I rang the bell. With my own heart pounding in my ears, I stood on the porch for ten minutes, but the door did not open.

House of the Sun

Just before my graduation from Boulder High, one of my teachers pulled me aside for a chat. After pleasantries, he said, "Gerry, when I graduated from high school, I thought I knew more about the world than at any other time in my life since."

I thought about this for a moment, then replied, "Meaning that's it's all downhill from here?"

Laughing, my teacher continued, "That's a bit harsh, Gerry! Slow down, or you will prove my point. I just mean that you still have a lot to learn. We never stop learning, you know."

"For a moment there, I thought I was in trouble!"

Continuing in a serious tone, my teacher said, "What I am really trying to say is, don't get ahead of yourself. Take your time and enjoy what you have today. There is not just a lot to learn, there are many life adventures out there. Don't spend all your time trying to be somewhere else. When an adventure comes to you, by all means seize it. But don't go so fast that you miss the merry-go-round. Gerry, don't run off the end of life!"

"Run off the end of life—that sounds prophetic. How does that happen?"

"That's one of the things you have to learn. Just be vigilant, so you can learn before you burn. Now, run along boy."

After the graduation ceremony, I lazed on the Boulder High lawn under perfectly blue, early June skies with my now staunch clover-questing companion, Gabe Lee, looking for that elusive four-leaf clover. My calculus class had taught me that I indeed had a lot to learn. I knew enough about academics from watching my dad's complicated research program to know that I was a babe in arms when it came to class work. The mountain of a university degree and then graduate school loomed high over my head. As I thought about my teacher's advice, I figured that it applied to my life's other arenas. My climbing was on a fast track to somewhere, but I was not sure where. I knew that I had a lot to learn in the mountains; they had been my best teacher so far. My nascent love life was a swirl of confused emotions powered by a passion that was controlling my feet, brain, and even my willpower right now. It was time to seize a ring and take a ride, but I wasn't sure which ring to grab.

Just then, I found a four-leaf clover. There it was nestled among a hundred three-leaf clovers, which themselves were lost in a sea of green. I gently pulled back the nearby grass to be sure, and yes, this clover had four leaves. I reached into its nest, plucked it ever so carefully, and pulled it up close to my eyes for a better look. Gabe, peering over my shoulder, said, "You got it, man! Now, what are you going to do with it?"

Then I saw my teacher walking out of the school toward his car and his summer vacation. I jumped up and ran after him, catching up to him in the parking lot. "Look what I found!" I announced.

Without breaking stride, my former teacher glanced at the clover and said, "Yes, you are a lucky kid, Gerry. That's why I told you what I told you!"

The first thing that I learned after graduation was that my father was smarter than I had given him credit for. Not just in an academic sense, as he had passed his competition years earlier in that department, which was why he was now the director of his own research empire. He was also smarter in the other areas where I needed his help more. My dad had watched my struggles and now saw a chance to help, so he plucked a ring for me.

His research program, which studied the airglow, was now in full flower. He was proving that the airglow, while not often visible to the naked eye, was nevertheless quite prevalent in the midlatitudes. His observatory on Fritz Peak, near forty degrees north latitude, had now collected a mountain of observations of charged particles zooming into our atmosphere, interacting with it, and giving off light. His study covered three different, important wavelengths. One of the three elements that my climbing attached me to was the atmosphere, so I was not just interested in the airglow, I also recognized the importance of studying it. I understood that charged particles coming into Earth's atmosphere from the sun, or anywhere else beyond Earth, and *changing* it, were well worth understanding. On a personal level, the airglow demonstrated changes in my greater mountain environment. I supported my dad's research, and I was probably just a little bit smarter than he gave me credit for.

With the midlatitudes well studied, his research needed an observatory farther south, in the subtropics. Just as I was good at reaching summits, my dad was good at securing funding for his research ideas. Tapping his usual sources and adding support from the University of Hawaii, he put together a grant to build a new airglow observatory on top of Haleakala on Maui. This extinct shield volcano is near twenty-one degrees north latitude, just over 10,000 feet high in the central Pacific's clear skies, and has a road to its summit and several other astronomical observatories nearby. The mountain provided a perfect platform to extend the range of airglow observations. Charged particles making themselves felt that far south were even more energetic, and thus, even more important to understand.

My dad's plan was to get the basic observatory building constructed quickly, install the photometers, and start collecting data in July of 1961. While the observers observed by night, the construction crew would put the finishing touches on the facility by day. Dad's clock was ticking, so he signed me on to the construction crew, and two days after graduation, I packed my bags for a summer on top of a Hawaiian volcano.

With only a couple of hours before my flight, I took a chance and stopped by Shirley's one more time. To my astonishment and ear-tingling delight, the door swung wide, and Shirley ushered me in with a flourish. "Oh, Ger! I knew that you would come! This is great! You have a grand direction for the summer now. You will be working, getting in shape, making money, enjoying Hawaii, falling in love, and best of all, living on top of a sacred volcano! How could you be so lucky?"

I had resolved, that if I ever saw Shirley again, I wouldn't ask her how she knew so much about me, so I just blurted out, "I found a four-leaf clover!" Then, fumbling in my pocket, I extracted a folded piece of paper, gently lifted the tiny talisman from it, and extended it toward her. "Shirley, I have my summer luck already! You take the clover now. Please. For both of us."

Shirley took my hand in both of hers, pressed it to her lips while looking me in the eye, took the clover from me, pressed it to her heart, and breathed in her husky tone, "Thanks, lover!"

Not knowing what to say next, I tried, "Shirley, it's really good to see you! Where … "

She cut me off quickly with, "Hush. I know that you don't have a lot of time, so let's just enjoy this moment." Then she turned up *Madam Butterfly* which was already playing, and independent of the music, danced around the room holding the clover in front of her. Astounded, I flopped into my usual chair and watched in amazement. Except for the cave, I had only seen Shirley in long dresses, but now she was barefoot, wearing only short shorts and a flimsy, loose top. Her unbraided dark-auburn hair was down, swirling about her waist like a grass hula skirt. Her hair carried several hundred swirls from being braided for so long, but for the moment, it was free. In the next two minutes, I saw more of Shirley's enthusiasm than I had a right to see in my entire lifetime.

Finally, she curled at my feet, rested both of her arms on my legs, and looked up at me. I tried to speak, but nothing came out. Before her tears could leave her face, she nuzzled her head into my lap. After lifting and stroking her hair for many minutes, I could still not form a single word. Knowing that I was late, I glanced at my watch; I had to leave in three minutes or miss my plane. Raising her head back toward mine, I slithered from the chair to sit with her on the floor. Stroking her arms while her hair encircled us both, I finally croaked it out. "Shirley, I suppose you already know that I love you."

I saw her mouth working and realized that she was also unable to speak. Licking away her tears, she finally nodded, then pressed her hand to my chest and nodded again. Just as the Humming Chorus started, I remembered my pledge of honor and struggled to my feet as she continued to hold me. Shirley's hands slid down my legs and across my shoes as I inched toward the door, while her hair clung to my pants and held our embrace until the last second. Outside, I shut the door ever so gently, but the click was still deafening.

▼ ▼ ▼

Sun was the Hercules of the Hawaiian heavens. Untouchable, he raced across the sky at will. No one, not even other gods, had ever gone near Sun and lived. The Moon, pale and dead in appearance, moved slowly, while mighty Sun, full of life and strength, sped along. Thus the days were short and the nights were long. Both were burdens to the Hawaiian people, as they suffered from Sun's fierce heat during the day and from his prolonged absence at night. The darkness was so great and lasted so long that fruits would not ripen and kapa cloth would not dry.

Seeing the suffering of his people, Maui, a demigod filled with strength and courage, schemed ways to snare Sun and slow his heedless haste. First Maui made snares from strong coconut fibers, went to the mountain where Sun would rise, set his trap, and waited until morning. However, Sun easily burst through Maui's coconut ropes and escaped into the sky, laughing. Maui made stronger ropes, but mighty Sun, who had sixteen legs, broke them all.

Then Maui thought of his sister's magic hair, which was long and beautiful. He cut some of it off and made a stupendous rope. This time he also took his enchanted club, which his grandmother had given to him. When Sun's first leg climbed over the mountain, it stepped into Maui's snare. Maui pulled his empowered rope tight and secured Sun's leg to a rock. Three more legs came over the mountain, and he snared each one. Sun raged against the tethers, but before Sun could break the rope, Maui struck Sun's trapped legs with his enchanted club and broke them off. Sun yanked his broken legs from the snares and escaped, but without all of his legs, he could not go so fast. This is how Maui slowed Sun and made him sail higher to escape further harm.

Haleakala means "House of the Sun" in Hawaiian. "La," along with its synonym "Ra," is the Sun's name throughout Polynesia, but Ra was also the sun God of ancient Egypt. Thus, the antiquities of Polynesia and Egypt touch each other, and today, nobody knows why.

▼ ▼ ▼

Double clutching down, I smoothly took the fourteenth switchback, then floored our VW combi van up the next straightaway. Mack always let me drive the combi up the narrow, convoluted Haleakala road, and I liked that, since it gave me a chance to perfect my driving skills and ascend a mountain at the same time. The road up Haleakala was a strip of pavement eight feet wide in 1961, which was just wide enough for one vehicle. When a car came the other way, I sent my outside wheels to the dirt shoulder and, without slowing, encouraged the oncoming vehicle to do the same. This was rarely a problem, since there was very little traffic on the road in 1961. Since Mack and I had been driving this road for several weeks now, we knew all the dangerous curves and utilized a special evasive maneuver if one of the wide-eyed tourists suddenly forgot how to drive.

Mack Mann and I were the observatory's "construction crew," and while our number was small, our output was potent. We had worked efficiently, and the ten-by-twenty-foot building was almost ready for the observers. One end of the building held a bunk bed for naps and a small kitchen table, while the rest of the floor space was filling with recording instruments. The photometers were destined for the roof, and we already had their casings in place. Today we would work on Mack's favorite project, building a lava wall in front of the observatory door. Its purpose was to block the incessant wind, since here at 10,000 feet Hawaii's trade winds carried a bite. However, when I had stepped off the plane at sea level, it had only taken me one inhalation of the smog-free, scent-filled air to realize that I was in paradise. After my first swim and snorkel, I forgot about the mainland, which of course was exactly what my dad knew I needed.

Since the commute up the mountain from our rented rooms in Kula was time consuming, Mack and I usually worked a two- or three-day shift on the mountain, then descended for a day to pick up supplies and swim at one of Maui's stunning beaches. Our favorite beaches were at Kihei on Maui's southwest shore, and our usual routine was to bump along the rutted dirt road until we found a deserted beach. If there was even one parked car, we moved on, since we could always find a beach with nobody on it. The beaches varied from intimate coves with a hundred yards of clean sand between two lava headlands to larger coves to long sweeps.

I quickly learned to dive under the waves, swiftly stroke far beyond them, then dog-paddle on my back while looking up at Haleakala. After this Karmic Rest, I would put on my mask and snorkel, flip over, and begin a search for shells. Of course, I hadn't completely forgotten about my mainland life, and this was my simplest way of connecting the mountain and water domains. After my finger-freezing, high-altitude snow climbs, I reveled in Maui's warmth. The discussion about which was closer to water, ice or snow, seemed remote, and in any case, I had a better touch here, since I was *in* the water. Perhaps I could connect the water to the mountain instead of trying to connect the mountain to the water.

While snorkeling, I savored the water's bobbing surface, and with a big breath and a little practice, I could dive down fifteen feet for a short visit to the underwater world. With all my training and a large lung capacity, I could stay down for a couple of minutes. During these brief excursions along the ocean floor, it dawned on me that perhaps the ocean floor was another domain, which was independent from the rest of the water world and Earth's land domains as well. While schools of multicolored fish ruled the water, corals, anemone, and shells graced the seafloor. I had seen nothing like this above sea level, so while the gentle swell above sent curtains of light rays down to dance through the coral, I added the ocean floor to my list of domains for a new total of nine. With lungs bursting, I pushed off from the floor, finned back to the surface, blasted into the air, and looked at Haleakala. Thus, in a few seconds, I touched five domains, the last with my eyes.

Day by day, I labored on the observatory and explored Maui's hallowed treasures while my body, mind, and spirit relaxed. I saw all the standard tourist sights during the first two weeks, and my stay here moved beyond a tourist visit toward a lifestyle. Most of the observers and their families were already on the island, and our outings were usually jocular, domestic affairs. Our picnic baskets held Hawaiian favorites including pineapple, guava juice, and sushi. Holding it in my hands, I learned to carve up a fresh pineapple while sitting on the sand, then handed out the savory morsels. Of course, dropping the pineapple into the sand was an unthinkable act, like falling off of a mountain, so I used my mind-control training to keep my handheld morsel from becoming buried treasure. Completing the messy affair, I stuffed the leavings into a trash bag, sprinted for the water, then, bobbing beyond the waves, I delighted in plucking a remaining strand of pineapple from between my teeth.

I never tired of the view from the top of Haleakala, which is the higher of two volcanoes making up Maui. During the crystalline dawns, I stepped out of the observatory, climbed on top of our sturdy lava wall, and gazed west-northwest down on the rugged escarpments of West Maui, the lower, older, and more heavily eroded volcano. Lava from the two volcanoes flowed together to form Maui's namesake valley, and the Valley Isle. It looks like a lopsided figure eight on a map, however with Maui spread out before me, I didn't need a map. Looking farther to the northwest, I saw the neighboring islands of Lanai, Molokai, and even Oahu, and to the southeast, the Big Island of Hawaii with its twin volcanoes, Mauna Loa and Mauna Kea. I resolved to get to the Big Island and hike up those peaks at my first opportunity. Falling away to the east of the observatory was the top of Haleakala's famous crater where Maui snared Sun, which we just called, "the crater."

On some of my days off, I elected to stay aloft on the mountaintop by myself while Mack descended. After hefting my pack, which still felt enjoyable, I strode down the Sliding Sands Trail into the crater. I took several extended hikes on the trails that wound among the many cinder cones, and I spent solitary nights in each of the three cabins that were strategically placed across the seven-mile-long crater floor. If I got up early in the Kapalaoa Cabin, I could hike out of the crater and be at the observatory to meet Mack at 8:00 A.M. One day, after hiking out of the crater before breakfast, I worked all day, then Mack and I descended to Kihei for a sunset swim. Surging off the ocean floor and blasting out of the water, I realized that I had improved on my five-domain touch. I had not kissed them all in just a few seconds, but I had done it in a day.

Haleakala's famous crater where Maui snared Sun.

Then, walking back to the car at dusk, I stepped on a Keeave thorn, which is a tiny, multispiked terror that, resting like a jack, always has one thorn pointed up toward the bottoms of unsuspecting feet. The Keeave trees commanded the strip of land between the beaches and the rutted road, and I usually wore flip-flops for this dangerous journey. However, this evening, flush with excitement from my five-domain feast, I had gone barefoot—and paid the price. After plucking the cactuslike cretin from my foot and pitching it toward Haleakala, I realized that the land behind the beach was a desert. While Maui's windward side held heavy vegetation, here on the dry side of the island it was very arid. So, without even trying, I had touched six of my nine domains in one day. Well, in the last case, the domain had touched me. I coined the new term "Karmic Touch" for this six-domain event and added it to my growing Karmic vocabulary. Limping on, I mused that this Karmic Touch would be better if I could do it all on foot, and if I could control all the touching.

One day in July, while I perched on the lava wall sipping some guava juice and eating my lunch, Mack walked up and said, "Hey, beach boy. I just opened a package from your dad. Most of it was observatory stuff, but he also included a clipping for you." As he held the folded newspaper toward me, he added, "You're not going to like it." Then Mack walked away, leaving me alone. Before unfolding the report, I saw that it was from the *Boulder Daily Camera*. Retreating into the observatory to escape the sun's glare, I sat down and read the account in disbelief.

Dave Roberts had gone climbing with Gabe Lee, my clover-questing classmate from Boulder High. Their objective was the left side of the First Flatiron, which is a complicated piece of rock. Trouble arose after they were 300 feet above the ground, when during a belay exchange their rope fell down the slab and hooked under a flake. Repeated pulling and flipping only lodged the rope tighter. After a discussion, Gabe—unroped and unprotected—started climbing down to free the rope jam. Before he reached the jam, he fell. Sliding flat-bodied for a few feet, he tried to stop himself, but one of his feet caught on a protrusion and he flipped backwards into space. He sailed through the air, crashing back onto the rock three times. After the third smash, he flew clear of the rock, ripped through the trees, and hit the ground with a heavy thud.

Horrified, Dave watched Gabe fall, then called to him repeatedly with no response. Unable to downclimb from his precarious stance, Dave soloed up to the top of the Flatiron, climbed down the back side, and rushed down the gully to Gabe's position. Before he could accomplish all that, help arrived from below. In those days, it was common practice for people in town to watch climbers on the Flatirons, and Baker Armstrong had seen Gabe's fall from his front porch. Baker called the Rescue Group, and my neighbor and Orizaba companion, Bruce Munroe, sprinted up the hill. Bruce was the first to reach Gabe. When I talked to Bruce later, he could barely choke out a brief description of Gabe's shattered head and badly broken body.

My reactions to Gabe's death went from disbelief to shock and sadness to anger. I felt that Gabe had taken a fall meant for me, but that I would have prevented it. I also blamed Dave for letting it happen. Carelessness caused the rope to jam in the first place. Even with the jam, how could there not have been enough rope available to rig a belay for the downclimb? Layton and I had solved this problem on T2, a much more difficult route. Dave was a better and more experienced climber than Gabe, so how was it that Gabe attempted the unroped downclimb and not Dave? Crushing the clipping, I could almost hear Dave berating Gabe with insults until he attempted the dangerous maneuver.

Gabe had taken the fatal fall that I had faced on the Fist's drainpipe crack where my brain screamed at me to retreat. Gabe's final consciousness must have progressed rapidly from surprise through alarm to terror and a mercifully short-lived horror. Alive and above, Dave had his separation, but with Gabe, not me. What had Dave thought when he was on the summit of the First Flatiron and Gabe lay dead below? In my worst moments I assumed that it was what Dave wanted, but I would never know, since Dave and I had now gone our separate ways. Much later, I talked to Geoff, who had spent many hours talking to Dave after the accident. Dave offered that Gabe had volunteered for the downclimb, thinking that his new, and for the era, hi-tech klettershoes would give him the advantage that he needed. Gabe had been dead wrong in his assessment, and like Prince, a momentary negligence had taken him.

Squinting tears, I walked out into Maui's subtropical sun, did a slow 360 to look at my now familiar view, then hiked east to Magnetic Peak, a place that I often used for meditation. As the rest of my life rushed through my fibers, I plopped down to stare at the House of the Sun. Still holding the crushed news clipping, I smoothed it out and read the account again, hoping that it might have changed, but of course it was the same. I wiped a lingering tear from my cheek and rolled the cheap paper between my fingers to smudge the newsprint. Looking at Haleakala's glory, I knew that the best thing I could do was to invent a climb and infuse its steps with joy in Gabe's memory. Perhaps in some small way, that would glorify Gabe's life. Perhaps others would follow in my footsteps and thus carry Gabe's spirit forward. With my last tear now dry, I looked at the Pacific shimmering beyond the crater and immediately knew what my climb had to be.

A month later I had my chance. Chuck Purdy, who was one of the observers, and his wife, Mary, dropped me off at the historic Huialoha Church on Maui's sparsely populated southeast coast. With Chuck and Mary watching, I put on my Kelty pack and marched down to the ocean's edge. Via my intended route, Haleakala's summit was twenty-two miles away and 10,023 feet above me. After getting wetter than I had intended to, I turned inland, waved good-bye to Chuck and Mary, and started walking toward the House of the Sun. I planned to ascend through the Kaupo Gap today, meet friends in the Paliku Cabin tonight, and hike with them to the summit tomorrow. I had heard about hikers crossing the crater and descending through the Kaupo Gap to reach the ocean, but there were no stories about anyone hiking from sea level *up* to the summit. I reasoned that I had to uphold my reputation as a mountain climber and not become known as a mountain descender, so I padded past the still-sleeping ranch headquarters at Kaupo on the King's Highway then, heading for the heights, left this modest civilization behind.

I was not quite done with civilization and soon reached a gate with a sign that read, "Warning! Do not enter this field unless you can run 100 yards in 9.9 seconds. The bull can do it in 10 flat." My record for 100 yards was 10.5 seconds, so I hiked around the field while the bull eyed me with interest. Above the pasture, I also left the ironwood trees behind, then climbed into a zone of ancient koa trees, which covered their territory with dozens of twisted, intertwined, moss-covered branches.

Above the koas, I entered Haleakala National Park and felt the embrace of Kaupo Gap's walls for the first time. The Haleakala Crater is a strange one in that it has not one but two large gaps in its otherwise continuous crater rim. Originating in the crater, great quantities of molten rock poured out through these gaps on a journey toward the ocean. The Koolau Gap is on the crater's northwest side, thus its lava had flowed toward the wet side of the island. There was no trail down the Koolau Gap, and I was curious about exploring it someday. In contrast, the Kaupo Gap is on the crater's southeast side, and its lava had toured Maui's dry side. Haleakala's remaining ramparts tower above each side of the lava flow that I was now walking up, and it felt like the God of Hikes had designed this enchanted, even-graded route.

At these low elevations, my lungs found plenty of oxygen, and I strode briskly up the trail through my lofty house. As I approached the entrance to the crater, I felt Maui's power, for this was the place where his mythical struggle with Sun occurred. Entering the crater, the bottoms of my feet tingled, which I assumed was from my long lava trek, but it could have been because the ground that I walked on was sacred. Still striding swiftly, I admired the clouds rolling over the crater's eastern rim, which looked like God's binkie. I walked under the fluted parapets of 7,553-foot Kuiki where Sun's first foot entered the crater on his fateful day, and I resolved to climb it someday. At midday, I reached Paliku.

The rustic Paliku Cabin nestles in grassy fields at 6,400 feet in the crater's lower, eastern end. Paliku is under the crater's eastern rim, which hosts wet-side clouds according to some cosmic whim. Sometimes clear, the crater rim stands above Paliku like a great green guard. Sometimes clouds roll over the rim to dissipate in the crater's dryness. These roller-coaster clouds can spin over the rim for hours while Paliku basks in the sun, then without reason or warning they will descend on the hut to unleash a torrential rain worthy of the deepest jungle. The Hawaiians consider that any rain on their islands is a blessing, for without it their life here would soon end. Thus Paliku is a well-blessed place, and the surrounding trees wave their thanks. As fast as they come, the clouds fly away, leaving their raindrops gleaming on the sun-blessed grass. I consider Paliku one of the centers of the universe.

With several solitary hours to enjoy, I lolled in the grass near the cabin and practiced blowing tunes on the reeds of grass just as Gabe had taught me to do on the lawn in front of Boulder High. Paliku's well-blessed grass provided larger, tougher reeds, and I soon tooted a passable tune, listening to the simple notes frisk the air then float away. The only thing that could improve my already sacred stay was laughter and love, and after three solitary hours on Paliku's lawn, I received just that. Looking up the trail, I saw the Andrews clan approaching at high speed. They were descending from the summit road to join me. Mark, the fittest of the four, was first to arrive, as usual. He zoomed in, piloted his pack to a perfect landing next to the hut, and quipped, "Hello, beach boy! You're kind of far from the surf, aren't you? What do you think you are, a mountain climber?" Used to Mark's needling, I just smiled and nodded, then turned my eyes back to the trail. When Mark saw me looking up the trail, he added, "Calm down, mountain man, she'll be here in a minute."

Seeing what I most wanted to see, I walked out onto the grass. When Terry saw me, she broke into a trot, rushed toward Paliku, dropped her pack carelessly on the grass, and leapt into my arms. After I picked her up and nuzzled her pretty, round face, she wrapped her tan legs around my waist as I twirled her in our usual greeting. Losing balance, we tumbled onto the grass and into each other's arms. Without hesitation, she pulled me close and said in her fervent tone that made every time sound like the first time, "Oh, Gerry! I love you so much!"

One of the things that Shirley had predicted for my summer was that I would fall in love, and once again, she had been correct. Terry and I were deeply in love and already talking about getting married, living on Maui, and raising a flock of kids. For our home, we had already picked out an isolated, idyllic peninsula overlooking the surf. I had not yet figured out how I was going to make money on Maui, but I was living here quite comfortably now, and being in love, financial futures did not matter.

A few minutes later, Terry's older sister, Ann, arrived and hollered, "Break it up, you two." Ann was the leader of the Andrews clan and a good friend. Moments later, Terry's other younger brother, John, arrived. John was not as fit as Mark, but he had been to Paliku many times, had tough feet from living barefoot on the beach, and he knew how to pace himself. Gently propping his pack against the hut he said, "Hey, Big Ger, you better head up the trail and rescue your boss. He's got bad blisters, and he's slowing fast. Besides, he has dinner in his pack. If you can't get Mack, at least bring his pack!"

I grabbed the first-aid kit and assured the clan, "I'll get both," then started up the trail.

I walked uphill for twenty minutes before I found Mack slumped on a rock with his feet sprawled out like lost legions. Nearby, his pack, which he had clearly tossed off in anger, sat nearly upside down against another rock. Used to being in control, Mack preempted me with, "Don't say a word!"

Of course I said a word or two, but I considered them carefully since Mack was my boss and Maui mentor. "You've got another mile to go, Mack. Maybe we should fix your blisters before we head on?"

"No, No, No! You can take my pack if you want, but it's my sacred duty to walk to this sacred hut for this sacred occasion, and my goddamned sacred feet are going to get me there!"

I had never seen Mack like this and didn't quite know what to say. After I got his pack on and readjusted it, I tried, "It really is beautiful there. You'll like it!"

"My feet are not gonna be beautiful, but I will sure like taking these boots off, I can guarantee you that! Now just march on!" As Mack limped toward the hut, I started singing the Hawaiian wedding song, but on the second stanza Mack hollered, "Oh shut up! This is not a luau!"

Safely ensconced in the hut, the six of us settled in for a joke-filled evening. Mack's blisters were open but not desperate, and after getting out of his boots and receiving some first aid, he felt much better. However, his boots sat in the corner reminding him of tomorrow's impending uphill hike. Eyeing his boots, Mack continually admonished the clan, which included me at this point, "Eat heavy things! I'm not hauling any food back up that hill!" Pouncing on Mack's pack, Mark, John, and I dug out all the heavy things, and we prepared a feast fit for Maui's family, which certainly included us at this point. After stuffing ourselves, there was still some heavy food left over, so when Mack wasn't looking, I moved his boots around a corner so that he couldn't see them anymore.

Terry and her siblings were Maui natives, and they lived next to the Kula

Sanatorium where their father was a doctor. The Andrews family had befriended me from the outset, and I felt like I was already part of this large family. I spent most of my nonmountaintop evenings in their gracious home, and they had fed me many dinners. Terry and I had fallen for each other instantly and had spent the rest of the summer getting to know each other. The Andrews had a rustic beach house nestled in the keeave trees behind one of the Kihei beaches, and outings to their place had replaced my searches for the perfect, deserted beach, as the Andrews' beach was always waiting for me. Having grown up on Maui, Terry and Ann knew more of Maui's secrets than any tourist ever would. After swearing me to secrecy, they took me to their special places, which always amazed me. I had not just fallen for Terry once, but a hundred times as she slowly showed me her paradise. Now, bonded at the family hip, our love was a Hawaiian wedding song just waiting to be strummed and sung. As our love and laughter filtered out into Paliku's night, Kuiki collected it and waited for Sun.

I got up early the next morning and prepared myself a bowl of oatmeal. When I sat down to eat it, Mack opened one eye, saw what I was doing, and hollered from his sleeping bag, "My God! You're eating oatmeal! That's light! Eat heavy things, man! Eat that canned ham—that's heavy!"

"Canned ham for breakfast? Nah, this oatmeal tastes good." As Mack opened his other eye, I assuaged him with, "Don't worry, boss. I'll carry the canned ham up the hill. We'll stow it in the observatory, and it will taste great later."

Later, striding toward the summit, I fell in behind Terry, which was one of my favorite places to be, since I could chat with my beloved and also look at her legs. Terry's strong legs always seemed to have another mile in them, and even on the longest hike, when asked how far it was to the destination, she always replied, "About a mile!" Today we were expansive as we chatted away about everything from Hawaiian myths to our unborn children's names.

The crater's rim now towered over us on two sides. To the south, the rim ran continuously from the Kaupo Gap up to Haleakala's summit. To the north, the Koolau Gap interrupted the rim over our heads, and this section of the rim culminated in 8,907-foot Hanakauhi, which I had admired all summer. Striding along with Terry on my sacred mission to carry Gabe's spirit from the sea to the summit, I had no idea that Hanakauhi would provide me with a future memorial climb.

Today we took the crater's northern trail, which took us by the Bottomless Pit, surrounded by a tourist-restraining fence. For the other's pleasure, Terry and I repeated the pit ritual. I started with, "Oh, neat! A *bottomless* pit. It must be so deep that no one can measure it!"

Terry continued, "Wait, let me check this sign over here! Oh, it says, 'Bottomless Pit—ninety-six feet deep.'"

"That's not bottomless! That's ninety-six feet!"

Terry finished the delivery with a flourish. "And so you see my mainland friends, thus it came to pass that Maui, a demigod of strength and courage, not only created the

A mature silversword
frames Hanakauhi in
Haleakala's crater.

islands, fixed the sky, and snared the sun, he also figured out the depth of the Bottomless Pit!"

Moving on, we took the Silversword Loop to admire this rare plant that only grows in the crater and in similar terrain on the Big Island. The plants sent a hundred gracefully curving spike arms skyward, each one seemingly dusted with silver. Each Silversword lives for many years then shoots a ten-foot stalk into the sky in its final, seeding glory. Being careful to look but not touch, we admired life's transient beauty in this otherwise lava-controlled place, then marched on.

At the Holua Cabin we stopped for a final break and refilled our water bottles from the cistern behind the cabin. The only source of water in the crater is from the three cabin's cisterns, which collect rainwater off their tin roofs. Mack and the clan had stashed the combi at the Halemauu trailhead, which at 8,000 feet instead of the summit's 10,000 feet provided a much easier escape from the crater. Our plan was that while I hiked all the way to the summit, Mack and the clan would hike to the combi, then drive to the summit to pick me up. Splitting into two groups, Terry and I took off at high speed while the others followed at Mack's pace.

With our legs pumping, Terry and I powered up the famous, and sometimes dreaded, set of switchbacks that climb from the Holua Cabin to the upper rim. It was easy to admire the crater as it slowly fell below and assumed its classic shape. Here on the rim wall, it was not hard to imagine the violence that Haleakala had used to create itself. I reasoned that if a mountain could make itself, then I should be able to climb it. Terry and I reached the trailhead together, and after grabbing a drink, I tossed my Kelty with its canned ham into the combi. Terry would wait here for the others and ride to the summit with them. She blew me a kiss and told me, "Hurry, lover! I want to kiss you for real on the summit at sunset!" This additional motivation sent me charging up the lava.

I did not follow the road from Halemauu but stayed on the lava near the rim, which was a shorter route with better views. Glancing at the lowering sun, I knew that I needed to hurry to make the summit by sunset, since I still had four miles to go. Putting my head down, I shifted into high gear. I was now on my own again in a rush for a Sacred Summit, and in a race with the setting sun. Glancing at the sun again and judging its rate of descent against my rate of ascent, I felt the sun winning, so I double clutched into overdrive and ran across the rough lava.

As I ran, I mused that I had a lot to be thankful for, but I was also carrying my lost friend's dreams, and at times like this, they pulled me to a different place. My friends were dying in the mountains at an accelerating rate—first Karl, then Prince, and now Gabe. Indeed, they had all made mistakes, but they did not deserve to die—especially not in the mountains, which were my growing fountain of joy. Confused, I pondered that it was not sufficient to just take greater care with my own climbs. My mountains were not only giving joy, but crushing it as well, and I knew that my growth needed to include another dimension.

My idyllic summer on Maui had given me a more relaxed perspective, but I knew that leaving the mountains completely was not a fulfilling solution. I had to stay true to my dreams but also carefully consider where they were leading me. Right now I was in love and full of plans for a family with Terry, and I did not feel a desperate desire to rush to the most dangerous heights. As Haleakala's rough lava raced by under my feet, I knew that I could stumble and cut myself, but that this mountain was not going to kill me. At this moment, Himalayan heights were not calling me, but I knew that I had to get off the spiral of ever harder and more dangerous climbs, for that could only lead to death or an abandonment of my mountains. Running even harder, I knew that for now, and in some measure forever, I had to embrace the gentle mountains as well as tougher ones. Haleakala had taught me that I needed not more intense love, but a broader base. Looking up from my meditation and seeing only the summit in the setting sun, I knew that Haleakala was just as good as Everest.

With Haleakala's familiar summit cinder cones in view, I heard the combi grind by on the road below. Terry would be on top waiting for me—I just had to get there. In the saddle below Red Hill, which is Haleakala's highest puu, I broke into a knees-up sprint as the sun puckered up to the Pacific. Digging deep, I dashed up to the summit just as the sun kissed the horizon. Breathless, Terry rushed up to kiss me while the sun embraced us and carried us across the threshold into our new home. Leaving me, Gabe's spirit flew ahead, set the sky on fire in a final salute, then moved on to climb clouds.

Haleakala was my eighth Transcendent Summit, and true to my new commitments, became one of my most visited summits over the years. For now, I was addicted to Maui's multiple rushes, and the Valley Isle was my new fulcrum. More importantly, my new Earth view would forever fly the colors from the House of the Sun.

chapter four

touching greatness

Talkeetna, Alaska

the Alaska Railroad conductor broke our reverie by barking sharply, "Talkeetna! You boys got three minutes to unload that stuff! We have a schedule to keep!" We jumped to the task as if a grizzly bear were chasing us, rolled open the boxcar door, and propelled our gear out into the rain. As fast as our four pairs of hands shoveled the gear out the door, a single pair of hands caught and stacked it outside the train. Counting as we shoveled, I hollered to my teammates, " ... 19, 20, 21. All pieces accounted for! Everybody out!" We hopped into the mud, and the train rumbled off immediately.

The single pair of hands that had collected our gear belonged to Don Sheldon. We had corresponded with Don and were eager to meet this famous Alaskan bush pilot, who was already a living legend. Even in 1963 the stories about Sheldon's heroic mountain flying feats preceded him. He was a short man with black hair, a perpetual twinkle in his eye, and an Eskimo appearance, especially when he wore his trademark parka with the fur ruff on its hood. We took a deep breath, but Sheldon was way ahead of us, greeting us with, "Yowsah! You're the track team from Colorado! You betcha!"

Overly eager, I blurted out, "When can we fly in? This weather doesn't look so good!"

Chuckling, Sheldon replied, "Patience, lad! The McGowan party waited ten days for good flying weather." While we groaned about this bad news, Sheldon backed his battered old truck up to our pile of gear, dropped the tailgate, and said, "Use this rig and run your stuff over to my hangar. That's where you'll be staying. Don't worry, men. The weather has gone ape, but this just looks like a three-day blow. I gotta go to Anchorage, you bet." Three minutes later, Sheldon's plane roared overhead.

We hustled over to Sheldon's red-roofed hangar just as the June rain doubled in intensity. It drummed on the hangar's tin roof as if God had released a bag of celestial marbles. Dick looked at our soggy, muddy clothing and shouted over the din, "Ha! We've been here five minutes, and we already need a shower and a laundry."

Mike replied, "Hey buddy, in Colorado, we don't do those things."

Geoff added, "You betcha, oh clean one!"

Trying to slow my companions down a little, I summarized with, "Welcome to Talkeetna, lads!"

Smirking, Dick regained his composure, grabbed his raincoat, and said, "OK, you Colorado hotshots. I'm from Seattle where it rains all the time. We never break stride for a little rain, so I'm going out to explore the town. Would you thinclads care to join me? I know Gerry will." We rose as one and marched into the rain.

We quickly explored tiny Talkeetna, which is an Athabascan Indian name meaning, "Where the rivers meet." Main Street ran for three long blocks from the train tracks to the Susitna River. The town runway went from the Susitna River, past Sheldon's hangar, across Main Street, and right up to the Fairview Inn, which held a soggy, limp wind sock. Wet enough, we returned to the hangar and examined Sheldon's yellow two-person Super Cub with its retractable skis. We would fly into the mountain in this plane.

External exploration over, we paced the hangar's sagging plank floor and, near one of Sheldon's workbenches, found a suitable bar for doing chin-ups. Naturally, we immediately had a contest. Mike, as fit and crazed as ever, won with twenty. I got second with sixteen, Dick managed fourteen, and Geoff twelve. Nothing had changed—I couldn't even beat Mike in a chin-up contest! As the rain continued to drum on the roof, I fell into a reverie about how the four of us had arrived in Talkeetna together to climb Denali.

Synergy

After graduating from Boulder High in 1961, I spent my freshman year at the University of Colorado. Then, eager to spread my wings, I transferred to the University of Washington in Seattle, where I met Dick Springgate and moved into Wilburs, which was a three-story house that ten climbers shared. Dick and I crammed into the smallest room in the house, a tiny basement hovel. My reward for the cramped quarters was that my room and board cost a mere $50 per month.

Dick had grown up in Seattle, and he quickly introduced me to climbing in the Cascades. When the weekend came, we always went climbing—rain or shine. With this tactic, we didn't have to understand the vagaries of the storm fronts that continually battered the Pacific Northwest. Usually it rained, but we still managed to make our summit most of the time.

Dick and I had one surprising thing in common for college roommates. We both liked grand opera. We pooled our money, bought an FM radio, and got a schedule from the Seattle classical station. Soon the passionate strains of *Carmen*,

Rigoletto, *La Traviata*, and *Madam Butterfly* filtered through our wet climbing gear and smelly socks. Our housemates upstairs thumped on the floor in time when we started singing along, and we all laughed when great groups of fat singers required twenty minutes to observe that the sun had risen. We also had the plots down pat. Act one: profess undying love. Act two: many complications. Act three: everybody dies. On Sundays we went climbing, and the steep, snowy slopes refocused my lust for the mountains.

When I went back to Colorado for Christmas in 1962, Geoff and I had an overdue Summit Club meeting. Once we were secure in our sacred basement office, Geoff was immediately serious. "Bro, I've gotten wind of something."

"Om belay. What?"

"Dave is going to climb McKinley next summer."

My neck hairs immediately tingled. "You mean Roberts, don't you?"

"Yeah. He and some Harvard hotshots are going to try some fancy new route on the north side."

I absorbed this news for a second, then looked straight at Geoff. "Well, we have to beat him up there."

Going right for it by offering a critical thumb up, thumb down choice, Geoff asked, "It's time the Summit Club did a big one, right? Climb zees mountain?"

Surrounded by our fading rope and old pitons, I looked at Geoff again then sealed the pact by going thumb up and saying, "What would Prince have us do? Climb zees mountain!" Then the Summit Club fell silent for a long minute. Finally I said, "What do we know about McKinley?"

Geoff continued, "Not much, but I have done some initial checking. The mountain is huge, and it's way up north in Alaska."

Remembering my Uncle Laurie mentioning that Alaskan mountains are white all summer, I exclaimed, "Alaska! How high is McKinley?"

"Over 20,000—20,320 feet to be exact. By all accounts, it's a real bear."

Reaching into my memory banks, I said, "Hmmm. I did see a slide show on McKinley years ago—back in 1953, I think. They had a big team and spent weeks on the mountain, but they made it."

Tapping his foot, Geoff asked, "Were they on the north or west side?"

"They were on the north side. I remember that the presenter had a shot of the mountain from the tundra. He got the audience all revved up looking at the mountain, then he said, 'But this wasn't the mountain!' Then, he traced his finger slowly up the screen, pointed to a patch of glacier peeking through the clouds, and said, 'The mountain was up here!' Everybody, including me, gasped. It was a great moment."

"Yeah, the mountain is huge. The Indians didn't call it Denali, or 'the Great One,' for nothing."

Now tapping my foot, I asked, "What about routes? Where is the standard route?"

Geoff had indeed done some checking. "The standard route is on the west side.

It's called the West Buttress. It's not the first ascent route, but it's what people are doing now that a pilot can land you on the glacier. More than a dozen parties have made it up that way."

Noticing that one of Prince's pitons was still on our wall, I asked, "And Roberts is going to be hanging by his toes on the north side?"

"Yeah. It's called the Wickersham Wall. It's really huge, and it's never been climbed."

Clapping my hands, I said, "Great! That will slow them down for sure. How much is their sham wall going to cost them?"

Rubbing his fingers together in the air, Geoff replied, "A lot. Apparently, there are some rich turkeys from back east putting this trip together. Roberts is sailing on their coattails."

Trying to be serious, I continued, "We can't get sucked into trying to outspend them, so we'll just outclimb them. Well, that's it then. We zip up the standard route and beat Roberts to the summit. With any luck, we won't see Dave up there—we'll just leave a Summit Club flag for him to discover!"

Still serious, Geoff continued, "Bro, we'll need more than the two of us for this one."

After staring at our old pitons for a brief moment, we suddenly looked at each other and cried in unison, "McCoy!"

With Mike, our high-school track chum, on board, I returned to Seattle, where I had no trouble recruiting Springgate, and we quickly had a team of four. We did research on the mountain, pooled our meager resources, bought used equipment, and called in some favors until our preparations became a frenzied fervor. When June finally arrived, Geoff and Mike drove Mike's battered station wagon from Boulder to Anchorage, while Dick and I flew from Seattle.

Sheldon's Wager with the Wind

The roar of Sheldon's plane returning abruptly broke my reverie. We chased after him, but Sheldon zipped across the runway, disappearing before we could reach him. Chuckling, we returned to our "Talkeetna Hilton," and plotted new strategies for catching up with Sheldon.

It rained for the next three days, but nevertheless, Sheldon was never in sight for more than ten minutes, so we thought of our questions before he reappeared. When he walked into the hangar, we fell in step and fired away. He was always going somewhere and seemed to be in the air more than he was on the ground. We listened to his plane roar off at 3:00 A.M., come back at 7:00 A.M. and blast off again at 8:00 A.M. In his brief appearances, he said things like, "Gotta go to Anchorage … Gotta run these supplies up the river … Gotta get those fishermen outta camp … You bet!"

We attached homemade traction plates to our wooden snowshoes with Sheldon's tools. Our system consisted of a metal plate bolted under the snowshoe's wooden cross member, which was just in front of the foot. We hoped the plate would give us

Dick Springgate

Mike McCoy

Geoff Wheeler

Gerry Roach

better traction on steep slopes. When Sheldon saw our system, he exclaimed, "Skookum! Grouzers! Why didn't I think of that? You can climb straight up the hill with those Grouzers. You betcha!"

Sheldon's stories of daring, skill, and bravery were often told, but Sheldon never told his own tales. He was too modest and always off making another story. In February 1954 Sheldon flew his Super Cub through heavy cloud and located the wreckage of an Air Force C-47 that had crashed sixty miles north of Talkeetna. He dropped a note to three staggering survivors directing them to an open meadow, then landed in oncoming darkness and a rising storm. After spending the night with the survivors, he evacuated them one by one the next day.

In 1958 he again flew through heavy cloud on Mount Iliamna, southwest of Anchorage, looking for a lost C-54 transport plane. The plane carried passengers, Christmas packages, and payroll for the troops at Shemya Air Force Base. As he approached the active volcano, the wind was "rippin' and tearin'," and his Super Cub "jumped like a scared cat." He played his hunches correctly in the swirling clouds and volcanic sulfur fumes and finally found the wreckage near the summit. This time, there were no survivors. Because of the location, the military did not try to recover the bodies. Six years later, it was Sheldon who stopped a scavenging treasure hunter from plundering the wreckage.

Sheldon took on another daring rescue in 1960—this one was on Denali. John Day, Pete Schoening, and Jim and Lou Whittaker completed a speedy climb of the mountain, but they took a horrendous fall while descending from Denali Pass. They slid at high speed down a long, steep snow slope before stopping at 17,000 feet. The fall seriously injured Day, and the others were in various states of disrepair. Another team from Anchorage had a seriously ill member at 16,400 feet, a woman named Helga Bading. The Anchorage party did what it could for the Day party, but the two stricken teams needed outside help.

Sheldon flew over the accident site and, horrified, saw the incinerated wreckage of a Cessna 180. A pilot from Anchorage had crashed in his attempt to aid the climbers. Both the pilot and his passenger were dead. Sheldon dropped emergency supplies to the Day party then returned to Talkeetna. Several rescue attempts by army helicopters failed, and the army grounded their choppers. Sheldon ferried a large rescue team to the Kahiltna Glacier, but the injured climbers were way above them on the upper mountain. John Day was immobile, and Helga Bading's condition worsened. Time was running out.

Via radio, Sheldon told the Anchorage party that if they could get Helga down to 14,200 feet, he would attempt to land there, even though no one had ever landed this high on Denali. While the climbers struggled down, Sheldon made multiple passes over a tiny patch of smooth snow trying to decide if it was big enough for a landing. It was minimal, but enough, so Sheldon made the first landing high on Denali and snatched Helga from the mountain.

Immediately after landing in Talkeetna, Sheldon refueled his plane and returned to the mountain. This time he flew cover for a plucky helicopter pilot named Link Luckett. Luckett's tiny chopper had a 16,000-foot ceiling, and John Day was at 17,200 feet. So, Luckett threw out everything nonessential, put in minimal fuel, started the chopper, then threw the battery out to save every possible ounce. Luckett and Sheldon flew up to rescue Day. Luckett made three landings at 17,200 feet and relayed the injured climbers down to Sheldon's landing spot at 14,200. Sheldon flew them out from there. Then, without a break, Sheldon flew out the rescuers. He made eighteen landings in this unbelievable marathon. Such stories had made Sheldon a living legend.

We knew all about the Day-Bading saga after reading a *Life* magazine article, which was complete with many gory pictures. We didn't talk about it much, but it struck terror into our hearts. On May 1, 1963, just a month before our departure for Denali, Jim Whittaker had become the first American to climb Mount Everest. The man who had carried the stars and stripes to the roof of the world had not been able to complete an ascent and descent of Denali under his own power three years earlier. We were trying to climb Denali, not Everest, and this realization only deepened our terror. We resolved to be very careful on the slope below Denali Pass where the Day party had fallen.

We knew Sheldon would get us to the mountain when the weather cleared, but when would that happen? We passed the time by practicing our crevasse rescue drill on Sheldon's runway. We roped up, walked down the runway, then at random, someone screamed, "Falling! Arggh!" The "faller" pulled crazily on the rope in some unexpected direction, while the other three fell down and controlled the craziness. Once the faller was tethered, the last person zipped forward, set an ice ax on the imaginary crevasse edge, attached a small rope-gripping prussik knot to the faller's rope, and pulled back with a two-to-one mechanical advantage. With one more maneuver, we had a three-to-one advantage and sedately pulled our kicking and screaming victim across the runway. We perfected our three-to-one drill so it took less than thirty seconds, all the while providing entertainment for the locals.

After our fourth day of waiting, a patch of blue showed through the clouds. We immediately tracked Sheldon down, pointed excitedly to the patch of blue, and asked him if he was ready to go. Without breaking stride, he replied, "Nope! That's just the eye of the storm comin' this way! Big wind blow'n up there now. Tear the wings right off the Cub!" Then, zoom, he was off to fly a fisherman over the river.

When the weather continued to improve, we soared into feverish excitement; this was not a time for analysis, since the mountain consumed all our energy. We would fly in one at a time in Sheldon's two-seat Super Cub, so we drew straws to determine our order. It ended up Geoff, me, Mike, then Dick. We felt sure tonight would be the night. Dozing fitfully at 3:00 A.M., I heard Sheldon's plane landing. Convinced that he was coming to get us, I lurched up from my sleeping bag and sprinted outside the hangar, while my stomach tied a bowline. Seeing the taxiing plane pushed me over my excitement limit, so I quickly changed course, sprinted around the side of the hangar, and threw up! While I cleaned myself up, the others fell in line with Sheldon, but all he said was, "Nope, gotta let the weather sober up over there. Maybe later today."

I just muttered, "Oh, blast," since I had been sick for nothing.

Finally, on our fifth day, Sheldon surprised us by striding up and saying, "Yowsah! Time to huckledebuck on up there! You bet!" Then he barked his orders, "Lookee! Divide your gear up into four equal piles. Make sure that each man has his own sleeping bag, snowshoes, and survival gear. Make sure that the first man has a tent, stove, food, and fuel in case he ends up on the glacier alone. Hike down the runway and cut fifty spruce boughs three to four feet long. Roll the hangar door back, but don't touch the plane yet. I don't know what to do with your sled. I'll be back in fifteen minutes!" This really was it, and we flew into frenzied activity. We had plenty to do now, and I controlled my nervous stomach.

Sheldon returned on cue and said, "Help me roll the Cub out and let's get her ready." While Dick cut spruce branches, Mike and I helped Sheldon gas the Cub. Sheldon carefully filtered the gas through a chamois to eliminate any water, then he washed the Cub's Plexiglas windshield. Geoff put on his mountain clothing and double boots. He looked strangely out of place on the tarmac, but in one hour he would be on the Kahiltna Glacier at 7,000 feet. Suddenly, we had to adopt a mountain mentality. Hat at the ready? Check. Sunglasses? Check. Camera? Check.

Sheldon carefully supervised the loading of the Cub. He didn't want the plane to get tail heavy, so he stuck a few light items in the back along with his own emergency kit. Geoff placed his pack on the floor where the passenger seat would have been if it were there, crawled in, and sat on his pack, then we carefully stashed gear around him. We placed a gallon of gas upright in a good spot, two five-gallon food cans between Geoff's feet, and another on his lap. At the last moment, we passed in a great wad of spruce branches. Sheldon would drop these one at a time over the landing site so he could see the glacier's surface better. Sheldon tied Geoff's long trail snowshoes to the wing strut—his own were already there.

Finally, Sheldon slipped into the front seat, prepared to pull the two-piece door shut, and said, "I'll be back in about two hours. Make sure the second man is ready to go. Blast off, you bet!" He fired the engine, watched his gauges come to life, spoke a few words into his radio, and taxied onto the runway. We ran along giving thumbs up and victory signs, but we had packed Geoff in so tight that he couldn't wave back. The overloaded Cub roared down the runway, and we wondered if it would lift off before crashing into the river. Pulling up in plenty of time, the Cub made a slow, climbing turn over the river, then headed north toward the mountain. We watched until the tiny plane slipped from our view and its sound faded into the Alaskan wilderness.

The next two hours seemed like an eternity. I was next! I put on my boots and mountain clothes, then paced around my pile of gear, sweating. If Sheldon came back alone, then Geoff was on the glacier and the flight had been a success. If Geoff was still in the plane, Sheldon had scrubbed the flight. What if Sheldon didn't come back at all? This was unthinkable, since Sheldon always won his wager with the wind! My stomach started acting up again, but this time Mike paced with me.

As soon as I heard the Cub returning, my mouth went dry. Sheldon feathered up to the hangar and hopped out. The plane was empty, and water still dripped from the skis. He had done it! Sheldon explained, "No sweat. It's a beautiful day up there! I did have a little trouble seeing the glacier's surface though. We'll take some more spruce branches on the second flight. I'll be back in ten minutes!"

After carefully folding myself into the tiny airplane and piling extra gear around me, my stomach acted up again. I groaned, "Oh no, not again! Not in the plane!"

Mike saved me in my moment of need. He ran up with starting line fever, thrust a bottle of Pepto-Bismol into my hand, and hollered, "Here, take this! I know just how you feel, buddy! You gotta hold it in, Gerry!" I chugged some of the pink liquid, burped badly, and just barely managed to retain my stomach's contents.

Welcome to the Kahiltna!

Sheldon strapped our sled to the wing strut, mumbling, "I don't like the looks of this contraption. Betcha it'll screw up the Cub's lift."

I insisted, "We need the sled, Don! After this five-day storm, we've gotta make up for lost time, and we need the sled to do that."

Finally, with a wad of spruce branches in my face, we accelerated down the runway with Sheldon bellowing over the engine's roar, "Blast off!" I kept the Pepto-Bismol handy.

We lifted off, turned over the Susitna, and headed for the mountain. I couldn't converse with Sheldon over the engine's noise, so I just sniffed the spruce branches and marveled at the Alaskan scenery. Below, a huge carpet of spruce trees reflected a thousand subtle shades as streams meandered through numerous small lakes. I thought about all the mosquitoes that must be down there.

We passed wooded lowlands, flew over the Peters Hills, and left the last green behind as we flew into the foothills of the Alaska Range. I would not see green plants again until I left the mountain. Sheldon circled once to gain elevation, then flew toward a narrow mountain cirque. I had assumed that we would fly up the Kahiltna Glacier from its snout and wondered where Sheldon was going. Straining for a view, I pushed the spruce branches aside. There was a pass ahead of us, but it was much higher than we were. Suddenly, Sheldon turned the Cub and headed west, away from the cirque. Sheldon summed it up with, "That pass is a one-shot deal. No second chance, no nuthin!" Then he pointed accusingly at our sled on the strut and hollered, "That's eatin' my lift. Gotta go the long way."

Suddenly the mountains of Little Switzerland surrounded us. These rugged peaks are not high by Denali standards, but my eyes still bugged out at all the ridges and faces. My mind couldn't process all the routes that we flew quickly past, but the sensory overload was grand.

Then we were over the Kahiltna Glacier, a prodigious river of ice that provides access to Denali through the lower peaks. Sheldon started pumping hard on a handle, and I realized he was lowering the skis. We looked out to verify that the skis were both down and locked in position. As we slowly gained altitude, the glacier rose up to meet us. Ahead, I saw a large icefall full of crevasses. We were too low to clear it, and Sheldon circled to gain elevation. At first I worried that he wouldn't be able to turn the plane around in the valley, but this turned out to be a silly fear, since the glacier is three miles wide and Sheldon turned the tiny Cub in a few hundred yards. He aimed straight at the mountain wall enjoying the scenery, then turned for another view.

After two complete circles, we still didn't have enough altitude to clear the icefall. As Sheldon banked for a third circle, he turned to me, pointed hard at the sled on the wing strut, and thundered, "She won't climb!" I felt guilty for insisting on the stupid sled, but said nothing.

After four circles, we made it up over the icefall. The snow looked whiter up here, and the peaks near the glacier no longer looked like foothills, but huge mountains. Straining, I could see Mount Foraker and Mount Hunter standing guard on opposite sides of the glacier. These two peaks are the next highest peaks in the Alaska Range after Denali. I couldn't see their summits from the Cub's cramped interior, but knew that there would be plenty of time for ogling the view later. I also knew that the landing site was just south of the national park boundary on the Kahiltna's southeast fork below Mount Hunter. We were almost there!

Turning, the Cub nosed up the Southeast Fork, and suddenly I saw Geoff running on the snow below us. He already had a tent pitched, and I saw ski tracks from the Cub's first landing. We barely saw Geoff's spruce branches on the snow, so Sheldon swooped low over the landing site several times eyeing it carefully. When we came close to the glacier's surface, the Cub seemed to be going very fast.

Sheldon pulled up and gave me our prearranged signal to prepare the spruce branches for pitching. Sheldon lined up for a pass over the runway and opened the door. An icy blast hit me like a piton hammer, so I gripped the branches tightly to keep them from ripping out of my hands. When Sheldon's hand dropped, I heard him holler, "Bombs away!" I popped the branches out one or two at a time as fast as I could. He raised his hand to wave me off, and I stopped throwing. After we repeated the process, we saw a neat line of dark spots along the "runway."

Our awkward sled on the strut still worried Sheldon, so we prepared to drop several five-gallon food cans to lighten the aircraft. Our timing on these drops was critical, since this was our food. If I mistimed the drop, the food could land in a crevasse, far from camp, or worse, hit the tent or even Geoff. Also, I had to propel each twenty-pound can cleanly downward so that it would not hit the plane's tail. We had attached long colorful streamers to our cans so we could find them after they fell into the deep snow. However, at launch time, the streamers had to be tidy so they wouldn't catch on anything in the plane.

This was not a time to enjoy the view, and as Sheldon banked hard I struggled to get the first can ready. Sheldon lined up on the drop zone then raised his hand in the ready position. Ignoring the wind, I clamped the streamer on the can and held it out the open door. I grimly hung on until I heard Sheldon bellowing in a huge voice, "Reaaadyyy ... Drop!" I pushed the can down clean and hard. Where it fell I knew not, but my job was to get them out clean, since Sheldon did the aiming. I had four food cans, so we repeated the process three more times. They were all clean drops. When Sheldon banked hard after each drop, I saw Geoff standing near the tent. We made one more pass, and I pitched out three bundles of wands that we would use later for marking our trail. The plane was now 100 pounds lighter. This was a significant savings since the Cub's empty weight was only 1,000 pounds.

Finally Sheldon lined up for the landing. He kept the engine rpm's high, and the Cub seemed impossibly fast as we approached the sloping glacier. He feathered the engine slightly then put the nose up until I could no longer see the glacier ahead. Sheldon couldn't see it either, so he looked out the side window and watched the snow come up to meet the skis. The skis touched the snow with a metallic hiss, and we slid up the glacier. Sheldon revved the engine, kicked hard on the left rudder, and maneuvered the Cub to a stop in a sideways position in preparation for takeoff. He hit the master switch, shut down the engine, and popped open the door. My Pepto-Bismol immediately fell out onto the snow, while Geoff sprinted up and hollered, "Welcome to the Kahiltna!"

I staggered out on shaky legs and mustered my best war cry. "Summit Club climb zees mountain!"

By the time Mike and Dick landed, Geoff and I had a better runway stomped out and a decent camp pitched. Without the sled, Sheldon had no trouble with the other landings, and fourteen hours after Geoff had blasted off from Talkeetna, we were all on the glacier. As Sheldon prepared to leave for the last time, he looked around at the mountains, the weather, the sky, then offered us his advice for climbing Denali. With his hand on the Cub's door, he said, "When the weather clobbers up, dig in and hunker down! When she clears up, go like a jackrabbit!"

Sheldon pulled into the Cub, strapped himself in, and fired the engine. While we pushed on the wing struts to get him going, he flapped the rudder and ailerons like crazy to pop the tail wheel out of the snow. As he started his takeoff run, we ran along through the deep snow pushing as long as we could, then, at the last moment, we jumped to the side so the tail wouldn't hit us. The track team gave Sheldon his best push ever! Sheldon's cub roared down the glacier in a prodigious cloud of blowing snow, lifted off, banked left, and quickly disappeared. The engine's sound echoed off the mountain walls for another minute, then it was very still. The only sound was our breathing as we lay panting on the snow. We were finally here, and we were alone. Suddenly, our pile of used equipment looked very small.

An imposing mountain vista surrounded us, and as we took stock of our position, we realized that none of us had ever been in such a beautiful place. We were at 7,300 feet, and Mount Hunter's 14,570-foot summit was only two miles away. The original Indian name for Hunter is Begguya, meaning "Denali's child." Hunter's north face rose abruptly from the Kahiltna's Southeast Fork in a sweep of rock, snow, and ice whose size we could not comprehend. The face rose well over a vertical mile at an average angle of forty-eight degrees. As we stared up in awe, a huge avalanche swept down the face then roared onto the upper Southeast Fork. We were safe at the landing site, but an instinctive fear tugged at us. If this giant was the child, what would Denali look like?

The main Kahiltna Glacier was a mile away down the Southeast Fork, and we gawked across the great river of ice. What a view! Mount Foraker soared above the far side of the Kahiltna, rising from 6,700 feet to 17,400 feet, a difference of more than two vertical miles. Foraker's summit was almost eight miles away, but the peak seemed impossibly close, huge, and beautiful. Staring, I knew that Foraker was the most beautiful mountain that I had ever seen. The original Indian name for Foraker

I immediately rejected all thoughts of ever climbing Hunter.

Photo by Dick Springgate

is Sultana, meaning "Denali's queen." For our stay in this white wilderness, Foraker was my fairy queen, and I gazed at her, trying to understand.

While Hunter inspired neck-bending awe and fear, Foraker transmitted beauty, power, and a regal grace. I immediately rejected all thoughts of ever climbing Hunter. However, even in '63, I found myself eyeing Foraker looking for routes. Even without having seen the mountain, Denali's greatness started to touch me. I felt that this special place was a womb between mother and child—a place of fertility and regeneration. Looking around, I knew that in this physically sterile land, the gift of life is given to the spirit of those who come here.

However, we had not come here to climb Hunter or Foraker. Where was Denali, the Great One? We looked toward Denali, but lingering clouds covered the intervening ridges, and we could not see him. Later that evening, the temperature plummeted, the clouds dissipated, and Denali appeared. Subtle shades shimmered across the gulf between the aloof summit and us as we stared in silence. We quickly grasped that Denali was farther, colder, higher, and larger than either Hunter or Foraker, and that Denali would not so easily reveal his secret splendors.

Denali's summit was more than eight air miles from where we stood, but air miles only have meaning for pilots in this serrated vastness. We were now on foot, and our climbing route would require seventeen horizontal miles, almost three vertical miles, and all our resources. My Pepto-Bismol froze during the first night, but it didn't matter, since I would not need it again now that I was in the mountains.

Ready, Shoot, Aim

June 20 dawned clear, and our first day on the mountain began with bravado. In a tour de force, we planned on using the sled and moving all our supplies ten miles up to Kahiltna Pass at the head of the Kahiltna Glacier. When Dick and I had discussed our plan with the veteran Dick McGowan in Seattle, he politely pointed out that we were nuts. He said, "You don't understand the distances up there. It's not like going for a run around Green Lake. You just can't make the same time that you make in Colorado or even in the Cascades. You better plan on a camp halfway to the pass and on doing at least one relay."

I stammered in disbelief, "But that would require four days to get to the pass!"

McGowan replied, "That's right."

We were young and out to prove McGowan wrong. We knew the key was to take just what we would need but no more. We had twenty-eight days of food in fourteen five-gallon cans. Since our college budgets didn't allow us the luxury of flying out with Sheldon, we cached four food cans and some fuel at the landing strip for our planned walk-out to Talkeetna. Then we loaded up huge packs and put everything else on the sled. Our packs weighed 80 pounds apiece, and the sled had 300 pounds in it. There was one food can left over. Dick picked it up and strapped it to his pack with much macho blustering. He baited us with, "You Colorado boys are wimps! The weather is always good there, so you never have to carry anything. In the Cascades, where the weather is tough, we heroes carry *big* packs!"

Dick's pack was now more than 100 pounds, and I said, "I believe in applauding heroes at the end of the show, not the beginning, so I'll talk to you tonight!" We put on our snowshoes, roped up, and pushed off. The first mile was glorious, since we went downhill to reach the Kahiltna at 6,800 feet. Because of the crevasse danger, we marched along in single file, spreading out at even intervals along our special 200-foot rope. Our sled coasted along in our tracks with almost no effort on our part as the entire expedition cruised along in the sun. This is what we had dreamed about. We were doing it!

Our bubble burst when we got to the Kahiltna, started uphill, and the sled bogged down in the deep snow. We pushed, we pulled, we tried several different

However, I eyed
Foraker, looking
for routes.

Photo by Dick Springgate

rope riggings, we just about blew our guts out, but we could not get the 300-pound
sled to go uphill. We had no choice but to leave it behind, and we planned to
return for it the next day. We marked it carefully with some of our four-foot wands.
"Well," I reasoned, "at least we can still make the pass in two days."

Free of the sled, we took off up the glacier with renewed vigor and soon had
our second surprise. Distances were indeed deceptive here. Since there were no
trees or man-made objects to give scale, the smooth glacier easily fooled our eyes,
and we marched as if on a treadmill. I led, bashing down the deep snow with powerful strides, while the others packed it down even more. We left a trough two feet
deep behind us. After two hours, we stopped, consulted the map and learned that
we had only covered a little over a mile. Used to going a mile in four and a half
minutes, Mike cried, "A half-mile per hour! After applying a McGowan factor, I still
figured we could make one mile per hour with the sled. Damn!"

I noticed Dick was not using the waistbelt on his frame pack to transfer weight
from shoulders to hips. When I asked him why he wasn't using it, he just hollered,
"Belts are for wimps!"

I put in a wand every rope length to guide us back along the trail in a whiteout. When the last man on the rope got to the wand, he sang out, "Wand!" So not
only did I have to break trail, I also had to fuss with the wands. I quivered them in
my pack and became adept at fishing out a new bunch without breaking stride. I
carried my ice ax in my right hand and the wands in my left hand. The paint on
the bamboo tomato stakes left my hands a bright green. As chief wandman, my
load got steadily lighter, and I learned to place the fattest wands first to maximize

the decline. It was small compensation for breaking trail, but it occupied my mind on the long march. As I led on through the deep snow, I became completely absorbed in the effort of leading and the task of going in a straight line. At first I had a hard time keeping the march straight, and my tracks looked like a drunk's. With a little practice, my tracks sobered up, and I was able to go for a half mile before looking back to admire my row of wands in a perfect line.

Occasionally the snow settled for hundreds of feet around us with a sickening thump. This is a sign of weak layers in the snowpack, but in the thump instant, we were never sure if we were about to plunge into a crevasse. The map indicated the worst crevasse patterns, and we plotted a course up the glacier designed to miss them.

In three more hours, we had only covered another two miles, and Dick prevented any discussion about what we should do by loudly proclaiming, "I can't take another step. We've gotta camp here!" I couldn't resist hollering, "Hey, hero! We're still a mile short of where we want to be! You should have used the wimp belt, you wimp!" The good-natured banter helped as we pitched camp at 7,400 feet. Our net altitude gain for the day was only a hundred feet, and we were less than halfway to the pass. Clouds brewed up late in the day denying us a view of Denali.

The next morning Dick declared himself sick, probably from his stupid overexertion. The good news was that Geoff, Mike, and I blasted down the trail to our sled in one hour. The bad news was that we had to move 300 pounds with only three of us instead of four. We put half the sledload into our packs and rigged the sled so that two people pulled and one pushed. I got stuck with the push end, which turned out to be a raw deal, as I ended up doing more than a third of the work. Nevertheless, we set upon the project like the well-oiled track team that we used to be, and the sled soon scooted up the glacier with much shouting, sweating, and swearing. In spite of a whiteout and fresh snowfall, we made a nonstop run and roared into camp frothing. Our rapid round-trip impressed Dick, and he made no further Colorado-wimp jokes. Nevertheless, we would leave the sled here, since it had not helped us.

The morning hours of June 22 were gloriously clear, and we had our first views of Denali since leaving the Southeast Fork. The Great One rose behind the Kahiltna Peaks and still seemed impossibly high. The Indians had named it well, and the mountain only needed one adjective: great. The sound of Sheldon's Cub buzzing up the glacier interrupted our solitude. He wagged his wings at us, but we had no way to talk to him. Landings are not permitted inside the park except in emergencies, and we assumed that something was wrong with either the McGowan or Canadian parties that were ahead of us on the route. We hoped it was not serious.

Seeing Sheldon's flight intensified our eagerness to reach the pass and find out what was going on, but when we reached 8,500 feet, it socked in again and snowed hard. Nonetheless we kept going using compass readings to find our route. Geoff led while I worked the compass, and I quickly discovered that without correction, Geoff veered to the left while leading into the whiteout. He walked forward in a great white globe like a blind man, while the rest of us could see Geoff, the rope, and the tracks, which made it easier for us to judge a straight line. I compared the compass bearing with the track's line and kept correcting Geoff. I had to hold the compass in my hand and take readings every few steps to keep us on course.

Foraker floating in the stark, snowy loneliness.

Photo by Dick Springgate

The leader's missteps seemed pitiful, but if anybody complained, he got to lead and see for himself what it was like to be on the sharp end of the rope. Since you can plunge into a crevasse with any step, you strain looking for clues but find none. After a while your equilibrium goes, you adopt a stumbling step, and circle one way or the other. People really do go in circles when lost.

My altimeter nailed down the third dimension, and I took readings every fifteen minutes. When we reached 9,000 feet, it started to blow and snow in earnest, so Mike and I got the map out of his pack. We had protected our maps with plastic for just such an event. We turned our backs to the wind to read the maps and quickly saw that we had only covered three of the remaining five miles to the pass. There was no way we could push another two miles into this maelstrom. We remembered Sheldon's advice: "Storm? Hunker down! Clear? Go like a jackrabbit!" We quickly made a cache for our loads then taped some four-foot wands together to make a seven-foot wand. We pushed the seven-footer into the snow, leaving four feet exposed. We had to find this cache later or our climb would be crippled. Relying on the wands that we had placed on the way up, we turned and did a snowshoe shuffle-trot back to camp.

The next day it stormed hard, and we hunkered down. We welcomed the rest after our exertions of the last three days and enjoyed eating, reading, and cracking jokes. We lived in an appropriately named McKinley tent, which had a six-by-eight-foot floor and a single center pole. Since we were college students used to living in basement hovels, the cramped tent did not bother us.

In the late evening, it cleared. I stood up in the tent, peeked out the tiny vent at eye level, and saw a surrealistic scene. Storm cloud remnants swirled around nearby peaks creating backlit halos as Denali, floating behind, was swathed in a deep-blue radiance. I watched for several minutes as the subtle shades shifted. The storm was over. Suddenly, I had a deep desire to get going. Not tomorrow, but *now*. The others were already sacked out, but I reasoned that, if they understood the beauty outside, they would jump up and we could make the pass in a few hours. This was speech time. "Ahem," I began simply as I peered out for inspiration. "You guys gotta see this! I can see all the way up the glacier. I can also see Kahiltna Dome and Mount Crosson, and beyond Crosson, beautiful alpenglow is bathing Foraker. I can see the Kahiltna Peaks with cotton-candy clouds on them, and beyond that I can see Denali. The Great One is clear and beautiful in its stark, snowy loneliness. In short, gentlemen, the storm is over. If we start now, we can be at the pass in a few hours!" Finally I paused for dramatic effect. When I received no response, I looked back into the tent. Gentle snoring wafted up to greet me—I had only succeeded in lulling them to sleep with my speech. Chagrined, I tried a more direct approach. "Hey, heroes! We've gotta get going *now*. It's clear out!"

Springgate stirred and mumbled, "Shut up, Roach! We're trying to sleep. We'll get going in the morning!" He cinched up the drawstring on his sleeping bag hood and rolled over. As the snoring increased, I peered back out at the fading glory, felt a lump in my throat, and wondered if I was the only one up here who wanted to climb this mountain. Up to this point, our fun-filled adventure had been grand, and I had indeed come a long way from my Great Wall of Paris. However this was *the* Great One, and I knew that our real test was much higher, on the upper mountain. I was eager to be there, but also concerned, even terrified, at what we might find. Denali had already demonstrated great power, and it was clear that the mountain could snuff us out in a second, especially if we offered it momentary negligence. And yet powerful urges drove me upward toward the unknown heights. I believed that we were simply not going to make a mistake that would turn us around down low. I was nearly dead wrong in this assessment.

The unknown can be both terrifying and joyous at the same time. I watched the long Alaskan twilight until a deep blue gripped the glacier and the heights reflected a lighter azure. Leftover moisture condensed in the cold air, and tiny crystals floated down through the frigid sky. If I listened carefully, I could just hear them tinkling on the tent. After my eyebrows sagged below the vent, I lay down, snuggled into my sleeping bag, and fell asleep instantly.

Kahiltna Pass

I woke the next morning to Dick's sarcastic voice. "Wake up, Roach! It's so very delicately clear, and we've just gotta get going right now!" I guess I deserved it; I probably shouldn't have put in the part about the stark, snowy loneliness. Nevertheless, today was our fifth day, and we were still trying to reach Kahiltna Pass. McGowan had won, and worse yet, we would have to face him at Kahiltna Pass.

During breakfast we looked up at the glacier and to our surprise saw eight figures descending on skis. We assumed that it was either the McGowan party or the four-man Canadian team that we knew to be ahead of us on the West Buttress Route, but it was neither. When the large group skied into our camp, Hans Gmoser introduced himself, and we quickly heard their incredible story. This team of six Canadians and two Americans were descending the lower West Buttress Route after having climbed Wickersham Wall. Geoff and I immediately pricked up our ears, as that was the wall Roberts was climbing. They knew about the Harvard expedition, but had not seen them. They estimated the Harvard team to be three weeks behind their schedule.

The Gmoser team had climbed Wickersham Wall's western edge, and three of the party had made it to the top of Denali's North Peak, which we knew to be 850 feet lower than the South Peak. After fighting the storm that had held us in Sheldon's hangar, they traversed to the top of the West Buttress and descended with McGowan's party to Kahiltna Pass. They were now bolting for the Southeast Fork and the pleasures of Talkeetna. After Gmoser's team left, Geoff and I shot each other a Summit Club glance. The Gmoser team, not the Harvard team, had just made the first ascent of the Wickersham Wall. Better, Roberts was well behind our schedule. Barring disaster, we should be able to beat him to the summit.

Turning to our own task, we were worried about finding our cache in all the new snow, since our tracks and wands from two days ago had disappeared. Following Gmoser's trail, which was different from our earlier trail, we pushed up the glacier as fast as we could. It socked in at 9,000 feet right on cue, but this time we were determined to reach Kahiltna Pass. Finally, we found Sheldon's Cub tracks, so we knew we were close to the camps at the pass. When we decided that we must be near the McGowan camp, we pitched our tent in a whiteout at 9,800 feet. Kahiltna Pass, at 10,300 feet, separates the southward flowing Kahiltna Glacier from the Peters Glacier, which flows to the northeast. The West Buttress Route doesn't cross Kahiltna Pass but takes a hard right just below the pass and climbs onto Denali's slopes for the first time. Denali's summit is five miles east of Kahiltna Pass, but even at this significant distance we still felt close to the Great One.

The next morning was clear, and I had fun rousting Dick from his bag with a hearty hero's yodel. Squinting in the sun, we saw the West Buttress up close for the first time. It was a large triangular rockface flecked with patches of hard snow. We knew that the top of the face, which hid Denali's upper slopes, was at 16,000 feet. It loomed over us just as impressively as Hunter had from our landing camp, and this was just the shoulder of the Great One. Little by little, Denali was revealing his secrets.

We also saw McGowan's camp a few hundred yards away. Tom Nash, one of the guides, came over to our camp and told their troubled tale. I think that he was glad to have some fresh people to talk to. They had cached their snowshoes near here at 10,000 feet then climbed above Kahiltna Pass on hard snow. After locating a camp above the headwall at 16,200 feet, the now famous five-day storm hit. After the storm they were out of food and energy, and one team member had serious frostbite. They descended to 14,200 feet and discovered twelve feet of new snow. With no choice, they plowed down without snowshoes. To make matters worse, when they got to Kahiltna Pass, they couldn't find their cache. It was now days later, they still didn't have any snowshoes, they were almost out of food, and the expedition was in disarray.

The morning that Sheldon had flown over our camp he landed at their Kahiltna Pass camp with much-needed food supplies. Unable to take off, Sheldon spent two days on the glacier sitting out the most recent storm. He had only gotten off the glacier this morning after mumbling, "Kahiltna Pass is a bad spot for a pick up, you bet!" Nevertheless, knowing Sheldon, I figured that he was chuckling when he said it. McGowan's team had still not found their cache, so we lent Tom our collapsible avalanche probe. He probed a huge area looking for several thousand dollars worth of equipment, but they never found the cache. After probing for two days, Tom had tears in his eyes. When we talked to McGowan, he never said anything about how long it had taken us to reach Kahiltna Pass, since the mountain had hit him much harder than it had hit us.

We still had to descend and find *our* cache. After talking with the McGowan team, we got a late start but finally zoomed off around noon. We broke a new trail down the glacier for two miles to the area where we knew our cache was, but there was no sign of it. The stark, snowy loneliness stretched to the edge of the glacier in every direction. We had cached in a whiteout with no landmarks to help us. Now we had to spot our seven-foot wand or we too were going to end up a crying, probing failure. It tugged at me that perhaps there was a scenario that could turn us around down low.

We went to the most probable spot and walked in an ever-widening spiral for over an hour without success, then it started socking in again. This was getting damn embarrassing. If anyone found these tracks, they would surely form a dim opinion of the track team. More important, we only had a few minutes left before we were in a complete whiteout. We stopped and stared into the gathering gloom, looking for the wand. We stared hard.

Once again this was Geoff's day. His eagle eye spotted something and he hollered, "There it is!" The rest of us looked where he pointed but couldn't see it. Geoff took off at an all-out snowshoe-trot, hollering insistently, "Follow me! We have to get to it before it socks in!" After 200 yards we couldn't see anything, but Geoff kept going into the whiteout on his chosen bearing. We could only go like this for a minute or two before Geoff would lose the line. There was no time for the compass, and I didn't have a bearing anyway, so we just ran into the white snowy loneliness. We ran hard.

Then we stopped. There, at Geoff's feet were the top three inches of our precious wand! We were only three inches from crying, probing failure, and only the simple act of taping two wands together and Geoff's eagle eye had saved us. Our most probable spot was off by 200 yards, which was not much in this huge place. One more storm would have committed our success, and perhaps even survival, to the Kahiltna's eternal snows. We quickly dug down six feet and retrieved our vital food cans. Feeling like a cat that has just caught a bird, we marched back to camp with our precious find. It had taken us six days to get everything to Kahiltna Pass, and we had been so sure that we could do it in one! We had heard many first-person horror stories and were taking copious mental notes. We were learning fast, as Denali easily lived up to its reputation.

June 26 dawned clear, and the Kahiltna Pass camps buzzed with activity. Sheldon flew in and landed with snowshoes for the McGowan party, then he loaded the frostbite victim into the Cub and managed to take off with another spirited push from the track team. That was before breakfast. After breakfast we left to carry our advance relay up to 12,400 feet under the West Buttress. The slopes between Kahiltna Pass and the West Buttress were significantly steeper than anything that we had encountered on the Kahiltna Glacier. The snow was very deep, so we continued to use our snowshoes, but for the first time, we put on our Grouzers.

The plates gave us good traction, but they were too long. Mike put on the best show, tripping, slipping, and doing painful face plants into the deep powder. Mike usually won his races, and he hated slowing the team, especially since the rest of us barely controlled our smirks while he wallowed about trying to get back up. During each thrashing, Mike's cursing rose in intensity until the air around us turned blue. His awful oaths reached the heights, but Denali simply echoed the sentiments back to us. We were the ones struggling here. Finally we stopped, took the traction plates off, and just left the bolts sticking down. Thus we created Baby Grouzers, and they worked much better. Their traction was sufficient, we didn't trip anymore, and soon the track team was again moving gracefully uphill.

We reached 12,400, and cached our loads. After our near disaster with the glacier cache, we marked this stash with multiple triple wands, then feasted on raisins and the beautiful view. Foraker, rising behind and much higher than Crosson, drew my eye as usual, while the impassive West Buttress soared far above us. The northern view opened for the first time, so Geoff and I looked down on the upper part of the Peters Glacier that flows under Wickersham Wall. We knew that Roberts was over there somewhere. Beyond the Peters, holes in the clouds below us revealed the Alaskan tundra, where dozens of small lakes reflecting low sunlight dappled the distant green carpet. The sight of white mountains, open water, and distant wilderness tugged at my emotions. Never mind Roberts; our climb now had a growing sentience of its own. Descending back to camp, I felt strong, lucky to be alive, and elated to be here in the white open wilderness, or the "WOW," as I now called it. That night, the weather clobbered up.

In the WOW.

Photo by Dick Springgate

By morning it was snowing heavily, and we couldn't see anything. This was a real storm, so we hunkered down. McGowan's party had descended before the storm started, but a four-man Canadian team was now in camp with us. They had reached the summit on June 20 and were now descending. We enjoyed talking to them during the leisure hours that the storm forced on us, and they gave us good information. One of the Canadians had frostbite on his hand, so we got our first close-up look at a frostbite blister. They had also lost their snowshoes in the big storm. Everybody descending the mountain had quite a story to tell, and we couldn't help wondering how our story would end.

It was not a violent storm, but it moved into a second day and snowed hard enough to threaten the tents. After shoveling out the camp, we cut up our paperback books, passed around the pieces, and read everything at the same time. We had to be careful not to reveal the endings, but usually "who-dun-it" was common knowledge before the fourth guy finished. We read fast, since we would not carry our finished tomes any farther.

As the four of us sat in the McKinley tent reading on the storm's third day, Geoff surprised me by asking, "Hey, bro. What ever happened to your Hawaiian girlfriend, Terry? Weren't you going to get married and have kids? How come you're here on an Alaskan glacier instead of tending to your garden on Maui?" Mike and Dick immediately put their books down, since a discussion about a guy's love life was always far more interesting than fiction.

Putting my novel down as well, I began with, "OK, but this is tent talk, right?"

Mike blurted out, "What's tent talk, Roach? Just spill it, man!"

Geoff replied, "Mike, now we know why you won all your races but never had a date at Boulder High. Tent talk means that the tent's walls contain the talk."

Getting excited, Mike exclaimed, "You mean I can't tell my girlfriend?"

Groaning, I said, "Mike, you don't have a girlfriend. But even if you did, you couldn't tell her or anyone else." Dick just shook his head as his book jumped up and down on his chuckling stomach. When Mike didn't say anything else, I pressed him with, "Tent talk, right?"

Scratching his hairy ear, Mike stammered, "You actually want me to agree to it out loud?"

I said evenly, "Yup. That's the tent talk rule, Mike."

After several silent seconds, Mike finally said, "OK, OK, tent talk. Now spill it, man!"

I turned to Geoff and Dick in turn, and only after acknowledging their solemn nods of agreement did I begin. "Ah yes, Terry. If I close my eyes, I can still see her blond hair framing her pretty face. Yes, we did have plans to get married. If we had done that, then kids would have been a given."

Mike, more agitated then ever, said, "Out with it, man! Did you get laid or not?"

Dick, who was my college roommate and hence knew my story well, set his book aside and admonished Mike, "Shut up, Mike! If you ever hope to get a date, get laid, get married, or raise a family you would do well to slow down and listen a little. Gerry doesn't know all that much about it, but he knows a heck of a lot more than you do!"

With an uneasy calm in the tent, I continued. "OK, here it is. After the rush of our first summer love, we had to face some realities. Terry and I were working on university degrees in different states, and we hardly saw each other. We made phone calls and sent letters galore, but that's not the same. I was so in love with Terry that I spent a second summer on Maui. I had another great summer, but Terry and I became deeply frustrated with our impending separation for years to come and the impossibility of a sex life."

Mike interrupted with, "Impossible sex life? How can that be? You just ... "

Geoff cut Mike off with, "Mike! For Pete's sake, you of all people know all about impossible sex lives! Now let's hear the story."

With marginal order restored, I continued. "Terry is a Catholic—the whole Andrews family is Catholic. With a lot of encouragement from her folks and several priests, Terry believed that thou shall not have sex before marriage, and once married, thou shall not use birth control. It wasn't reasonable for us to get married for several more years, especially since we both want to go to graduate school. Also, because of the birth control commandment, we couldn't get married until we were really ready, because the kids would have come right away. In the meantime, the no-sex commandment drove us batty to the point that we started to become dysfunctional as a couple."

Dick asked, "Good grief, man. Couldn't you talk her out of that one?"

Lowering my eyes, I said, "No. Trust me, I tried for two years. On top of that, there was another problem."

Mike just couldn't sit still and interrupted again. "What could possibly be worse than no sex life?"

Used to Mike's excesses, I said, "Well, if you would just hush, Mike, I'll tell you. The other problem was that I am not Catholic. That one didn't rear its ugly head until it was clear that Terry and I really were serious about getting married, then her parents made a fuss. They were just as adamant about my needing to be Catholic as the other two commandments. The only way out was for me to join the Church."

With his elbow back on his sleeping bag, Geoff asked, "So, did you?"

Fidgeting, I continued. "Well, believe it or not, I actually looked into it. I took what they call instruction, meeting once a week with a trained layperson to discuss the next chapter from this fat book that they gave me. Everything was moving along logically until I hit a big snag."

Dick piped up, "What was the snag?"

Sighing, I went on. "The snag was the leap of faith. I reached a step in the sequence of beliefs that I could not take, because there was no logical bridge. With no rational support, I was supposed to leap across a chasm on faith alone. The landing site on the other side looked inviting, so I looked everywhere for a bridge and talked to my instructor about it for two painful months, but in the end I could not accept the leap of faith. I walked away from my instruction. With all the other problems, the relationship collapsed soon after that." After rubbing my head through my hat, I continued. "After Terry, I reconnected with climbing big time and realized how important the ascent is to me. People and relationships can disappear, but the rocks and mountains have always been there for me. For now, climbing is the best therapy."

Geoff added, "So that's why you are here on the Great One. Well, bro, now you have new insight into the term 'faithful'!"

Pouncing on his opportunity to say something, Mike said, "So, you never got laid, huh? Not even once?"

Helping me out, Dick said, "Mike, for heaven's sake! You have your answer. Anyway, when I heard this story, I immediately fixed Gerry up with a non-Catholic cutie in Seattle so the poor guy could finally have a sex life!"

Turning around, Mike said, "Geoff! Think we can swing through Seattle on the way home? I'd like Dick to fix me up with a hot date! Wait 'till I tell … "

We sang in chorus, "Mike! It's tent talk!" Then I looked at Mike and added the universal symbol of two fists breaking a neck.

"Oh yeah, I almost forgot." Then Mike added the universal sign of a zippered lip. Fortunately, Dick took over at that point, and entertained us all with ribald stories for several hours.

When we got hungry the conversation turned, as it always does, from women to food. In particular, we talked about what we would eat when we got back to Talkeetna. For now, all we could do was sample the various goodies that we had scored from the McGowan and Canadian teams. A goodie was as simple as a bag of lemon drops or as glorious as a package of black bread. We knew that it was important to keep our energy and spirits up while we were still low on the mountain, since the higher altitudes would reduce our appetites. Nevertheless, after three days of sitting in the tent, we were eager to quit yakking and face the test.

Alone on the Mountain

After depositing three feet of new snow, the storm broke on June 30. With all our sopped-up energy, we prepared to go like jackrabbits. Before we launched, Sheldon flew over and dropped snowshoes for the Canadians, who quickly packed up and descended. We were now alone and would not see another person or plane until the end of our climb. One of the joys of climbing Denali in 1963 was that we had the upper mountain to ourselves. We had heard the horror stories and seen people probing for lost caches, relying on Sheldon for emergency airdrops, then flying out with frostbite. Our apprenticeship was over; it was now our turn. We had our experience, our passion, and our plan. We figured that we could be on top in six days.

We carried our camp to our cache at 12,400 and kept going. At 13,200 feet, we reached the famous Windy Corner where the route sneaks around the lower end of the West Buttress. We thought about camping here, but remembering a story that McGowan told about six out of seven tents failing in a storm at this windy spot, we kept going.

The weather socked in, but we just plodded on into the whiteout. I led, straining to see the crevasses that I knew were on the slopes above Windy Corner. On a traverse I spotted one ten feet in front of me, so I stopped instantly and hollered, "Whoa! Crevasse!" There was another one below me. I started slowly forward and out of the corner of my eye saw something suspicious on my right. I quickly backed away shouting, "Back! Back up!" What had at first appeared to be a crevasse below me shifted when I moved until I realized that I was on the edge of a big drop-off. I was off route and couldn't see anyone behind me, so I just yelled back into the gloom, "There's a big crevasse network here! Have Dick lead through from the rear on a new line higher up to the left. Be careful!"

We snaked around and reversed the rope. Dick got past the first crevasse higher up, then spotted another one. Now it was Dick's turn to holler back into the gloom. "I've got another crevasse! There's an old wand in the middle of a snow bridge, and I'm going for it! Keep the rope tight!" We inched forward. When Dick was in the middle of the bridge, the snow fell away under his snowshoes until he stared into a black hole at least sixty feet deep. The old wand tinkled down into the blackness. Dick froze, supported only by the front few inches and long tails of his snowshoes. Should he go forward or back? Before he could make up his mind, he thundered, "Yeow! Deep hole! Rope tight!"

We had a mission to climb this mountain, so Dick decided to lunge forward. The rest of the bridge broke away as he made his move, and his legs started down into the abyss. But Dick was strong, and gravity was not going to take him so easily. With most of his upper body on the far side, he jammed in his ice ax, outmuscled the obstacle, and crawled up on the other side. All we heard in the rear was a protracted, "Arrgghhhh!"

After Dick caught his breath, we found and crossed a better bridge still higher on the slope. Dick led for another 400 yards into the persistent whiteout then stopped at the edge of another crevasse. We had all had enough of this dangerous game, so I yelled, "Hey, heroes, what's for dinner?" That did it. We dug out a deep platform and pitched our tent on the spot. My altimeter read 13,700 feet. We had chicken noodle soup, a huge spaghetti feast complete with Parmesan cheese, and banana cream pudding for dessert.

The next morning, Dick said, "If we work like demons, we can move everything up to 14,200 today!"

After pondering this for a moment, I replied, "How about splitting up into two teams of two and each team does a double carry?"

Mike boasted, "No double carry. We'll just carry big packs and do it in one trip!"

"Mike," Geoff reminded, "the last time you had a killer pack on, you spent a lot of time on your face. You'll need more than Baby Grouzers today."

In a poor attempt to keep the peace, I replied, "OK. I'll go down with Mike. You heroes move camp up. Just have soup ready for us when we arrive with the killer packs."

The wind blew sixty miles per hour as Mike and I went down around Windy Corner, and it was at our backs while we descended to the cache. Could the two of us make good on our boast and carry four loads?

The wind had blown the formerly copious new snow away, leaving only blue ice and a few rocks. Mike and I struggled in the wind for an hour to get our packs loaded for the big carry. We couldn't set anything down or it would blow away. When ready, our packs weighed 110 pounds apiece. Even helping each other, we barely got them on our backs. We staggered slowly upward into the wind, taking one step at a time, then bracing and balancing ourselves. I expended most of my energy fighting the wind and had little energy left over for upward movement. Worse, rime ice formed on the rope until I dragged it along behind me like a pipe of penance. When I floundered in the breakable crust, it was my turn to hurl oaths at the impassive buttress.

Somehow we made it up to Windy Corner where we promptly collapsed. Mike tried to convince me that we could make it up with everything, but I talked him out of it. "We have to be smart, Mike. If one of us falls in a crevasse with a killer pack on, we'll be in big trouble. Why do you think it's called a *killer* pack? This is a long race, buddy. No sense dying just to make good on a stupid boast." This logic, plus a final look at his pack, convinced him. I took the extra food cans off our packs and carefully cached them in the rocks. At least we had brought them up part of the distance. Then, dodging the crevasses that had plagued us the evening before, we continued up with mere ninety-pound packs to our new camp at 14,200 feet. We dropped our semikiller packs into the powder, then plopped on them to remove our crampons. This was our toughest day so far, and we needed no further boastful banter. The mountain was teaching us a lot, but there was still much mountain ahead of us.

Voices

Geoff emerged from the tent with chicken noodle soup, and we remained perched on our packs through dinner as the warm food and growing beauty salved us. We watched subtle hues dance and play on the peaks in the long Alaskan twilight that never becomes night. Pulling on our down parkas against the growing cold, we watched as Hunter's twin summits nudged Denali's long shadows. Foraker passed through a colorful kaleidoscope in the lowering sun before settling into a deep blue. We could not faithfully reproduce these colors with our cameras, so we just photographed the scene with our eyes. I looked at my teammates and said, "We've come to a fairyland, lads." When the cold crept inside my parka, I crawled into the tent and drifted into a dreamless sleep.

The next day we split up again. Geoff and Mike went down for the food cans at Windy Corner while Dick and I broke a trail through new snow up the much-talked-about headwall between 14,200 and the top of the West Buttress at 16,200 feet. At forty-five degrees, the upper headwall is the steepest part of the West Buttress Route. Since our Baby Grouzers were no match for a forty-five-degree slope, we left our snowshoes at 14,200. Our worst fear was that the headwall would be an ice sheet, but instead, Dick and I sank up to our knees with each step. We alternated leads every three wands, but after three leads Dick pooped out, so I led the rest of the way.

After five and a half hours of exhausting work, we reached the top of the West Buttress. There, for the first time, we felt Denali's cold nipping at our toes, so our first chore was to warm up Dick's feet. Even with no wind and the sun shining, our feet had been buried deep in our steps where the temperature was much lower. Dick and I wore a civilian version of military mouse boots. The original, thickly insulated rubber mouse boots are effective on Denali, but we were not sure about our cheap imitations. McGowan had looked at them and proclaimed them OK, but sitting at 16,200 trying to warm his feet, Dick was not so sure. While Dick sat in the sun, I dug our precious cargo into a secure cache.

While we worked, we enjoyed a jewel-studded scene to the north, where still peeking through clouds thousands of tiny tundra lakes reflected the sun in concert. Like the ending of a Bach chorale, it was fundamental. We felt empowered, and with summit fever surging, we wanted to go higher. When I saw Dick looking up at the route ahead, I said, "We can be back here tomorrow and be on top the day after that. Soon, buddy, soon."

That evening, with all our loads above Windy Corner and an advance relay at 16,200, I finally felt committed to Denali. With the Kahiltna Glacier well below us now, the lower world faded in our minds as the climb became consuming. After dinner Geoff pulled me aside and said, "Hey, bro, you and I gotta climb together on the summit push. It's time for the Summit Club to swing into action! We're going to need all of our climbing instincts up there, and we'll be stronger as a team if you and I go first." Geoff was right—it was time to marshal and organize our strengths. The crevasse danger was less on the upper mountain, so we decided to climb on two ropes of two. Geoff and I would go first and alternate leading.

▼ ▼ ▼

An expedition to climb a great mountain develops a certain life of its own. As the expedition ascends, it starts to move with an energy that is greater than the sum of its members' passions. In short, it develops momentum. One of life's extant experiences is to be on an expedition where the energy is positive and the momentum is always accelerating toward the summit. In spite of a million variables, most expeditions pre-ordain their success or failure long before summit day. We didn't know it yet, but we had created positive momentum. It didn't have anything to do with banter and boasts. The way we did it was by each of us carrying just a little more than his share. The difference between a little more and a little less than your share is trivial, but that small difference controls an expedition's spirit.

▼ ▼ ▼

In the middle of the night, I lay in my bag listening to the signature of the wind that I knew was filling in our tracks up the headwall. I knew Geoff and I would do the exhausting lead up the headwall again, but this time we would continue up to our high camp at 17,200 feet, then it was summit day. We would be starting in a few hours—could we do it? Out of my inner night space a line popped into my head from Mendelssohn's *Elijah:* "Then, *then* we shall see whose God is God the Lord."

The morning was clear and bright, we were now above any clouds, and good weather was settling in on the upper mountain. Trimming our supplies for the summit push, we left behind our snowshoes, some food, fuel, and our spare gas stove. We would rely on the two butane-cartridge stoves that we had used up to this point. To make sure that we could find our cache at 14,200, we marked it with a compact snow pyramid ten feet high. Then we took thirty wands and taped together several multi-stage monsters. We jammed a twelve-foot wand onto the ten-foot pyramid, and placed other monster-wands around it. There would be no crying, probing failure here!

I led up the slope for an hour, post-holing up to my knees with every step. When I got disgusted with the deep snow, Geoff came roaring by fresh as a well-napped lion and led for another hour, while I followed easily in his steps. When Geoff slowed slightly, I charged ahead and led for another hour and a half. Geoff polished off the steep part of the wall with another forty-five-minute lead. When Geoff and I convened on the ridge at 16,200, I said, "This is the old Summit Club teamwork!"

Geoff replied, "We knocked more than an hour off yesterday's time!" Mike and Dick soon joined us, and we fell into our usual banter. Things were going well when we were in banter mode, and I considered that trouble lurked when we fell silent. One thing we did not have trouble with was the altitude. We all felt fine, our spirits were soaring, and the weather was still perfect. We were twenty-four hours from the summit.

The route above 16,200 follows the crest of the upper West Buttress for a thousand feet to a small plateau at 17,200, where we planned to place our high camp. This is the route's most spectacular section, and the views were indeed stunning. I led up the ridge as afternoon slipped slowly into evening, the temperature dropped to minus ten degrees Fahrenheit, and the outer world fell farther below us.

My crampons squeaked as I crunched up the hard, wind-packed snow. The cold, clear, still air tingled with an intensity that I had never experienced before. Suddenly, alpenglow bathed the upper mountain, infusing the snow with intense color. A deep red was below us, at our feet, high above, and somehow, in the air. We climbed on into a fairyland that photographers would turn triple flips for just to see from below, but this time we were in the photo. We were privileged passengers in a fleeting mountain rapture. I looked at my boots, and seeing that the color was even in my footsteps, I felt as if God was embracing this mountain for a few special moments. We did not need to speak, but we did stop to stare at the splendor and let it embrace us. It was beyond human power.

Too soon the glaciers and lowlands dissolved into darkness far below us and only the highest peaks remained in the alpenglow. We now felt completely detached from the lower world as our eyes wandered over the surreal scene of red summits, pink skies, and beyond, the black of space. Geoff, Dick, and Mike stood poised behind me on the ridge. Beyond my companions I saw only one other peak that rose high enough to remain in the hand of God: it was Foraker—Denali's queen. While the alpenglow bathed Foraker's north face, I noticed a long straight ridge radiating upward in the center of the face. This beautiful ridge drew my eye directly to the queen's summit, and I knew that I had discovered my future Foraker route. In that instant, I understood that Denali was only a beginning—I would always have to touch great peaks. In the next instant, a strong voice spoke directly in my mind, "Don't have an accident!" Was this my old brain voice? A warning from Prince? From God?

Three seconds later, I heard Dick bellow, "Oh, no! No, no! *Stop!*" I turned to see Dick dash behind a boulder and assumed that Mike had fallen off the ridge. Fear stabbed at my sternum, then I saw Mike running after Dick, so they were both fine. What on earth was the matter? As Geoff and I raced down, we knew that it was still big trouble. At first we didn't see what was wrong, then Mike ran up wild eyed, hollering, "My pack! My pack fell off the ridge!"

Stove or Summit?

Dick and Mike had stopped for a rest and piled their rope on the snow between them. Unfortunately, they put their packs on top of the rope pile. When Dick took a few steps down the ridge to get a picture, the rope from his waist pulled on the pile and tossed Mike's pack off the far side of the ridge. It was a steep slope, and the pack vanished in a flash. Dick and Mike dashed over and watched it bounce down for a thousand feet. Then, to their continued horror, they watched the pack's contents spill out and roll down the slope in all directions for another 600 feet. One by one, little black dots came to rest in the glacier basin between the West Buttress and Denali's northwest ridge.

The loss of Mike's pack stunned us. Trying to think, I looked at Mike. "We have to keep our cool, man. What important things were in your pack, Mike?"

Mike thought carefully, then replied, "Two sleeping bags, parka, pots, and both stoves."

We all gasped, "*Two* sleeping bags? *Both* stoves?"

Mike went on, "Yes. Both stoves. I traded out some heavy stuff with Dick for bulky stuff, trying to get a better-balanced load." An old "gotcha" had us—we had put all our stoves in one pack. We could improvise for missing sleeping bags, parka, and pack, but we had to have at least one stove. Without a stove, we could not melt snow for water, and without water, we would not survive long. The mountain had played a very big card, and suddenly we were in trouble. Mike started moaning, "It's all my fault! Both stoves gone, and I did it! I've blown the summit for the whole team! It's all my fault!"

This emotional outburst startled Dick, but Geoff and I knew Mike. We shot each other a quick Summit Club look, then launched into our well-oiled starting-line routine. I began with, "Hold it in, Mike! It's not your fault. It's not anybody's fault. It just happened, OK? Now you've got to hold it in or we really will have a problem!"

Geoff continued the patter. "Now we're going to solve this dilemma and go on to the summit. We have our spare stove down at 14,200, and maybe we can climb down to get the lost stuff."

Mike blurted, "I'll go! I've gotta go!"

I replied in my best voice, "Hold it in, Mike! We've gotta think this through. For starters, let's go see what the downclimb looks like." Mike was calmer when we walked over to the edge, focused on the physical problem, and analyzed our position. We had to have a stove, so we had to go down one side of the ridge or the other. The advantage of going back to 14,200 was that the route was already in and we knew that we had a working stove there. The disadvantage of this scenario was that we would still be short two sleeping bags, pack, and parka. The advantage of going down after the pack was that we could recover most of the vital stuff. The disadvantage was that it was new territory with unknown dangers.

In the fading light we peered over the edge for a better look. We saw little black dots on the glacier below, and there was a smooth snow slope all the way down to the dots, so it was no worse than the headwall. After a pregnant moment, we decided to go after the pack. Mike piped up instantly, "I'll go!"

I countered, "Slow down, Mike. We don't all need to go down. We should divide our strengths. Two of us should move all the loads up to 17,200 and set up camp while the other two go for the lost gear."

Geoff continued, "Dick has more experience on crampons then you do, Mike. He should go down. We need your strength up here to move the loads. Dick and I are going down, and you and Gerry get camp set up."

So it was that in the middle of the Alaskan night, Geoff and Dick started heeling down the unknown side of the mountain at high speed and were soon out of sight. Mike and I rearranged our remaining loads then started up. I thought that we were past the ridge's difficulties, but we soon came to a buttress that nearly blocked our passage. We climbed around it on the left by clambering up a steep trough. We did not know at the time that this was the fabled Washburn's Thumb. Above this obstacle it was hard work with our heavy packs, and we climbed for a long time over and around rocks on the ridge.

After almost an hour, Mike and I pulled up onto the edge of the small plateau at 17,200 and saw Denali's upper slopes. I stared, but the Great One was no longer beautiful; a very cold, impassive Denali stared back at me. This stark view jolted me, and the seriousness of our position began to sink in. Mike and I dropped our packs and perched on a rock without speaking. I stared at the mountain and tried to think it through again.

It had taken us longer to get up here than I had hoped, and there was that tricky buttress on the ridge. Geoff and Dick might not be able to add another tough hour to their already heroic effort. Worse yet, what if they didn't find a stove? We would then run back to 14,200, and the camp here didn't make any sense. Looking at Denali, I said, "Mike! This is too far up, and we're getting too strung out. Let's leave some stuff here but take the tent and bags back to 16,800. Geoff and Dick will be exhausted, but I think we can pitch the tent on the ridge right where your pack went off. If they have a stove, we can brew up, sleep for a few hours, then come back up here. If they have no stove, we'll run back to 14,200."

Much calmer now, all Mike said was, "You're right. Let's get going."

We cached some food, fuel, and wands, then started back down. When we got back to the spot where the pack fell, we looked down for Geoff and Dick. They were still far below but were moving slowly up, so at least they were OK. We pitched our four-man McKinley tent right on the ridge. There was barely room for it, and we couldn't walk around the tent on one side. We did our best to anchor the tent into the hard-packed snow with ice screws, but it was a precarious camp. I knew that a strong wind could blow us right off the ridge, but hopefully we would only be here for a few hours. I scanned the horizon carefully. The weather was still perfect, and the sky was lightening for the new day. It was July 4th, Independence

Day, and just maybe, summit day. Exhausted, Geoff and Dick made it back to the ridge at 5:00 A.M. "We found most of the stuff, but only one stove," Geoff said as they dove into the tent.

I said, "That's great! One stove is all we need. Get into your bags, and we'll brew up!" I fished the precious stove from Mike's icy pack, handed it to Mike, and said, "Get this going while I unstuff the bags."

Two minutes later, Mike announced, "The stove doesn't work!"

I stammered, "What? Gimme that thing!"

Mike persisted, "The stove won't work, since there's no flame spreader." I examined the stove and confirmed that the flame spreader was indeed gone. Geoff and Dick were already asleep, but we roused them and asked if they had the flame spreader.

Geoff awoke long enough to explain. "We were lucky to find one stove. It was just sitting there in its bag. We grabbed it and put it in the pack. If the spreader isn't in the bag or loose in the pack, then it's gone!" I carefully examined everything in the pack, but there was no flame spreader. During the long fall, it had slipped off the stove's stem and escaped from the stove bag. Without the flame spreader, gas shot out in a dangerous stream, and we could not ignite it without creating a Roman candle.

After climbing all day and all night, we were very thirsty, so as Mike and I went to work to solve the stove problem, I just said, "This is a different kind of race, Mike. We've got to be creative, since we have no choice. Hold this spoon over the gas jet while I try to light it." To our amazement, it worked. Well, sort of. If we held the spoon perfectly still, a flame appeared around it. If we moved the spoon, the flame popped out, leaving gas jetting into the tent, which was a formula for another disaster.

Hunched in our bags, the four of us gathered around our broken stove like a bunch of hungry hobos. Right now, we would settle for a cup of cold water each. One of us worked the on-off knob, one held the spoon, one worked the lighter, and one held the pot over the precious flame. The spoonholder had the toughest job, as he had to hold the spoon perfectly still. We took turns at spoonholding for two hours and managed to get two cups of water. We each got a swallow, which was better than nothing. At 7:00 A.M., no one could hold the spoon steady anymore, so we decided to get some sleep. We stuffed snow into our water bottles, wiggled deeper into our sleeping bags, pressed the bottles against our empty bellies, and dozed fitfully.

I stirred at 11:00 A.M., and tried to focus, but had a bad case of cotton mouth and dehydration. Miserable, I thought that we should go back to 14,200, get the spare stove, and start another summit push. Mike, already wide-awake, sat bolt upright and roared, "I've been thinking about it all night! *We've gotta go for it!*" I undid the tent door and looked out as fresh air smacked me in the face. The weather was still perfect, and there was no wind. If we went down, we might not get another chance, and we all knew that this was the pivotal moment of our trip.

There are times to be careful and times to go for it. On this memorable occasion, we went for it. We forced a little cold lunch food down our parched throats and got another swallow from our water bottles. We stuffed hard candies into our pockets, collapsed the tent, put on our crampons, and started for Denali's summit at 1:00 P.M.

Touching Greatness

Geoff and I went first on one rope, while Mike and Dick followed on a second rope. I led up the now familiar ridge to our cache at 17,200, where we picked up some extra wands and grabbed a few more candies. After Geoff post-holed across the small plateau, I attacked the long slope leading diagonally up toward Denali Pass. This was the slope where John Day and the Whittakers had fallen three years earlier. We had not forgotten, and we went into our Summit Club climb mode, banishing all extraneous thoughts and focusing only on the climb.

As I led up the slope, I steadily felt stronger and more determined. Looking to the north, I only saw tundra, lakes, and an occasional cotton-candy cloud thousands of feet below. The tundra was so far beneath us that it looked like a work of art. I felt like the rest of the world was the painting now, and that it was sitting still watching me—the Earth's only living creature. Looking west and south, I saw Foraker and open skies beyond, which meant that the weather was still perfect. I started a long ascending traverse to reach the pass, but about halfway up I paused and stared up the slope at a great shortcut. The shortcut was steeper, but the snow was good and I felt stalwart. I looked back at Geoff and said, "Why go all the way over to the pass when we can just climb straight up?"

He gave me all the encouragement I needed when he said, "Summit Club forever! Summit fever! Go for it, bro!"

Starting up the fall line, I responded with our old club call, "Squirrels gonna climb zees mountain!" Kicking steps up the perfect snow, I sucked either a piece of ice to get some liquid or a hard candy to get some sugar. My strategy paid off, and I continued to feel better. Geoff's yodel gave me our signal that he was ready to lead, but without breaking stride, I waved him off and hollered back, "I've got it to the top of the slope! You take it to the summit from there!" This was the crux, it was my lead, and if required, I would kick steps for twenty hours to get to the top of this slope. I settled into a rhythm and climbed on into the Alaskan afternoon.

We passed 18,200 feet—the elevation of Denali Pass between the north and south peaks—and pressed on. There is a dream that makes people come to the heights, and I was living the dream. It was summit day, I forgot about the lower world, sun was on my back, and I felt fantastic. The snow sparkled as it flew away from my boots in graceful arcs. Step by shining step I approached the venerable upper slopes on one of Earth's great peaks. Afternoon was slowly slipping into early evening when Geoff and I pulled up onto the crest at the top of the steep slope. As we sat at 18,700 feet, well above Denali Pass, Geoff said, "Our shortcut worked!" The comment needed no reply.

The view down the other side startled us. We had been living with the same views for two weeks and now reveled in our new, chimerical vista. For the first time, we had a clear view of Denali's North Peak. It was two miles away and still higher than we were. Its graceful summit ridges crowned ramparts that fell away into the Harper Glacier basin below. The Harper drew our eyes to the northeast where Denali dropped for miles into deep shadows. Beyond the shadows lay the painting-perfect tundra with its jeweled lakes. Roberts was down there in the shadows somewhere, but we were up here in the light.

Geoff and I were now as high as Mexico's Orizaba, the highest peak the Summit Club had climbed. Our eyes traced a long line up nature's screen to the summit of the Great One, which was still a mile away and 1,600 feet above us. We were poised to smash our altitude record. With crampons squeaking on the hard snow, Geoff led us up into the evening light.

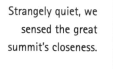

Strangely quiet, we sensed the great summit's closeness.

Photo by Dick Springgate

A subtle pink glow infused the snow as we passed Archdeacon's Tower. When stopped to eat some candy, I noticed that we were now higher than the North Peak, which, impressive as it was, was just a false summit. Now only the highest snows in North America remained above us. Mike and Dick had fallen behind, and for the moment, Geoff and I were alone. As we sat together munching and eyeing the final, 700-foot slope to the summit, we felt our old Summit Club companionship. The weather was still perfect, and we sensed the great summit's closeness. We were strangely quiet, as our usual banter and macho blustering were completely unnecessary in this sacred place.

The hard snow here was unlike anything I had seen below. It was not clear like ice, but it felt just as hard. Unknown winds had scoured these slopes for centuries leaving graceful, curving ripples. Calmed, I sensed a permanence in these snow slopes, as if the rest of the land was soft and might suddenly wash away, whereas these sculpted slopes were here forever. The rigid ripples caught the evening alpenglow as Geoff and I continued up into another colorful fairyland. Denali's summit slopes became my entire universe; I could no longer even see the painting that represented the rest of the world, and this new, detached dimension captivated me. Halfway up the final slope I wondered if this mountain would ever stop going up, but I did not break stride. We were on a mission that could no longer be denied.

When Geoff and I stepped onto the summit ridge, the view down the south face made our toes tingle, but with the summit so close, we still did not break stride. We danced up the concluding ridge in a state of rapidly compressing space, time, and experience, and in the final intoxicating steps we executed an old Summit Club routine. Without slowing, we each coiled half the rope and arrived at the highest point together. We just stood there puffing until Geoff broke the silence by hollering, "Highest point in North America! Yowsah!"

Geoff on the summit
in film-cracking cold.
In all of central Alaska,
we were the only
people still in the sun.

This time a reply seemed necessary, so I let out our Summit Club yodel, "WheeeeeHonken!" then, for Sheldon, added, "You Bet!" It was 10:00 P.M., and with the sun kissing the northern horizon, we took some pictures before the light faded. In all of central Alaska, we were the only people still in the sun. It was windless, but our thermometer read minus sixteen degrees and was dropping at an alarming rate. Cold, we pulled on our down parkas.

When we saw Mike and Dick approaching the summit ridge, I let out another "WheeeeeHonken" to encourage them. When they joined us on the summit at 10:30, Mike cried, "We did it! A clean sweep!" Geoff and I tried to unfold our frozen, homemade Summit Club flag, but I had to pry the prize with my ice ax to finally get it open. The ink had bled through the cheap cloth, so our flag looked like a double exposure, but we posed with it like heroes anyway. Then we tied it to a wand and plunged it into

Our flag looked like a
double exposure, but
we posed with it like
heroes anyway.

Photo by Dick Springgate

the highest point for Roberts to find. The gesture seemed silly, since our presence here was triumph enough.

I tried to absorb all the views and understand the message, but there was too much to take in. The Alaska Range swept away to the east and west as far as I could see. There were more peaks than I could count, but we were higher than all of them. Deep blues folded into darkness in the chasm below Denali's south face. I saw Hunter and Foraker, but they were far below and strangely distant. This was Denali's moment. My only perception was that we were touching greatness. We had not conquered the Great One, but we had kissed it. This, the thirty-fourth ascent of Denali, was my ninth and highest Transcendent Summit, and my most sublime so far.

Just before we put the thermometer away it read minus twenty, and Dick complained that his feet were cold. Mine were too, since our boots were marginal. It was time to move. Starting down a little after 11:00, Mike and Dick zoomed off to see if Dick's feet would warm up. My feet warmed as soon as I started moving, so Geoff and I followed at a more sedate pace. Reluctant to rush away, we soaked up the Alaskan night.

Descending the shortcut slope, I kept repeating my new mantra, "Don't have an accident—don't have an accident!" Step by step we moved carefully down the mountain. We stopped at our precarious high camp at 16,800 and slept for a few hours. Dick's feet warmed up in his sleeping bag, and in the morning we had our next surprise: Dick had some frostbite on his toes. We were still high on the mountain, and our new mission was to get Dick down before frostbite blisters formed, which would render him immobile.

We shot down to 14,200 and melted snow with the spare stove until we had consumed a gallon of liquid apiece. This was our first real liquid in forty-eight hours. Then we hurried around Windy Corner and continued down to make camp at Kahiltna Pass. As we started to prepare our first solid food in three days, we spilled some gas on the tent floor. We waited a long time for it to evaporate, but not long enough. When we set the running stove down, the whole tent floor burst into flame! This was the disaster we had worked so hard to prevent at high camp.

Dick was in his sleeping bag, but still opened the door and slithered out in two seconds. I followed him out and threw snow back into the tent. Geoff had his boots on and stomped like a dancing dervish while Mike grabbed the down gear. A few seconds later, Mike and Geoff tumbled out of the tent in a cloud of smoke. We sat outside in disarray and realized that the mountain was still in command. It seemed as if Denali was determined to continue teaching us lessons. We inspected the damage and discovered that the fire had not destroyed anything. However, our new problem was that Geoff had bent the stove stem in his wild stomping! Now even our spare stove didn't work, and we sacked out again without getting our hot meal.

The next morning, Mike and I sat down with the spare stove and repaired it, since we had no choice. We had to bend the stem without breaking it, so we carefully bent it just far enough so that it worked and no farther. There was no margin for error. Then Mike and I cooked up a huge meal while Geoff doctored Dick's feet. He still didn't have frostbite blisters, so we set off down the Kahiltna.

Escape

We still planned on walking all the way to Talkeetna, but by the time we reached the Southeast Fork it was clear that Dick's feet could not handle the journey. In our absence, a team had flown in and was busy climbing Foraker's southeast ridge, which was only the second ascent of Foraker. They had left a radio in basecamp, but after many attempts, we still had not raised anyone. Where was Sheldon when we needed him? After a day of discussion, we decided that Geoff and I should walk out so that the four of us would not be stranded here forever.

Geoff and I left that night on hard snow with seventy pounds in the sled and light loads on our backs. We were now past the solstice, so it was noticeably darker at night. Our reward was that as we walked, the moon rose, framing the peaks on both sides of the glacier. As Geoff and I cruised down the glacier, we felt expansive, and started thinking about re-entering the rest of the world. After six miles crevasses appeared in the glacier, and for some time we snaked through giant chasms with fragile snow bridges over them. Reaching a precarious overlook point, we looked down the glacier and realized that there was no way we could get through this maze. We needed to be on the glacier's edge, but even that route didn't look very likely. The Summit Club was in over its head on this one, so we turned around and slogged back up to the Southeast Fork. Even Denali's lowest slopes held lessons, and we were still detached from the lower world.

We had climbed the mountain, but could we escape it? We sat around for two days trying to make the radio work. Then on July 9, as we lay dozing in the tent, Mike suddenly bolted upright and screamed, "A plane! A plane! I hear a plane!"

The rest of us didn't hear anything and thought Mike was dreaming or losing it completely. We started with, "Hold it in, Mike! You're dreaming!"

Mike emphatically said, "No! I'm not dreaming. I-hear-a-plane! Listen!" We fell silent, cocked our ears, and there was the faintest, sweetest sound that we had ever heard—a tiny engine purring up the huge glacier. Somebody had indeed heard one of our radio calls, and when Sheldon got the word, he was zooming through the air within ten minutes.

Racing down the Kahiltna Glacier after taking off, Sheldon roared, "So, she was a howling success, eh?"

Wanting to verify that the track team had really climbed Denali but unable to discuss it in the roar of the plane, I just bellowed, "Yowsah!"

Back in Sheldon's hangar, our physical escape was complete, but we had one more problem: we were starving. Pacing the hangar floor in the depths of night, I said, "What time does the Fairview open?"

Pacing with me, Mike grumbled, "Not 'till six."

"What time is it now?"

Mike's voice cracked when he said, "Only three!"

Holding my stomach, I replied, "My God, we'll never make it."

Proving that he was not asleep, Geoff piped up from his sleeping bag, "The Fairview doesn't open until seven."

Without showing his head, Dick rumbled from inside his bag, "We'll head over at five and wake 'em up. Now shut up!"

At ten to five we could wait no longer. When the Fairview's proprietor came to the door in his bathrobe and slippers, we quickly explained our climb, the loss of stoves, and our current hunger. The man eyed us and seemed ready to tell us to come back at seven. We held our breath.

Then an Alaskan twinkle came into his eyes, he swept the door wide and said, "Come on in, men. It's going to take a little while, but I'll fix you the breakfast of a lifetime. Sit right here." We tried to sit in the tiny anteroom, but when sounds and smells came from the kitchen, the only way we could contain ourselves was to pace in small circles, holding our tortured tummies.

When the food started arriving, we dove into it, but our culinary savior said, "Pace yourselves, men. There's plenty. The slower you eat, the more you can get down." Heeding this advice, I ate a dozen eggs, six slabs of ham, eight pieces of bacon, four pieces of thick sourdough toast slathered with butter and jam, seven glasses of orange juice, six buttermilk pancakes overflowing with syrup, a plateful of home style potatoes, two glasses of milk, and a large cinnamon roll.

The Great One introduced me to the WOW and taught me more lessons than I could easily count. I just summarized them into one big "U" for *Understanding*, which I added to my "WHO CLIMBS UP" acronym for mountaineers. It had been

years since I had added a letter, and it felt good to be back on my learning program. Moreover, I knew that if by some life turn Denali were my last major climb,
then all my years of training would have been worth it. However, there was one
letter left before my acronym was complete, and I knew that I would have to
attempt at least one more climb to discover it. I could not know that it was the
most important letter.

Eclipse

*I said my good-byes to Dick, Mike, and Geoff, then traveled alone into Alaska's interi-
or to spend the rest of the summer working for the Geophysical Institute at the
University of Alaska at Fairbanks. Sixteen days after standing on Denali's summit, I
waited in an Alaskan meadow watching white puffy summer clouds. A total solar
eclipse was coming, and no human force could stop it.*

*As I lay on my back feeling the grass tickle the back of my neck, the moon slowly
made love to the sun. Imperceptibly, an accelerating sensory rush occupied my meadow.
It was not like twilight, not even a long Alaskan twilight. The landscape gradually
took on an eerie hue. As queer shadows crept across the meadow, a large hole opened
in the clouds as if by some celestial command. Birds on the wing sang their night
songs, then all was silent for a hopeful moment.*

*An abnormal pallor overtook the countryside as the totality shadow raced
across the northern land. A tiny whirlwind tugged at my sweater then vanished. For
a figment, cosmic fear seized me, since the moon's movement was so powerful and it
was not to be denied. This event was from beyond the realm of the living, and I felt
compelled to learn from it. Something tangible enveloped bird, man, and meadow as
moon and sun united. Awe overtook my fear as I merged with the prime mover.*

*The sun's last salute was Baily's beads, flashing for three suspended seconds, then
the sky was dark. The sun was gone. Simultaneously, the sun's corona and stars
appeared. I stood transfixed by the celestial spectacle, while solar coronal filaments
played with the edges of my mind. A frightened bird fluttered overhead and a flower
started to close, yet I felt strangely peaceful. This was not a summit, but my spirit
was in alignment with Denali's family of summits. This eclipse was a supreme syzygy
of Summit, Self, and Sun, and I stood at its zenith. Just as Denali's Transcendent
Summit had done, this Transcendent Sight was engraved upon my memory forever.*

chapter five

d a s   c a v e

The Color of the Mountain

Mount Rainier, at 14,410 feet, is the highest peak in the Pacific Northwest and impresses all who see it. Unlike Rocky Mountain peaks that rise from high, dry plains, Rainier is a coastal mountain and receives the brunt of the frequent storms that rake the Cascades. Rainier supports three summits over 14,000 feet and twenty-six named glaciers, which plunge more than 10,000 feet before spawning the swift, deep rivers surrounding the mountain. If you sliced off Rainier at 13,000 feet, the resulting summit plateau would cover two square miles. Refusing such a surgery, this enormous volcano's summit broods in a domain far above the Cascades' lesser peaks.

▼   ▼   ▼

on the rare days when the rainy coastal weather clears, you can see Mount Rainier's striking slopes from Seattle, and locals spread the joy on such glorious days by saying, "The Mountain is out!" Rainier is so impressive that a broad corridor on the University of Washington campus purposely points toward it. As I walked to my math class, I made my daily stop at the top of the "Rainier" corridor hoping for a view, but as usual, clouds obscured everything except the campus buildings. Entering class, I picked a desk by the window, since even if the classroom faced the wrong way, I could still keep track of the weather. It was late May, a grueling year of classes was almost over, and I was twitching to be outside. As I leaned toward the glass, the old chair I was sitting in, which was reminiscent of the old milk truck navigator's chairs, squeaked beyond its normal "snik," letting out a loud "snarrrrk!" The professor shot me a sharp glance, then started his math lecture. My body felt trapped in this classroom, but my mind was still free, so I propped my elbow on the windowsill and let my mind wander across an imaginary glacier.

My heavy class schedule caught up with me: I fell sound asleep and had a short but vivid dream about falling into a crevasse.

When my supporting elbow fell off the windowsill, I sputtered back to reality and yanked myself up from a twisted position below the window. Dr. Zukerman glared at me and said in a steady tone, "Care to join class, Gerry?" Wincing, I reassumed my stiff, studious posture with note-taking pencil at the ready as Dr. Zukerman continued his lecture in his steadily rising classroom tone. "In coloring a geographical map, it is customary to give different colors to any two countries that have common boundaries. It has been found empirically that any map, no matter how many countries it contains nor how they are situated, can be so colored by using only four different colors. It is easy to see that three will not suffice. Consider the following ... " As Dr. Zukerman's now flying fingernails clacked across the board sending a chalk dust cloud into the room, his pitch went up an octave as he pounced on his punch line. "It has been proven that five colors suffice for all maps, but it has not been *proven* that four will likewise suffice." Dr. Zukerman's copious white hair oscillated with excitement as he did his best to inspire his students to conquer mathematics' mountains. This was his Everest.

In 1964 the famous four-color problem was one of mathematics great, unsolved problems, having baffled famous mathematicians for 120 years. I had worked on the problem and believed that it would be solved not by an astute proof but by a computer program requiring many steps and great perseverance. However, my main interest in the problem was not to prove the theorem, but to relate it to the rest of my life. The four-color problem raised many other interesting questions, such as which colors? When? Why *colors*? Why the number *four*? Can you *smell* a color? If so, what does it smell like? Could you feel it or describe it? I believed that there were always many metaphorical connections between math problems and slices of life. In this case, could I link the four-color problem to my consuming passion, mountains?

I already had an A nailed down for this class, which was not bad since I was sure that my IQ-testing fourth grade teacher still considered me an idiot. As "Dr. Z" lectured in his high-pitched voice, my brain wandered out the window again. Ignoring the squeaky chair, I leaned sideways for a better look. The sky, its usual Seattle gray, seemed lighter—brighter. Somehow I just knew that the sun illuminated a glaciated slope and was beaming on Rainier's summit. The bell ended class precisely as Dr. Z snapped his book shut, but my mind was on top of Rainier. The four-color problem could wait, as Rainier was a mountain worth coloring, er climbing, right now. Walking back to Wilburs, I stopped at the top of the corridor and stared—the Mountain was out, gleaming on the horizon.

I quickly joined a team of six headed for Rainier. Our goal was simple. We planned to climb the Nisqually Icefall Route, traverse over the highest summit, and descend the easier Ingraham Glacier Route. The Nisqually Icefall is a slowly cascading jumble of frozen ice blocks that look like suspended chaos, and it is one of the more difficult routes on the mountain. I had no trouble convincing my roommate and Denali companion, Dick Springgate, to join us. His Cascade experience and gregarious personality always proved invaluable. Tom Stewart came with his strength, experience, and cool head. In a week Tom and Dick were leaving for Mount Logan, Canada's highest peak, and they were steeling themselves for a big one. Bill Hauser, another Wilburite, brought his keen insights and sharp wit, and Bill was all revved up since he was leaving for Denali in a week. Don Gordon added his bull-like strength, and Herb Staley was an experienced Rainier guide who had climbed the mountain forty-two times.

On Saturday of Memorial Day weekend, we arrived at Paradise, the traditional starting point on Rainier's south side. Pristine white snowbanks rose fifteen feet above the recently plowed parking lot, hemming in both cars and climbers. Next, we checked in with green-collared park rangers who carried out their bizarre ritual of jumping on our ice axes. If an ax broke, its owner could not climb. It was never clear whether this was because the ax would have been too dangerous or simply because you no longer had an ax. One by one we held our breath as the fierce ranger pounced on our precious wooden axes. Our axes held, and I smiled when the ranger bruised his foot on mine.

We shouldered our packs, left civilization's little indignities behind, and started our long trek up to Camp Muir at 10,000 feet. This traditional high camp for summit climbs on the Ingraham Glacier Route would be our launching point. On our long hike up the Muir Snowfields, we met several descending climbers who had failed to reach the summit because of deep snow, but the weather seemed good. In 1964 we did not have detailed, satellite-generated weather forecasts, and in any case, this was our sacred Memorial Day weekend, so our confidence stayed high.

Critical Closing Colors

A near-black, starry sky greeted me when I woke at 2:30 A.M. With youth's enthusiasm surging, I quickly banished sleep to prepare for our big day. I put my lunch into my heavy, gray canvas daypack, which was just right for a math major, since I had bought it from a friend for four dollars. Ready, I strapped on my crampons and walked away from Camp Muir on squeaky snow. A half-mile traverse took the team to the base of the icefall, still looming unseen in the dark. We crunched up steepening slopes as purple dawn flecked the sky. After the sun found us creeping into the pink-white chaos, the team solved the icefall's problems easily until a steep section threatened to stop us. Don led us along the left edge of a huge ice block, and we got around the obstacle. With this difficulty behind us, I felt committed to the upper mountain. The color was pure.

By noon the icefall was below us and the summit was in sight. However, there was little joy in this fact since the weather was rapidly deteriorating. Worse, Herb's unexpectedly poor condition slowed the group to a crawl, but I had no thoughts of turning around to descend the difficult terrain below us. We had to get over the summit and descend the easier route, so we continued nervously upward. When we reached the summit at 3:00 P.M., visibility dropped, white turned to gray, the wind came up, and it started to snow.

We were on Rainier's highest summit, Columbia Crest, which is on the west of a shallow, quarter-mile-wide crater. On the summit we met Carl and Sally, who had just finished a laborious ascent of the Ingraham Glacier Route that we now planned to descend. We joined forces with them, since Carl's knowledge of the descent route would be a big help for us, and six strapping men appearing out of the mists was a happy sight for them. Our summit celebration was brief. Now eight strong, we started across the crater floor with Carl and Herb in the lead. With the wind ripping at our backs, we climbed a short rise to the eastern crater rim and dropped onto the mountain's east side.

Visibility and color vanished, and I hoped that Carl or Herb could follow the route. At first we descended rapidly, but our progress soon slowed. With the storm deepening, Carl was having difficulty finding his ascent route, so we held a huddled conference. Herb warned us about crevasses near the 13,000-foot level, and we crept down again as the slope grew steeper. A crevasse appeared off to the right, then another to the left. Finally, a large crevasse appeared below, and we stopped. Carl had not passed through this many crevasses on his ascent—we were off route.

Like it or not, we could not descend on this line. With eight of us spread out over 200 feet on this steep slope, it was almost impossible to communicate, and because of the crevasses, we couldn't risk getting everyone together for a conference. In any case, this was not a good time for a committee decision. Even though I had never been here before, my sixth sense told me that we were too far north, and I felt that we should retreat back up the slope a short distance, traverse south, then descend again. Communicating my sixth sense to seven strong-willed people spread out on a steep, storm-raked slope high on Rainier was impossible. My nervousness turned to alarm.

Critical decisions in the mountains often hinge on a momentary flash of inspiration, but desperation may have motivated ours. From somewhere above, I heard shouted commands that we were going back up to the summit to find a steam cave. Head back up a mountain in a storm? It didn't make sense to me, since I had never heard about caves on Rainier's summit, and even if there were caves, how could we find one in such a storm? As we started back up, the whole tableau felt wrong. In moments of doubt, it is easy to be swayed by action, and I lost myself in the bizarre chore of reclimbing the mountain. With each upward step, I entered a new dimension, as the cold intensified and the day's colors slipped away. Recrossing the eastern crater rim and descending into the volcano's crater, I felt a dark door closing behind me.

I didn't know what a steam cave looked like, but I was certainly keen on finding one. No one questioned the insanity of looking for a cave on a high mountain summit in a raging storm at dusk, since we had to find a steam cave or die. After crossing to the base of the final summit slope on the crater's west side, we poked pitifully at the featureless white slope with our ice axes, but found nothing.

However, Herb had a nose for sulfur, and he shouted, "I've found one!"

Rainier broods in a domain far above the Cascades' lesser peaks.

We all rushed to the spot to behold our salvation, but my heart sank, since it was nothing more than a small black hole in the snow. Herb's enthusiasm was enormous compared to the opening's size, and he dug furiously. Soon he burrowed into the snow like a mole and disappeared. Curious, we followed. After wiggling through a ten-foot tunnel, we emerged, to my amazement, into a small, black, windless room. All eight of us crowded into the dank room and stood transformed. A moment earlier, we were fighting for our lives in a desperate whiteout, and now all we heard was our breathing and a dull dripping sound emanating from the cave's blackness. Our binary transition from white to black was like the click of a light switch—Rainier had used two colors. Would it take four or five colors to complete this climb? I knew it couldn't be done with only three, so either way we had at least two colors to go.

Our cave was warm. I sank down against the pumice floor and felt the warmth with my bare hands. It was Mother Earth's warmth, and realizing that I was touching an element from one of my least explored domains, I embraced it. With senses slowly returning, we took stock of our position. Rainier is a dormant volcano, but dormant is not the same as extinct. Heat escaping from small steam vents in the summit crater had melted the snow to form our cave, which had a sloping pumice floor and a six-foot-high snow roof. Sometimes, steam caves connect to form a long network of passages under the crater's snow surface. I sensed that this might be my tenth domain, since within a few feet, it synthesized the three elements of air, earth, and water. Perhaps there was a fourth element, fire, but I was touching that as well. My brain had warned me years ago on the Fist that there cannot be synthesis without antithesis, and on this voyage, I would finally learn what my brain's warning meant.

Tom produced a headlight, and we explored our sanctuary. Still in our crampons, we scratched deeper and discovered that the room was at least twenty feet long. The cave seemed to end there, but a deep, black hole disappeared in the back near the dripping sound. There would be time for exploring this unknown passage later—for the moment, we were delighted that there was room for all eight of us.

Our desperate gamble had worked! For the first time in several hours, we talked to each other without shouting. We spoke in low tones, since the cave seemed to demand it, and quickly decided that we would spend the night here. With Tom's light reflecting eerily off the snow roof, we settled uncomfortably onto the sloping, rust-colored pumice. There was little preparation for the night besides taking off our ropes and crampons. I rummaged in my gray pack for the remains of my lunch, found a single raisin, and popped it into my mouth. That was dinner.

After Tom switched off his light to save the battery, I lay against the blackness, and drifted into an uneasy catharsis. Amazingly, in the middle of the night, my butt got too hot. Some places were warmer than others, so I scooted over a few inches and crammed my trusty canvas pack under me. Listening to the others' breathing, I pondered our problem. My feeling was that we would descend in the morning, but what if the storm continued? A third color clouded my mind, but I pushed it aside. Calming myself with my now fervent feeling that we would descend in the morning, I drifted away again.

The Color of Hell

A vague light filtered through the snow signaling that it was dawn. I sat up and listened, but could not tell if it was sparkling clear or pure hell outside. I needed to go out to check the weather. While the team's disturbed breathing filled the cave, my stiff muscles creaked across it, and I crept into the entry tunnel. As I crawled through, my mind's scientific half knew that the storm could continue for days, but my mind's youthful, optimistic half willed it to be sparkling clear outside so we could descend in the sun to tell of our grand adventure. I reached the end of the tunnel, pushed away a foot of new snow, and saw the color of hell.

Science had made a mockery of my will, but I still couldn't believe it. With the storm lashing at my eyes, I optimistically thought that I might just be in some surface spindrift, so I wiggled farther out to be sure. My will was nowhere in sight; it was indeed hell outside. If anything, the storm was wilder than yesterday. To make matters worse, my clothing held a lot of moisture from the warm cave, and now, with the wind blasting on my parka, I felt an instant, deep cold. Aided by wind and moisture, the cold penetrated fast as a pang of red-hot fear stabbed deep inside me. There *was* a third color, and it was the color of hell. This was not just a painting of hell; this was a gushing, gurgling, sighing, dying, red-white-black, hot-cold hell. Answer in hand, I wiggled back into the cave's sanctuary and gasped, "It's hell out there! Go see for yourselves!" The rest of the team stirred, and several of them ventured into the entry tunnel. They all returned adding their own adjectives, but confirmed my observations.

I rummaged again in the remains of my lunch and this time found nothing. That was breakfast. With the murky half-light filtering into the cave, a long discussion followed. Our voices were very animated now, since we had much to talk about. We were safe in the cave for the moment, but we were still on Rainier's summit in a storm. We had no way of knowing how long the storm might last, but we knew that it could go on for days. The cave kept us alive, but it also kept us wet. If we decided to wait in the cave and the storm lasted for days, we would be very weak and wet when we finally descended. If we attempted the descent right now, we would be stronger but must face the storm. We had attempted the descent yesterday, had failed, and were in worse condition today for our effort. Drawing on Herb's detailed Rainier knowledge, we debated alternative descent routes, but none of them solved our basic problem: we remained trapped on Rainier's summit in a raging storm.

Occasionally a temper flared, but these outbursts came from fear, and our large group's calming effect minimized machismo. For the most part, our conversation was very analytical, and I wondered what Dr. Z would do to solve this problem. Doubtless, he would just scratch his talon fingernails on the board and come up with a brilliant, colorful conclusion. After several hours of intense debate, we decided to go for it and attempt the descent. It was a difficult decision, but in the end we felt that action was preferable to inaction and voted for strength over patience. We worked out a detailed plan since, once in the wind, we would not be able to communicate. If our plan worked, we would be off this hellish mountain in a few hours. As a backup, if conditions became too difficult, we could abandon the attempt and return to the cave like yesterday.

We completed our preparations in a few minutes, since all we had to do was strap on our crampons, collect the ropes, and crawl out of the cave. We knew that it was going to be tough and steeled ourselves for the wind's frigid blast. We had difficulty with the icy ropes but soon started across the crater. Herb had the most intimate knowledge of Rainier, so he led while Don, Dick, and I followed him as a rope of four. With the wind blasting on our backs, the other four followed on a second rope.

The motion felt good to my stiff muscles, and I was just starting to generate some heat when the rope stopped. Herb's crampons had come off, so Don and Dick moved up to help him get them back on; they would be essential once we left the crater and started the steep descent. The rest of us just stood with our backs to the wind and endured the tempest. After five long minutes, I became impatient and advanced to Herb. His crampons were back on, but he was crouching in the snow trying to talk with Don and Dick. We had already had our conversation, and shivering badly, I knew that we had to move fast, so I motioned to Herb to get going. Herb got to his feet and moved forward again, but he only went another rope-length. From my position at the end of the rope, I watched Herb wandering into the whiteout. It was important that we cross the eastern crater rim in exactly the right place. On a symmetric volcano like Rainier, a small directional error descending from the summit would magnify to put us on a completely different route lower down. We had a compass but couldn't use it in the howling wind.

Finally Herb struggled back to Don. It was no good—we couldn't even find our way across the crater, much less descend the entire mountain. We would freeze if we didn't get back to the cave fast, so we turned into the wind, bowed our heads to the tempest, and struggled back. When we reached the cave's vicinity, we could not find it. The cave had vanished!

We didn't need to talk, since we all knew what to do. Still roped up, we spread out, then started probing and digging. After many finger-freezing minutes, Bill found the entrance, wiggled in, and pulled the rest of us in on the ropes like a catch of fish. We shivered and fumbled badly for a long time in our black sanctuary. Our gamble had failed and our penalty was reduced strength and another night in the cave, but at least we were still alive. The cave was quiet, but it now smelled like hell, and this was the first time that I had ever smelled a color. It was a combination of sulfur, snow, sweat, shit, and fear.

The prospect of spending another night slithering down the sloping cave floor was grim, so after testing the slope with an ice ax, we hacked away at the wretched, friable pumice and slowly created a crude platform. The activity warmed and energized us, since at least we were doing *something*. After a debate we decided not to toss the debris into the black hole at the back of the cave. The hole appeared useless and was dangerous, but we were leery of losing any possible advantage, since we might still need the hole.

Dick, Bill, and I lay down on our new pumice platform while Carl and Sally clung to each other near the tunnel entrance trying to breathe nonexistent fresh air. In the back of the cave, Don, Herb, and Tom settled painfully above the black hole. We didn't have the energy to be hungry. The light faded along with our conversation, since we had little left to talk about. Perhaps my willpower was feeble compared to the storm, but it couldn't hurt to exert it, so I willed that it would clear tomorrow and that we would descend. The already dim light faded to black, then each of us faded into our own private stupors.

At first the heat felt good, but after thrashing around for a half hour, I realized that my butt was *too* hot. When we cut into the slope, we had increased the size of the tiny steam vents, and they now created a new and unexpected hazard: burns! After locating the worst vents and avoiding them, I folded my canvas pack twice and perched on it. As the steam, sulfur, and pumice ground into it, the smell of the color of hell infused my pack's canvas until the canvas *became* the smell and the color. Now, I smelled a fourth color.

We roasted on the bottom and froze on top. Somewhere in the night's nadir, I heard Sally's sobbing voice, "Ow, I'm burning! Oh, I'm freezing! Oh! Ow! Ow! Oh! ... " It was miserable: a thin snow film settled on us, melted into our clothing, and kept us soaking wet. I heard dripping from new parts of the cave and poked a finger into the now sodden snow roof. The blackness enveloped me, and I patiently perched, since this was not a time for brilliant solutions. This was a time for perseverance and I was about to relearn the importance of the "P" in my "WHO CLIMBS UP" acronym. My brain voice was groggy, but it did manage to remind me that here, on a steep, high, snowy volcano, I had my best opportunity for Karmic Gain. At the time, this thought only seemed like a taunt, but as usual my brain was ahead of the moment. After slowing my breathing, I gradually fell away into convoluted, four-color dreams.

The Color of Death

I drug myself from a stubborn stupor, and even before I mustered the energy to open my eyes, I knew something was different and very wrong. Then I felt the cave with my eyes, ears, and nose. There was only a vague luminescence, and it was deathly quiet. Was this the fourth color? Quiet? Death? Indeed, were we all still alive? As I rose on my elbow, my head hit the cave ceiling, and I silently cursed the soggy snow that fell in my lap. My heart took off abruptly when I suddenly realized that the top of the cave was lower! There was now too much heat, and with at least twenty feet of snow over our heads, our cave was turning into a tomb.

Perseverance time was over, so I jostled Dick and Bill, but they barely stirred. Head low, I moved over Sally and Carl toward the tunnel entrance. There was snow everywhere, and there was no tunnel. It had drifted in. Suddenly feeling trapped, I began scrabbling at the snow like a cornered cat until I could just wiggle through the snow-choked tunnel. I focused on the thought that in ten more feet I would breathe real air and see blue skies. As I burrowed, I reasoned that if the wind had shifted to drift us in, then the storm must be over. It *must* be over—yesterday was to build character, but today was the real thing. With all my powers, I willed the sky to be blue.

The tunnel's last section was steeply uphill, and I grunted with my effort. *Three feet to go.* Blue skies meant life, and white skies meant death. *One foot to go.* I pulled my head out and brushed the snow off my goggles. *One foot to go.* There was so much new snow that I was not yet out of the tunnel, but it didn't feel good. Pushing hard and realizing how weak I now was, I got my head out of the snow, and once again brushed the snow off my goggles.

Death. Stinging death. I pulled myself farther out to be sure. Death! The storm raged worse than yesterday, and the lashing wind froze me instantly. Now, I smelled the fourth color. The color was death, and it tugged at my weakness. No! I didn't have time to bleed or die, and I certainly had no energy to cry, since my tears would have frozen anyway. I slipped down and swam back into the cave as new drift snow poured in all around me. I was wild awake now, but the others were still in a stupor, since the cave's air was bad. Bonking my head on the sodden ceiling, I guessed that we had one hour before the cave's roof met the floor. We were in a shrinking tomb of doom, and I vowed that I would not die in a cave. I would go out, face the storm, and make one more attempt to descend. I would not die here—not like this. Like Prince, I would die trying.

I shouted, but nobody moved. Was everybody dead? I needed help, so I crawled to Bill and shook him hard. He was groggy, but OK. I said urgently, "Bill! It's still storming out, but we've got to get out of here!"

Bill pulled some colorful gunk out of his mouth and replied, "Unnh? We should stay here until it clears."

I insisted with, "Bill! Crawl through the tunnel and take a look for yourself. The cave is collapsing, and the tunnel is drifted in." Something in my voice moved him.

As Bill swam into the tunnel, I cleared the snow from behind him so that he could get back into the cave. More drift snow poured in with Bill when he came back sputtering, "You're right, Roach! We've gotta get out of here!"

I replied, "Good! Help me. We've got six more people to convince." Sally and Carl stirred, since we had nearly buried them with all the snow near the tunnel. At least they were alive. Bill and I shook Dick, and I went straight for it by insisting, "Dick! Crawl into the tunnel and take a look. Let me know what you think!" I knew that once Dick realized our peril, he would be very persuasive with the others.

Solid white, Dick came back roaring, "Yeow! We *have* to get out of here!"

Tom, Don, and Herb, who were at the back of the cave where the ceiling was a little higher, still did not understand the problem. Bill and I worked at keeping the tunnel open while Dick worked on Herb, who still insisted, "We *must* stay here until the weather clears!"

Without a word, Tom crawled out of the cave and did not return. Was he lost? Delirious? Dead? We did not know. We had one direction to move the drift snow that poured in—to the back of the cave. Quickly, the now doubly shrinking cave had only fifteen minutes before it collapsed.

The hole! We could stuff the excess snow into the black hole. Don was now wild awake and began cramming snow into the hole as we dog-paddled it back. With snow reaching the back of the cave, Herb finally understood the problem.

Sally shouted, "I've lost my ice ax and crampons in the snow near the tunnel!"

I told Carl and Sally, "There's no longer room for all of us. Get out while you still can and I'll dig for the equipment. I know it's essential." Carl was just able to paddle out. Sally got stuck in the tunnel, but Carl was able to reach her from above and pull her out.

It was impossible for two people to go through the tunnel together, since each person sent volumes of snow back into the shrinking cave. Those remaining worked feverishly to get the snow into the black hole. Then, as Bill battled through the tunnel, the black hole jammed full—our last ace was in the hole. There were four people left inside and ten minutes of cave left.

As each person crawled through the tunnel, the light faded. The signal for the next person to start was a blast of light as the tunnel cleared, and it was important to go instantly before the tunnel clogged. The exit got harder to negotiate for each successive person. As Bill popped out, Herb dove in. Dick, Don, and I dug frantically for Sally's ax and crampons. We had other problems waiting for us outside and needed the equipment. We dug all the way to the pumice but found nothing. Then we faintly heard Herb calling from the middle of the tunnel, "Help! I'm stuck! Stuck!!" From below, there was nothing we could do for him, and suddenly, one of our companions had trapped Dick, Don, and me in the cave.

We waited, since Herb's only chance was if the others could reach him from above, but had they even heard him? The seconds ticked like seasons. We had strong companions out there, and our only hope was that they would rescue Herb. While the seasons ticked, we crouched.

Finally there was a blast of light. Herb's rescue from above was complete, and Dick was into the tunnel like a driven demon. As Dick swam, I tried one more time to find Sally's ax while Don moved the snow back. I could not find the ax, and worse, our tomb was almost full. Only Don and I remained in the cave. By pre-arrangement, Don would go next and I would go last. As Don crouched for his launch, I smelled it—Don had taken a giant shit in the back of the cave. As light came into the tunnel, he paused for a second and said woefully, "Sorry. I had to." Then he charged into the tunnel leaving me alone. I held my breath for as long as I could, while my season-seconds seemed suspended. But this was no time to set a breath-holding record; I knew that I needed to oxygenate my muscles for my upcoming struggle, so I exhaled. Then I inhaled the fourth color, and knew that the smell of shit had become my color of death. It was only marginally better than no air at all. Barely breathing, I crouched in my tenth domain and waited for the light.

After two eternities, light appeared, but it was faint. I knew that the snow had nearly clogged the tunnel and that this effort was for my life. I launched, swam like a medal-bedecked Olympian, paddled like a kayaker fleeing Victoria Falls, then roared like a clever bull escaping a matador's death blow. At the elbow where everyone had trouble, I summoned absolute rage. This mountain would not consume me! Not here, not now, not ever. Wailing, "I must *climb*," I flailed up the last vertical section and popped out like a rogue rocket.

The storm still raged back at me, but at least I saw the third color again. As I came into the storm, I held my soaked mittens in a near fist so that they would freeze in a position that would allow me to grab my ice ax. Tom appeared from behind a small boulder—he was OK, but had simply decided that he was not going back into the cave. We had put our crampons on in the cave, but not the ropes, which was a mistake. Now we were all outside trying to tie into frozen ropes. I picked up a steel-stiff rope and, realizing that a regular knot would not work, took a huge bight, wrapped it around my waist, and with some effort, managed to complete a single half-hitch. We now had to make the descent that we had failed to do on each of the last two days, but we were now far weaker and wetter. The difference was that we were now fighting for our lives and had no choice. Knowing that this time we could not return to the cave, we shuffled resolutely across the crater without looking back.

After a rope length, our procession stopped as it had yesterday. This time I went forward immediately to see what the trouble was. Herb had crumpled onto the snow, and the team gathered around him. Still believing that mere encouragement would help, I railed at Herb, "Get up and move, man!"

Herb sagged lower and looked up at me with a face of death, sobbing, "*My-hands-are-freezing!*" It was the last coherent thing he said. We could not leave Herb. Or could we? The thought startled me and shook me to the core. I had never had that thought before in my life, but never before had my life been in such jeopardy. Then honor tapped me on the shoulder, and I snapped back. To abandon a companion would be the ultimate dishonor. Herb might not make it, but I knew that just as I had already chosen to die trying to save myself, I now needed to make the same commitment to save Herb's life. I would *try* to get him down.

With Herb beyond mere encouragement, it was now time for a different kind of action, one that helped everybody's odds of survival. After a struggle, I got my hand out of my mitten and reached into my shirt pocket for two tablets that I had carefully stashed there before leaving the cave. I ordered Herb to open his mouth.

As he mumbled, "Whaa," I stuffed the stimulants into his mouth, then quickly forced my nearly frozen hand back into my grotesque mitten. Tom frantically rummaged in his pack and triumphantly produced a pair of dry down mittens that he had carefully saved. We gathered around Herb, and with a considerable team effort, got the mittens onto his hands. Herb was incoherent, but we got him onto his feet. With Tom supporting him, he was able to stagger ahead, since his primal instincts were still good.

We stumbled forward, but could still not see enough to get our direction. The problem that had stopped us yesterday was stopping us today, but we had no choice, so we crept forward into the howling white wilderness. Rainier had spoken, and I had my antithesis. This was forever known as the "HOWL," which is the antithesis of the "WOW."

The Poetry of Antithesis

At our moment of deepest despair, Rainier relented. The clouds suddenly ripped apart, and we saw blue sky. The first blast of blue was heaven sent, and a few moments later, we saw the crater rim. Fearful that the clearing might only be momentary, we moved with renewed vigor toward the eastern rim. When we reached the rim, we blinked and looked all the way down the mountain. The storm was over, and the summit had been the last place to clear. After two nights of looking inward in a dark cave, the sudden, blinding view was overpowering. After our tears of joy froze, the view reminded us we were still on Rainier's summit, and we still had to descend.

Preparing for our final ordeal, we split our liabilities between the two rope teams. Tom led, Dick supported Herb, and Don anchored the two of them on the end of the first rope. Carl led the second rope followed by Sally. I belayed Sally and

Bill backed me up at the end of the second rope. Just before starting down from the rim, Bill hollered, "Gerry! My crampons are clogged with ice. Help me!" I quickly retreated to Bill and pried huge ice cakes away from his crampon points with my ice ax. He bellowed, "Thanks, Roach! Now I can belay the whole team!" I felt a tremendous surge, and as we started down, I believed that we could make it.

Different problems consumed each rope team. When Herb could not stay on his feet, Tom, Dick, and Don pulled and lowered him like a bag of marbles. It was hard work for them, but each foot down was a victory. Without ice ax, crampons, or sunglasses, Sally fell repeatedly. She courageously attempted each slope with arms spread wide for balance, but then her feet slipped, her knees buckled, and she shot down the slope like a tiny torpedo. I continually braced myself and held her on the rope. On the steepest slopes, Bill gave me a reassuring tug from his anchor position. With each step down, I felt stronger, and life's other colors slowly returned. Like a tattered old prayer flag, there was the poetry of prayer in our motion as we crept down the mountain.

Somewhere in the depths of the night, we slipped back into Seattle and Wilburs. Our housemate Newell Mack was asleep on the couch waiting for Dick, Bill, and me. As we whooped and roared, Newell grabbed me and held me for the longest moment. It was over.

Many years later, the four-color problem did fall to a computer proof. It fell to perseverance, not inspired insight or greatness. Likewise, our survival on Rainier was largely because of perseverance. I have returned to climb Rainier several times over the years, and each time the mountain has tried to kill me. Each time Rainier has demanded perseverance. Stuffed in the corner of my tiny Wilburs room sat a reminder of how I had learned to relate color to my mountains. My gray canvas pack held Das Cave's smelly colors forever.

Return to Antithesis

A week after escaping from Das Cave, I was back at 13,000 feet on Rainier in a whiteout, wondering which way to go. A bit of the, "Get back on the horse after you fall off" mentality motivated my second climb. Also, while I had climbed the mountain, I certainly hadn't experienced the mountain as I had hoped. There had been too many committee decisions that led us to Das Cave, and our party had been so large that, while strong, it sagged under its own weight. I wanted to climb Rainier on my own terms. Not surprisingly, none of the other Das Cave escapees shared my desire to head right back up there, so this time I went with three friends from the UW hiking club with whom I had done many weekend climbs during the year.

Having seen Rainier's south and east sides, I chose the Emmons Glacier Route on the mountain's northeast flank. Compared to the Nisqually Icefall, the Emmons Glacier is an easy route, and I looked forward to a normal climb where I could turn around if need be and descend my ascent route.

Much of our Das Cave malaise was rooted in the fact that we were committed to a traverse, which always greatly increases the risks on a big mountain. Indeed, when the weather had turned bad above the Nisqually Icefall, we found our retreat cut off and were forced to continue up into the storm. I also felt that our Das Cave horrors were rooted in Das Cave itself. I questioned our choice to head back up to the summit in the storm but had been outvoted by the committee at the time. I felt strongly that if we had worked harder at completing the initial descent, we would have made an earlier escape. The fear at the time was that someone might plunge into one of the crevasses, but we had to face this hazard sooner or later to get off the mountain, and with eight of us, we could have protected each other against this feared fall with the ropes. This is what Geoff, Mike, Dick, and I had done when we reversed the rope in the crevasses above Windy Corner on Denali.

On Rainier we were almost a thousand feet below the summit when we made the fateful decision to climb up into the storm for a *second* time. While there were some crevasses there, it was early season, and with a little work, I felt that we could have skirted the crevasses and completed the descent. Geoff, Mike, Dick, and I had spent many hours on Denali feeling our way in whiteouts, sometimes in crevasse zones, and I knew that some whiteout time can almost be expected on a high coastal mountain. Even if we had been trapped by crevasses on our first attempted descent from Rainier's summit, perhaps we could have sheltered in one of the crevasses. We would have been a thousand feet lower in any case. Another party had done just that and completed their escape during a slight lull in the storm, which of course we could not see from inside Das Cave. Also, such a lull might not be visible from the summit at all. I knew that such critical choices are situation dependent and that often all of the choices are dangerous. So seeking more experience to help me make these critical choices, back up Rainier I went. I would not have to wait long to increase my knowledge.

With my new team in tow, I packed up to Camp Sherman at 10,000 feet under the Emmons Glacier. The weather was better now, and we all looked forward to a fun-filled climb. Indeed our climb toward the summit the next morning was sunny until we reached 13,000 feet. Crevasses form near the 13,000-foot level on Rainier because this is where the glacier's critical mass pulls away from the relatively stable summit snowcap. Just as I had seen on Rainier's other sides, there were more crevasses here on the Emmons as well. Since it was still early season, which meant that the crevasses were mostly covered, I had no difficulty in maneuvering through them. However, once again, the weather was deteriorating rapidly. So just one week after crawling from Das Cave, I was once again at 13,000 feet on Rainier facing the same critical choices.

This time, however, there were three big differences. Back in Seattle, I had already made one critical choice, and that was to ascend the Emmons, which did not require a traverse. On the Emmons, I had the option of turning around and racing back down my tracks. The second big difference on this climb was that I was the leader and I did not have to face the committee. My companions were less experienced than I was, and they were willing to abide by my choices. Of course this meant that I had to factor their needs into my choices. As the clouds lowered toward the summit, I sprinted ahead to at least get a view of the upper slopes. Right after I got my view, the clouds descended upon us, visibility dropped, white turned to gray, the wind came up, and it started to snow. I felt a shiver race through me and didn't know if it was from the cold or from the memory.

While the first two differences protected my retreat, they did not ensure that I could reach the summit, especially in a storm. However, the third difference did. This time I had brought a large bundle of wands. I had been placing them for some time, and with my retreat now doubly protected, I continued up into the storm. Looking down to make sure that my companions were OK and that I could indeed see my wands, I kicked on through the soft snow until I reached the crater rim. The wind was ferocious here and visibility was only a few feet, but we were close. Turning right and feeling my way along the rim, I found the summit after a few more minutes. To be back on top of Rainier in another raging storm so soon after Das Cave was surreal, and I felt demons nipping at my heels. We whooped and roared and even managed to get a frosty photo, then I looked for Das Cave.

Das Cave was near the junction of the flat crater floor and the mostly pumice slope leading from the crater floor up to Columbia Crest, which is Rainier's highest point. From the high point, I climbed down the slope looking for any trace of Das Cave, but saw nothing. But I could smell it—the smell of the color of death was still here. I crept closer for a better look but still saw nothing. When I was twenty feet above the snows of the crater floor, I stopped. I could not see the cave, but when the rest of my senses told me where to look, I finally saw it. The otherwise feature-less snow held a faint swale where Das Cave had been—the cave had indeed collapsed. I thought about going out onto the snow to see if I could find Sally's gear, but a primal fear tapped me on the shoulder and said no. A new cave was probably already forming, and I might plunge into a new trap. The thought of once again thrashing through choking snow in a fight for my life sent more than a shiver through me. While my retreat might be doubly protected, I was now doubly extended, and I knew that my quest for additional experience was complete. Hearing my companions on the high point hollering for me, I quickly retreated up the pumice to the summit's sanctity.

Back on the summit, I realized just how ferocious this new storm had become, and suddenly, with father fear still tugging, I knew I had seen sufficient storms on Rainier's summit. It was now time to utilize my retreat protection. Without wasting another moment, the four of us hustled along the northern crater rim, spotted my wands, and plunged down the mountain.

Return to Alaska

A week after my second descent from Rainier, I was in Alaska. After Denali in 1963, I spent the rest of that summer working for the Geophysical Institute at the University of Alaska in Fairbanks. I loved the place, the people, and the work, and watching the total solar eclipse had been icing on my summer's bountiful cake. My college education was largely self-financed, and my main source of money came from my summer jobs. I had now spent three consecutive summers working, two on Maui and one in Alaska, and I needed one more summer job to see my degree through to tassel time. When I contacted the Geophysical Institute, they indeed had a job for me, but it was not what I expected.

The Institute was one party to a large research grant whose purpose was to study high-altitude health issues. The research needed to take place on a high mountaintop, and they needed a high-altitude facility with a support staff. The Institute had already picked a snow-free site near the summit of 14,163-foot Mount Wrangell, which is at the western edge of the Wrangell Mountains, 200 miles east-northeast of Anchorage, and they planned to build a hut there. With my experience in both mountaintop construction and mountaineering, I was a shoo-in for the job. The pay was good, and I reasoned that having spent one summer on top of a mountain in Hawaii, I should spend another on top of a mountain in Alaska. But this time there was a catch.

My roommate and now long-time climbing partner, Dick Springgate, had planned a trip to climb a new route on Mount Logan, which is the highest peak in Canada, and he wanted me to join the team. Having climbed Denali and Orizaba, the lure of Mount Logan was strong, since it would complete North America's big three—the three highest peaks on the continent. Dick had done his research and had picked out a beautiful unclimbed ridge on Logan's north side. An unclimbed route on a major peak was now more important to me than it had been when Geoff and I roamed around in the Flatirons. Dick's Logan expedition would take longer than our Denali climb had, and I would not be able to do the climb then zoom to the job as I had done in 1963. I had to choose between the two.

Each had their pluses, and the choice tormented me through the spring. Dick continued to hound me to go on the Logan trip, while the Institute's ring rolled by on the merry-go-round. If the Institute job had been behind a desk in Fairbanks, I would have gone to Logan. However, the job, while not a climb, was a significant mountain adventure, and it would pay me more than enough to complete my degree. I had invested heavily in college, and sensing that I would have future opportunities to climb Logan, I chose the Institute job.

When I arrived at the Glennallen airfield, I saw not one but three significant mountains to the east and knew that it was going to be a good summer. Arrayed from south to north were the curious Mount Wrangell, 12,010-foot Mount Drum, and 16,237-foot Mount Sanford. Rising in a long, low sweep, Wrangell was the least impressive of the three peaks. Since Glennallen is only at 1,500 feet, I found it hard to believe that Wrangell is more than 14,000 feet high. While not steep, Wrangell is indeed a high, snowy volcano, and I liked that.

Cupping my eyes for a better look, I saw that Wrangell was very white and held features that had escaped my initial glance. After consulting the huge wall map in the pilot's lounge and realizing that Wrangell was fifty-seven miles from the airfield, I knew that these were all huge mountains. Looking again at the map, I saw that these peaks were just the western sentinels of the vast Wrangell–Saint Elias Range that extended for 400 miles to the east-southeast and contained Logan, Mount Saint Elias, and a host of other high peaks. On Denali I had been focused on three great mountains, but here I sensed that I had an entire new universe to explore. I paced the edge of the runway, nervously waiting for my chance to begin.

The Institute had chosen Wrangell, a dormant volcano, for one simple reason. The volcano's heat had melted the snow along one of the ridges near the summit, and this pumice platform provided a snow-free place to build the research hut in an otherwise glaciated landscape. Having just emerged from Das Cave, I was skeptical of this plan. How could the temperature be just right? What if it was too hot and the building burned up? What if it was too cold and the snows returned to bury the building, or worse, to create steam caves? I knew that we would have to dig into the pumice to create a level foundation, and this would increase the emerging heat. Squinting again at Wrangell, I saw a plume of smoke—or perhaps it was steam—emerging from the southern end of the summit plateau. After a closer look at the map, I realized that Wrangell had an inner, more active crater at the south end of a five-mile-long caldera, and that the hut ridge was at the caldera's higher, northern end. Still smelling Das Cave, I knew full well that dormant is not the same as extinct. What if the volcano erupted? Immensely eager to get the answers to all these questions, I paced the runway at high speed then broke into a run to relieve the tension.

After several days of waiting, my runway sprints had slowed back to walks. The major party to the research grant was the army, and they were going to supply the helicopters and pilots for the airlift of men and materials to Wrangell's summit caldera. But where were they? While waiting at the airfield, I got to know Jack Wilson, the civilian glacier pilot who was the Sheldon of the Wrangell–Saint Elias Range. Jack did not sprint across the runway and disappear like Sheldon had, and I found it easy to catch him. When he sauntered up puffing on a pipe, he usually went into the hangar to fiddle with his Super Cub then retired to the pilot's lounge to get a donut, cup of coffee, and refill his pipe. All I had to do was stake myself out in the pilot's lounge, open the window, and wait for Jack to come to me. Once I had him in the lounge, I just pointed at some new part of the giant wall map, which covered most of the Wrangell–Saint Elias Range, and asked, "What about this peak?" Then, stirring creamer into his coffee, Jack would look intently at the map, and with a faraway look in his eyes, tell his tales. Jack had as many stories as

Sheldon, and I was fortunate to hear them firsthand, since in 1964 Jack knew more about the great range than anyone. I suspected that, like Sheldon, Jack would win his wager with the wind. After Jack left the lounge to fiddle with his Cessna, I remained with the map and planned a hundred future expeditions. I had no idea that events half a world away were delaying my Wrangell adventure.

When an old army helicopter did arrive for a reconnaissance flight over the mountain, I immediately dashed up and asked to go along. The crew, while sympathetic, denied my request, since the insurance agreement between the army and the Institute was not yet in place. I paced along the edge of the runway in bitter disappointment while the chopper rumbled off toward the peaks. When the crew returned, they told me about Wrangell and also about the new Vietnam War that was consuming the army's best efforts. Now I knew what had caused the delay, and it seemed to me like the world was speeding up. First, we barely escaped from the Cuban Missile Crisis in October 1962, then Kennedy was assassinated in November 1963, and now there was a brand-new war to go get the Reds. The pilots also told me that all the best choppers were already in Vietnam and that this project would have to be accomplished with old equipment. That was a problem, since their current bucket of bolts had not been able to fly over Wrangell's summit. After the crew hopped back into their aging machine and rumbled off, leaving me alone again, I paced the runway, knowing that the Cold War was heating up.

Finally the army did appropriate two tougher Huey helicopters and some experienced pilots who were under the orders of Colonel Allen. After a weeklong flurry of noisy, dangerous, blade-spinning excitement, I was on top of Wrangell with a six-person construction crew and a small mountain of equipment. Not surprisingly, after flying from 1,500 feet to 14,000 feet, the rest of the crew immediately disappeared into our tents to nurse their altitude headaches. This was the research program's first result—such a rapid ascent is not a good idea. After my recent camping expedition on top of Rainier, I had no trouble with the altitude and took advantage of this benefit by organizing my new crater camp.

For 1964 our prefabricated hut was quite an ingenious arrangement. The sixteen-by-twenty-foot hut had eighteen separate four-by-eight-foot panels, which connected edge to edge by a clever hook-and-grab system that we tightened with a special tool until the two panels were seamless. Four of the wall panels had double-pane windows. The ten-panel flat roof was supported in the middle by two ten-foot beams and a center column. The roof and sides were insulated, but the plywood floor was not, in hopes that the volcano's heat would travel through the floor and heat the hut. Before leaving Seattle, I had visited the factory in nearby Everett that had built the hut. In the flat, warm warehouse at sea level, my trial assembly of the hut had gone without a hitch, and I had assembled it in half a day. On top of Alaska's mighty Mount Wrangell at 14,000 feet, the assembly would take us two weeks.

After several back-wrenching, lung-straining days, we had a large, hand-dug

An aerial view of the snow-free ridge where we built the Pumice Palace.

foundation pit for the hut. As I once again found myself hacking away at the pumice trying to create a level place to sleep, I couldn't help thinking about Das Cave, especially since our construction site smelled very similar. The smell of desperate fear and death were not here, but the rest of it was. Our young expedition still held many unanswered questions, and this new volcano definitely had my attention. Once again I found myself peering into the underworld looking for steam vents—and finding them. I was now an expert in producing pumice platforms. At least this time there was no snow over my head, and if I needed fresh air, I would walk away to one of the nearby snowy summits and perch there. I had no interest in revisiting my tenth domain, and I carefully scanned the surrounding terrain for any sign of Das Cave II.

After we assembled the walls, we discovered that the hut was not square and would not accept the roof panels, since the clever attachment fittings needed to line up exactly. Our foreman, Eldon Thompson, tackled this challenge like an Everest. After setting several anchors, we cranked the hut into shape with a come-along until the hooks settled into their slots with a satisfying click. The next day we hung the front door and moved into our "Pumice Palace," just as a vicious storm started. The tents were still pitched, and for the first time in my climbing career, I stood at a window in my T-shirt watching a tent bending in a raging white wind. The tents survived, but after the storm we discovered some bent poles and packed the no longer–necessary tents away. After sealing the hut, adding an enclosed entryway and a volcano-heated snow-melting system, the Pumice Palace became a home.

On its appointed day, a large army plane flew over to drop us some fifty-gallon fuel drums. We heard the plane's roar, but could not see it due to some pesky clouds that liked the summit as much as we did. After several circles, the plane discharged its precious cargo into the clouds, and we spent several days finding and retrieving the drums from their ten-foot-deep craters. One by one we ferried the drums back to the Palace on the Arctic Cat, which was an early version of a snowmobile. With this basic construction complete, the crew was ready to head back to Fairbanks for R&R.

Several days later, Colonel Allen made several valiant attempts to reach the site in his Huey, but once again, clouds ruled the runway. He finally did land in a near whiteout and hollered, "It's really too dangerous to take any of you off, but if one of you wants to try, hop in!" Of course, I hopped in. After I strapped myself in, Colonel Allen hollered one more instruction: "Don't touch anything!" Because of the high altitude, the Huey had to slide down the runway like an airplane to get airborne. To escape the storm, Colonel Allen turned back toward the obscured summits, which we were below, and I suddenly realized the peril we were in. Flying by the seat of his pants in a complete whiteout, Colonel Allen flew through the small valley between two summits and emerged into open skies. Releasing a huge sigh, I realized the tension that Colonel Allen had been under. I resolved to be a little less hasty next time in my dash for comfort.

Back in Fairbanks, I became an army laboratory guinea pig, a duty that the Institute's job description had not mentioned. First I had a detailed physical, then suffered through a max O_2 test. With a tube-infested, heavy wooden box over my head, I was instructed to pedal a stationary bicycle at a steady rate while they steadily increased the resistance. A rolling-pen chart recorded what percentage of the available oxygen my lungs were able to extract. After 50 percent, the effort became more interesting, and I started concentrating. At 60 percent, I was working hard and cursing the box on my head. At 70 percent, I was only able to steal an occasional glance at the chart, but I was still able to curse my horrible hat. At 75 percent, the tester ran from the room to call some other officers, since he had never seen a reading this high. At 80 percent, I was in a froth, while a collection of officers huddled around the chart ignoring my pain. At 85 percent, they pointed excitedly at the chart, while I roared in my headdress, nearly expiring from my effort. That was as far as I could go, and the research program had another data point. I knew nothing about these numbers, but gathered that mine was a high reading.

Later, the army treated me to another unique experience—a cold test. Wearing only a lightweight, sensor-riddled mesh suit, I had to lie still on a hole-infested cot in a forty-degree room for three hours. The first hour was not too bad, and I enjoyed the rest. After an hour and a half I was stiff from my unflinching position, but when I tried to shift slightly, the tester roared at me from his heated observation room to remain still. After two hours I was shivering, but I took my mind away from my misery by concentrating on the fact that I had to pee. When I announced my dilemma to the tester, he announced that I had to hold it until the end of the test. After two and a half hours, I announced that they either bring me a bottle or I would let 'er rip. That did it. Fearing that I would flood some of the sensors and spoil the test, a bottle appeared. After the tester allowed me just enough movement to accomplish the task, I lay back in considerable relief, only to remember how cold I was. I wondered what percentage of my remaining body heat had departed in the bottle, and knew that, while I had reduced one discomfort, I had only increased another. After three hours, I thought that this was quite a sadistic test and vowed to never do such a foolish thing again. Immediately upon emerging from my cold cell, the testers announced that I would have to repeat the cold test at the end of the summer to see if life on Wrangell's summit improved my adaptability to cold.

I armed myself with a pack full of books, which included Hemingway's *The Snows of Kilimanjaro*, then Jack Wilson flew Eldon, Emil Peel, and me back up to the Pumice Palace for the rest of the summer. The Vietnam War was now tugging harder at the army's resources, and Wilson would supply our air support for the rest of the project. Jack enjoyed the extra cash that his contract provided and promised to take good care of us. Back at the Palace, we had an answer to one of our questions—the Palace had not burned down. Carefully opening the door, we felt a rush of hot air and immediately wondered if it was too hot. The initial temperature in the hut was eighty-seven degrees Fahrenheit, but after airing it out, we had it back to our usual, comfortable sixty-five degrees. On this second visit, we had many additional tasks to accomplish, including building a generator hut and installing a wiring system. After we installed a generator, we had much better radio communications with the base station in Glennallen, but the first report we received shook us to the core. Colonel Allen was dead.

Colonel Allen had one more flying job to do before heading for Vietnam, but this time, the cloud he flew through had a mountain in it. His fatal flight was unrelated to our project, but huddling in the Pumice Palace, tweaking the radio dial to better hear the shocking news, I felt the Vietnam War's long finger pointing at me. All the voice behind the finger said was, "Your turn will come!" Not ready to face the rest of the world, I just grieved for Colonel Allen.

As summer rolled into August, we had more free time and our summit explorations went farther afield. One day we went as near as we dared to the steam-spewing southern crater, but with dips, pits, and holes everywhere, I felt like I had arrived in Das Cave Land, sometimes called the tenth domain, and was happy to leave this devil's playground unexplored. However, it seemed determined to explore us. When the crater's stinky steam cloud roiled high into the air over us and blotted out the sun, we retreated back to the Palace. The next day the cloud boiled higher still, and we wondered if the Palace was far enough away. As the cloud consumed the sky, we felt like our five-mile separation was indeed insufficient and wondered if the mighty Mount Wrangell was coming to life for a major eruption. The towering cloud worried us for three days, then it slowly calmed down. What we saw was steam, not ash, and it is likely that a huge collapse occurred in the depths of Das Cave Land, sending enormous volumes of snow plummeting down into the underworld and onto the hot floor of the mother of all Das Caves. As I fearfully watched this impressive display, I knew that Das Cave was still with me, and I resolved to make no further explorations toward the mother cave. However, my next trip in the opposite direction gave me another shock.

Determined to get a good look at Wrangell's north slope, I drove the Arctic Cat through the valley of fuel drum fame, then when the slope became too steep for my machine, I parked it and continued down to the north on foot. It was a nice day, and the view of Mount Sanford from here was stunning. Below me I also spotted Wrangell's

Digging for
Das Cave II.

northern outlier peak, 13,009-foot Mount Zanetti. Even though I had explored all of Wrangell's summits, I did not consider that I had climbed Mount Wrangell, since I had been airlifted up there. I was itching for some untainted action. Squatting, I studied the smooth slope down to the Wrangell-Zanetti Col, which was not steep enough to require crampons. Suddenly I jumped up and strode off down the slope in climb mode, figuring that I could climb Zanetti and get back before Eldon or Emil missed me. I was alone and unroped, but we had been running around on these smooth slopes unroped all summer.

Partway down, I felt the snow give way under my feet, and falling, I thought I was a goner. I assumed that I was plunging into a crevasse, but after three feet, I stopped. The THUMP-Thump-thump of settling snow radiated from my position in a receding wave as far as I could discern. I had just experienced the mother of all thump-instants. Unstable snow below the surface had given way, dropping the harder wind-packed top layer down. Normally, these settlings only drop a few inches and stay within a few feet of the person who sets them off, but they clearly are a weak snowpack talking. In this case, perhaps heat from below the surface had weakened the snow-pack. If so, this was Das Cave talking. I was fine, but I could not convince my trembling legs of that, so without another glance at Zanetti, I turned and climbed back to the cat, knowing that there would be no further explorations toward Zanetti either.

I spent my remaining free time perching on one of the two easy summits that flanked the Palace, and on good days, even read my books there. I never tired of looking southeast toward the interior of the Wrangell–Saint Elias Range. From my "Perch Peak," I had a good view of 16,390-foot Mount Blackburn, and knowing that this was one of the range's stellar summits, I studied it carefully looking for routes. Of course, by the end of summer, I had resolved to climb it someday. Beyond Blackburn, I had only distant glimpses of North America's greatest mountain playground, but from my map work, I knew that Bona, Lucania, Logan, Saint Elias, and a host of other peaks were out there waiting. I felt that this range was full of potential Transcendent Summits and knew that I had a destiny there.

Wilson flew over the next day and dropped us some supplies. Jack preferred to drop us care packages rather than land, since a landing at 14,000 feet with his small Super Cub was still a big event. It was always a cheery sight when Wilson flew over wagging his wings, and his care package sailing through the air made me feel like Christmas. This time his present contained ice cream, but Eldon and Emil thought that eating vanilla ice cream on a glacier made no sense, so the half-gallon became mine. I ate a little bit and found it to be the most wonderful thing that I had tasted all summer, so I carefully stowed the remaining treasure in the snow. To my horror, when I checked it a few hours later, it was melting! Das Cave's fingers were in the snow, and it was not cold enough, so I cursed Das Cave, then immediately had my revenge by eating the rest of the half-gallon. Thereafter when Wilson's packages sailed down, I applied the pacing tactic that I had learned in the Fairview after Denali and ate the entire half-gallon in one sitting.

With the days rapidly becoming shorter, we needed light in the late evenings to illuminate our Hearts games. In between hands, our conversation sometimes dwelled on the cold test that waited for us back in Fairbanks. It seemed ridiculous to us that the first thing we had to do after leaving the top of the mountain was to shiver in a cold room for three hours. We dreaded the test and schemed ways to get out of it, but we knew that one does not say no to the army. Nevertheless, I had a secret strategy.

A week later, I did my last 360 on Perch Peak looking at the splendor that had held me all summer. Wrangell was not a Transcendent Summit, but it was the first time that I had enjoyed a Karmic Summit Rest. In spite of various adventures and misadventures, the summer had been wonderfully peaceful. I knew that the rest of the world would soon consume me, but for the moment, I was alone and free and exactly where I wanted to be. Only when I heard Wilson's Cub coming for me did I descend from Perch Peak. Folding my lanky torso into the tiny Cub one more time, I waved good-bye to the gleaming Pumice Palace and fastened my seat belt. In sharp contrast to the noisy army choppers that had originally brought me up here, Wilson's Cub seemed like a silent winged angel as it lifted off and banked over Das Cave Land. As Jack turned toward Glennallen and put the Cub's nose down for our descent, I also waved good-bye to Das Cave.

The first part of my cold-room strategy was obvious—I didn't drink anything for several hours before the dreaded test. After the first easy hour, I discovered that I didn't yet need my second strategy. After the second, not quite-so-easy hour, I applied my tactic. Slowing my breathing as I had done in Das Cave, I purged all extraneous thoughts from my overactive brain, counted backwards through the colors, and when there was only one word left, I silently repeated my secret mantra over and over to myself. After three comfortable hours in the cold room, I rose refreshed. The army recorded a data point that I had indeed adapted to the cold, but I knew that Das Cave had taught me transcendental meditation and that my exploration of the tenth domain was complete.

Another Canyon to Bridge

Only when I thought about it later did I realize that my Rainier summit achieved during the Das Cave incident was my tenth Transcendent Summit. That was not a human hand of honor that touched me at the critical moment, when I might have chosen differently and left Herb behind, but it was God's honor guard speaking. On that fateful day, God touched me because I chose to die trying to save Herb rather than abandoning him to save myself. I believe that the honor of that choice touched my companions as well.

The "H" for *Honor* was the last letter in my "WHO CLIMBS UP" acronym for mountaineers, and it became the most important of the eleven words, Weather, Honor, *Om*, Conditions, Leadership, Inspiration, Mantra, Balance, Strength, Understanding, Perseverance. My mom had told me that mountaineers are people of honor back in 1953 when I first read the *Life* magazine story of Hillary and Tenzing's climb up Everest. Now, eleven years later, I had my own story and the knowledge that my mom had been right.

▼ ▼ ▼

Of course, my Transcendent Summit on Rainier was very different from the others, which had all been expansive, inspiring, and, to some, more obviously transcendent. However, there are no human rules or choreography for Transcendent Summits, since they indeed transcend human plots, foibles, desires, or even conceptualization—and that's the point. There is no rule that says a Transcendent Summit will be comfortable or even life sustaining, as my Rainier experience nearly proved. It is possible that my Transcendent Summit on Rainier is the most easily identified of the ten, and some might argue that it is the only one that I had experienced, but that would be applying human opinion to God's business. I believe that all ten were genuine and equally important, however Rainier did give me a new perspective on the others.

As a man of math, I have always looked for a logical bridge to lead me to a new belief, especially when the new belief does not readily support itself. Indeed, it was the lack of such a path that prevented me from becoming a Catholic and perhaps marrying Terry to start a family, which certainly would have changed my life. In this case I sought to understand why it cleared when it did on Rainier. The default answer is that it was a mere coincidence, and that our providence was delivered by what some would call "dumb luck." Thus the gauntlet is thrown down for me to provide a logical bridge to support my belief in Transcendent Summits.

I find that the clearing, which occurred only a few minutes after I made my commitment to save Herb, cannot be completely explained by a Western conception of luck, which removes both human and God's will from the determination of the outcome. Certainly, some of the coincidence can be accounted for by science, but the probabilities still seem a zillion to one against that exact sequence of events occurring. Perhaps for some, it is a simple leap of faith, but one bridge for me is that God had a hand in both our deliverance from Das Cave and the attendant Transcendent Summit, and that in this case, they were tightly connected.

There is no way I can bolster this bridge with an astute proof that would fit in the margin of a math textbook. I offer my probabilistic bridge to support Transcendent Summits in the same way that we assume there to be other life in the universe, not because we have seen it but because the probabilities require it. Given enough time, I do believe that I could bolster my bridge that Transcendent Summits exist because the probabilities require it, proving this with a computer proof that would be just as compelling as the now accepted computer proof of the four-color problem.

Setting my probabilistic bridge aside, a second approach to defining a Transcendent Summit is to simply define it by example. Until God tells me to stop or graduate, I will continue to climb and will submit my examples to nudge us all closer to a better understanding of Transcendent Summits.

Transcendent Summits are not an academic exercise requiring a quest for proof. Transcendent Summits are also not an intellectual exercise, and perhaps I am guilty of having thought about them too much. Perhaps most surprisingly, Transcendent Summits are even a spiritual quest. If you recognize that you have experienced one, then you will likely be spiritualized by it, but you cannot script one to occur at the end of a quest. I say to the believers and skeptics alike, be open to the possibility that Transcendent Summits exist, then go climb your mountains. Perhaps, just perhaps, God will honor you in a way that surprises you—and makes you tingle forever.

chapter six

currency exchange

The Eleventh Domain

As we all know, Einstein figured out the physics of the A-bomb and distilled it to essentials in the most famous equation of all time: $E=MC^2$. Einstein figured out a lot more than the equation.

After World War II, Einstein helped form a group called the Emergency Committee of Atomic Scientists. With their considerable and collective wisdom, they declared three things. Point one is that making the A-bomb is no secret and that other nations could and would soon have it. Point two is that there is no defense from the A-bomb and that there never will be any physical defense from the bloody bomb.

Point three is that, because of points one and two, the only path to world peace and justice is to establish a system of universal, enforceable world order to outlaw war and settle disputes through world courts—not bombs and battlefields. Einstein's point three is the thesis for humankind. Not maybe, not just for this year or the next, but for all time. Physics wins. Einstein's equation signifies and triggers the new equation for humankind. Einstein is gone, but he did his work on both sides of the karmic balance sheet; now it's up to the rest of us to carry his peace flag forward.

▼ ▼ ▼

for me, the point in my life when I thought that I knew the most was not when I graduated from high school, but when I graduated from the University of Washington. My former Boulder High teacher had been right in warning me that such a moment was nigh, but he was one degree off.

Taking twenty-one credit hours per term to pull ahead of the four-year plan, I graduated two quarters early from the University of Washington. I didn't know it yet, but when I left Seattle with my degree in December of 1964, I ran off the end of college. Back in Boulder with my tassel tucked into my well-notched belt, I showed my degree to my dad. He examined it carefully, then nodded his approval. He still wanted me to go to graduate school, and I still assumed that I would do so, however I told my dad that I would be taking a break for a while because I had other pent-up passions. Something deep had been gnawing at me for years, for a heartbeat still resonated in my ears. Less than a day after arriving back in Boulder, I found Shirley's new apartment, stepped up onto the porch, and rang the bell.

When the door swung wide and I saw her smile spread across the room, it was as if no time had passed. "Come on in, Ger, I've been waiting for you!"

Standing in Shirley's living room, I felt surrounded by something, but could only stare at her face. "My God, Shirley! You look great! How have you been? What have you been doing? Where … "

Giving me her million-dollar sparkle, Shirley said, "Ger, have a seat and slow down. Now that you have your degree, we have a little time. I'll go start the tea."

I stammered, "How did you know that I graduated?"

Peeking out through the kitchen door, Shirley just gave me her twinkling, all-knowing smile.

"Oh, *that*. I forgot. My *God* Shirley, it's been a while." While Shirley prepared our tea, I sat back into the cushy chair, shut my eyes, and let her fragrance find me. I let it tickle my nose for a minute then breathing deep, it drummed on my diaphragm. Suddenly, I dozed.

Shirley roused me with, "Ger? Here, drink this." After I hunched forward to accept the tea, Shirley settled onto the carpet at my feet and propped one arm across my knee. Sipping and twinkling, we sat like this for five minutes. Finally, Shirley said, "Love, I thought that it would be best to start with a Karmic Rest."

Then, setting my tea aside, I rested my hand on her arm and said, "Shirley? What about Jim?"

"I'm alone, Ger, and have been for some time now."

"Once you told me to tell you when I was ready." With my heart pounding in my own ear, I said, "Well, I'm ready."

Shirley set her tea aside, then carefully placed her second arm over my hand, looked me in the eye, and said, "I know."

We rested like this for a while longer before I said, "Listen, Shirley, this is off the wall, but I have an idea for us."

"Ger, if it's from the heart, then it's never off the wall."

Blushing, my soul flipped, and I found a new room in my heart that I did not know existed. "Shirley, you also told me once that you wanted to go climb Kilimanjaro. The big, high, steep, snowy volcano, remember?"

Squeezing my hand, Shirley said, "Of course. I think about Kilimanjaro often. I just shut my eyes, and there it is."

"Well, Kili is far away and expensive, but if we could get our hands on a car, we could be in Mexico and on Popo in just a few days. You've never been there either—can you see it?"

While Shirley had her eyes closed, I watched her eyelids flicker. When she opened her eyes, she said, "Yes, I see us there. Let's go!"

"But we need a car. Do you have one?"

"That's my Ger, always worrying about the details. No, I am as poor as ever, and I know that you are too. Didn't your dad buy a second car?"

Chuckling, I said, "Yes he did, and God forbid, it's another Nash. This one looks like a box of crackers, but at least it's red."

"What about the Bathtub?"

"I already checked. That's my mom's car now, and anyway, the Bathtub is just a rollover waiting to happen. I'm afraid that the Roach Nash collection is off-limits to me right now, at least for what we're talking about. Where's the milk truck when we need it?"

"Ger, I've got an idea, and I'll make a phone call in a bit, but right now, let's rest." After arranging her head in my lap, we rested while I cradled her shoulders. Finally, after opening her effusive smile, Shirley rubbed my legs with an urgency that transcended the cloth and said in her low, love voice, "Soon, Ger, soon!"

Thus it was that a day later Shirley and I sped south in a powerful Ford that Shirley had been able to borrow from a friend. To cut costs, we found two riders from the ride board in the CU Memorial Center, so with four drivers available, we pursued the white line through the night. When it was our turn to rest, Shirley and I cuddled in the land ark's large backseat, dozing against each other while the vintage American engine purred its pursuit. With the automatic transmission taking care of all the shifting, we smashed the milk truck's best time by ten hours and rolled into Mexico City in the middle of the night. Prowling the silent streets, we found our riders' destinations and dropped them off to their nocturnal fates. Exhausted, Shirley and I checked into a hotel and collapsed into the only bed that the cheap room offered. Sleep massaged us for a few hours, but when a ray of light nudged us awake, there we were, skin to skin.

Our lovemaking was not like the proverbial rocket headed for the moon. It was not even like the first time, for indeed, we had been there in our minds for years. It was like the only time, and time was all we had. Driven by a passion from beyond, we made *love*, since love was all we had. United by our liquid love, we became one with our passion. Transcending passion, and permanently resident in each other's souls, we threw away the key.

Only after an angry maid pried us from the room at noon did we stumble down to a sun-drenched sidewalk café. Sipping fresh squeezed *jugo de naranja*, we lolled hand in hand in a brave new land. Some unions are greater than the sum of their parts, and with heads upturned toward the sun's full-spectrum light, Shirley and I rested on a Fat Karmic Line that led not just to the moon, but also beyond the stars. We knew that to start our journey, all we had to do was nod in our intended direction and God would speed us on our way. All things were possible. However, before we could wink our journey awake, God nodded at us, and we went back to our room for more Transcendent Lovemaking.

Two days later, or perhaps it was three, we found our way to the old Popo Hut, plopped in front of the great stone fireplace, and propped our feet up on the hearth. Thus nestled between the two mountain lovers of lore, we felt safe. Finally on our volcano, our opportunity rolled forward to open in our laps. After resting, dozing, and playing with each other, we finally found a little energy for conversation. As usual, Shirley opened to the core. "How many Transcendent Summits have you had now, Ger?"

"I've had ten. All different."

Closing her eyes to listen, she said, "List them for me. I love to hear the names."

"OK, here goes. Landscape Arch, Third Flatiron, Longs Peak, Grand Teton, T2, Orizaba, Ship Rock, which you know all about, Haleakala, Denali, and Rainier." While I spoke the names, I watched Shirley's eyelids flicker in the firelight.

Keeping her eyes closed, she said, "That's an amazing list of climbs and life experience, Ger. What do these summits mean to you now after all these years?"

"That's easy. A Transcendent Summit is like an Orgasmic Summit! They are life-changing at the time, and better, when I think about a Transcendent Summit years later, my toes still tingle, my skin still sings, and my hair feels like it's halfway to heaven!"

"Yes, I know what a Transcendent Summit feels like, but given that we're still here, what do they *mean*, Ger?"

Now it was my turn to close my eyes and lean onto Shirley's shoulder for a minute of thought. Then I continued, "They have defined who I am. I can't live normally with them, but I can't live without them either. Up until Das Cave, I assumed that they were about the creation of synthesis." Remembering Rainier, my eyelids started to flicker, but then, like bursting from the cave, my eyes popped open. "Das Cave changed everything!"

Opening her eyes, Shirley twinkled at me and said, "Yes I know, Ger."

"Now it's my turn. I love to hear you say it, Shirley, so tell me one more time how you know about Das Cave!"

"Ger! It was in the papers!"

Chuckling, I nodded, "Om!" then continued, "Anyway, Rainier was the antithesis of the others. It's too bad that we can't have synthesis without antithesis."

"Why? That's the natural progression, and whether you realize or not, there is antithesis in all your summits."

"Huh? Don't we want to get rid of antithesis?"

"Ger, you're not the first person to think about synthesis. The ancient Greeks worked on synthesis for a long time, and there is a lot of Buddhist and Hindu thought invested in it as well. You've made a good start, but are missing some pieces. Listen to me for a bit. I know how you like complicated things distilled to essentials, so here is what I can relate to you."

Realizing that Shirley was opening to a new level, I just squeezed her hand, looked her in the eyes, and said, "Go on, my love!"

"Ger, you need to back up a step. It all starts with thesis. You can't have either antithesis or synthesis without thesis. Now, the normal human progression is thesis first, followed by antithesis, followed by synthesis."

Squirming against the fire's warmth, I said, "Give me an example."

"That's easy. In your mountain climbing case, your thesis is simply to climb. Your antithesis is your struggle to get there, and the antithesis includes failure, and even death. There is no guarantee of synthesis, which is your summit. Now the thesis is of the mind, the antithesis is of the body, and synthesis is of the spirit. Ger, when you say, 'synthesize body, mind, and spirit,' you are close, but a more accurate interpretation would be that spirit is a synthesis of mind and body. If there is spirit, then there is synthesis. In these physical bodies that you and I are now enjoying so deeply, synthesis is all about the mind-body struggle. In your chosen craft of climbing, the struggle is started by your mind and fueled by your body. My struggles are more mental than physical, but trust me, there is always a struggle, and the end result can be very physical."

Staring at the fire, I said, "Shirley! Is that why you didn't answer the door sometimes?"

Looking down, Shirley breathed, "Oh Ger, yes."

When Shirley said no more, I looked at her and was astonished to see her face streaming with tears. Now it was my turn to slither to the floor at her feet, fold my arms on her legs, and gaze up at her. "Do you want to talk about it?"

"Ger, there's a lot that you don't know. I'll just say that the highs are getting higher, and the lows are getting lower. For me, it's no longer just a simple struggle of mind and body, but a matter of raw spirit. Sometimes I think that my spirit will either transcend or die. God Ger, I'm tired of my monkey mind taking me on this roller coaster."

"What about death, Shirley? Does it mean anything or is it just a bad ending? What about Prince?"

"I've thought a lot about that, Ger. Prince died for a reason. His death helps the rest of us understand more about life and hence pursue richer lives. That's our precious gift from Prince."

"The gift of life from the world of the dead. Their message is expensive but poignant. What about us, Shirley? Have you ever thought about your own death?"

"Of course. Ger, I feel that you are destined to endure. Your climbs will go on and on. Nevertheless, there are no guarantees. Be careful up there! For me, I'm not so sure." Then, after a pensive pause, Shirley added, "I think that I'm going to need some help."

"Does the fact that I love you help?"

As she pulled my face up, I felt her strength. "Yes, it helps tremendously! Why do you think I waited years for you?"

Wiping her tears away, I said, "Well, that's it then. I will love you forever, and that will make all the difference."

"I love you too, Ger. I've known for a long time that we would end up together. Let's rest now."

With my head buried in her lap, we welcomed the fire's warmth, then stiff from sitting on the stone floor, I rose, took both Shirley's hands, and said, "That's enough talk for now. Let's go to bed so I can sooth your spirit. Tomorrow we'll check out the volcano." Shirley rose, kissed me on the lips, then led me into the silent softness.

▼ ▼ ▼

Early in the morning, we crept from the hut to greet the dawn. Shirley would not climb with me since she had no crampons and it was not her need. As I loaded my pack, she said, "I'll climb with you in my mind, Ger. I've always been there, but perhaps this time you will know that I am there."

"Don't worry Shirley, after these last few nights, you will always be omnipresent in my being."

"At midday, I'll hike up toward Las Cruces and we can come down the last part together." Then, as if she were sending me off to work, Shirley kissed me and turned me toward Popo.

Striding briskly up the trail, I greeted my body, my breath, my motion, my mountain far above, the pumice under my feet, the cold, and the new day. I mused that those who have no clue as to why people climb mountains have probably never stridden forth into the dawn's early light with a keen intent to go all the way. At Las Cruces, I paused briefly to enjoy a distant, silhouetted view of Orizaba, then looking north, saw the new day greeting Izta. Turning back to my task, I climbed briskly up the pumice to the snow line, put on my crampons, and ice ax in hand, crunched up onto the ice.

For a while, I poured it on thinking that I might be able to break the three-hour, eleven-minute time that Geoff and I had set four years earlier. As it became apparent that I was in no shape to do that, I reflected that it had been an intense four years. Knowing that I had to let something go, I had not run track in college, but I had received more A's. I didn't know yet if that would prove to be a good trade as well. For the moment, I had the grades in the bank, and I was still climbing the mountain. Who would care if my time were a little slower? At the crater rim I was sucking wind badly and plopped down onto the pumice to collect myself. Looking north to Izta again, I realized that I was not acclimated at all. On the milk truck expeditions, we had always spent several days climbing Izta before tackling the higher Popo. I took the familiar right turn and held a more sedate pace along the rim up to Popo's highest point. Still invested in the comparison, I looked at my watch on the summit and learned that my third ascent of Popo had taken me four and a half hours.

Feeling older but better seasoned, I took a solitary tour of the summit, which I had to myself. Looking back at Izta, I realized that, once again, I had dashed up here only to discover that the woman was back there. Tingling, I knew that Shirley was with me in my mind, and that she would be waiting for me below. Perhaps I had rushed up here specifically to learn that it was now time to take the next step. Knowing that it was much more than corporeal, I hustled down the ice to be with Shirley.

I found Shirley on the slope above Las Cruces where we made ourselves a comfortable chair in the loose pumice and nuzzled into our nest for a rest. For many minutes, we just gazed at our view. There, beyond a maze of crosses, rested Izta with her face forever turned to the heavens. Behind us, Popo beheld us from his sentry position. Far to the east, Orizaba, where I had experienced my sixth Transcendent Summit, flew above low-lying clouds. When conversation came, Shirley started with, "How was it up there, Ger? Did you tingle?"

"Yes—a little. I assumed that it was you talking to me."

Then as always, Shirley surprised me with a profound statement. "Yes I was, but that's only part of it. Ger, you are a Transcendent Climber."

"Huh? What do you mean? I just march up the mountain like everybody else."

"Ger, listen to me. When you tingle, that's God talking to you. You've struggled to think about Transcendent Summits, and to the extent that you have realized them, you have become spiritualized. To the extent that you understand them, you have become a Transcendent Climber."

"Shirley, God gives me Transcendent Summits, and as I've said many times, I have no control over them. Wouldn't a Transcendent Climber have to exert and go beyond of their free will? Better, wouldn't a Transcendent Climber be able to climb clouds?"

Tipping her head back to scan the sky, Shirley said in her hushed, husky voice, "Climbing clouds is easy, Ger; I do it all the time. There! Look at the cirrus curling over Izta. Now, just visualize yourself turning that first step, then, ice ax in hand, crunching up the rounded slope to the highest point."

"Perfect! That's an easy one!"

"Now, look at the burgeoning cumulus over the Cuidad. How would you get up it?"

"Hmmm. There are a dozen routes to choose from. Ah! There it is! I would take the ramp on the left, contour back to that series of corners, then to avoid that bulging overhang on the ridge, I would have to find a secret cave in that shadowed recess. That would be the crux. Once above the bulge, I would be able to top out by following the ridge. Ta da!"

"You've got it, Ger; Climb it with your mind. Sometimes imagining things is almost as good as being there. Also, cloud climbers have a big advantage."

"What's that?"

"Cloud climbers can climb in three-dimensions; you are not limited to the surface of the cloud. Just tunnel through to the other side if you want! Imagine it!"

"Brilliant! That opens up another dozen routes on our cumulus!"

Turning toward me and squeezing my hands hard, Shirley exclaimed breathlessly, "Oh, Ger! Listen! It's all the same thing! You have been assuming that God is somewhere up there in the air above the mountain, and that by climbing high you are getting closer to God. That's a good first step, and perhaps a necessary step, but it's not the whole story. Oh, Ger! I've got to breathe for a minute! How high are we here anyway?"

"Almost 15,000 feet. That's your altitude record isn't it?"

"You know it is."

"Well then, this is my chance to tell you to slow down, Shirley. Sit up straight and breathe into the back of your body for a minute. Spread your breath, and it will all come back into focus." After a minute, I added, "Now, you were about to tell me that every time I breathe like this, I am breathing in God?"

"You're with me, Ger. Of course, it is God who is omnipresent. God is in all eleven of your domains. Most important for a climber, God is in the rock. When your feet tingle, you have established a direct connection. When you are climbing like that, every step is transcendent."

"Why do we need to go to the summit then? Why not just walk around in the park?"

"You answered that question for yourself years ago. It's your idea that each upward step garners a Karmic Point, and that higher is better. Now, it's time to move our understanding to the next level. As you climb toward the summit on God's rocks, you become more and more infused with God as there becomes less and less rock available. When the Transcendent Climber reaches the summit, God nods, acknowledging that there are no more rocks and that you may now move to the next domain. Since you can't flap your arms and fly, you either just rest, supported by God's rocky fingertip, then descend, or ... Oh! Gotta breathe!"

"Yes, me too! Breathe deep, and go on when you're ready, love." After a moment, I added, "Why am I still tingling?"

"Because we are about to make a Karmic Jump to another level!"

"We?"

"Yes. Ger, I have always been with you on your climbs. I see the summit with you, and I often recognized your Transcendent Summits before you did, especially the one in the blizzard."

Then Shirley gave me a look that I had never seen before and said, "Ger? Who do you think spoke directly into your mind on Denali just before Mike's pack went off the ridge?"

My short hair buzzed with electricity until I jerked around looking for a thunderstorm, but the serenading skies only held the dwindling cirrus and the distant, puffy cumulus. "Oh my God, Shirley! That was you?"

"Yes, Ger, I was worried about you. When I say that I'm with you, I really mean it. I especially know when you are in danger." After clutching my hands, Shirley continued. "Ger, when the Transcendent Climber reaches the Transcendent Summit, there is a higher synthesis that goes beyond the simple synthesis of mind and body. You are not just receiving God's nod of approval, you are receiving an offer."

Pursing my lips and exhaling sharply, I said, "You are offered a chance to really transcend?"

"Yes, Ger. The punch line is that you really can leave your mind and body behind. On a Transcendent Summit, your spirit is free to transcend synthesis."

Rearing my head toward the sky, I asked, "That's what Buddha did, right?"

"Yes, he did it, and that's what all the meditating monks are trying to do. But think about it; what could Buddha have possible done better?"

"Buddha could have done it quicker on a summit! The higher the better! Summits provide an easier path to transcendence, so no wonder only a few meditating monks down in the valley can do it. Ah, now I understand the image of the all-knowing guru sitting on a summit."

Grabbing my shoulders and gleaming, Shirley cried, "Ger, we're there! We're here! Right here, right now, this is a Transcendent Summit, and we're on it together!"

"So that's why I've been tingling since we got here! Now, I know that you've got one more thing figured out, Shirley. What's the eleventh domain?"

Cradling my face, Shirley twinkled through her tears. "I thought you'd never ask. Well, my love, we're just about to find out. For now, I have no intention of leaving my body behind, and I can see that you feel the same way. Kiss me, make love to me. Right here, right now, on these God-filled rocks. Let Popo and Izta hold us and be our witness!"

As Shirley urged me to lie back, I knew that there would be no jumping up and running away this time. Finally prone on the pumice, I whispered in her ear, "You're a goddess, Shirley!"

Our Child of Peace Is Born

When I could see straight again, I tried to prop up on one elbow, but fell back exhausted for another rest. Finally, on both elbows, I stammered, "Shirley, our eleventh domain was transcendent! I'm amazed that we're still here on this mountain."

"Yes, and on our eleventh Transcendent Summit to boot. Just like climbing clouds, our transcendence doesn't have to be forever, Ger. This time, we came back."

Flopping back to the pumice to rest, I squinted down toward the Ford for several minutes. Then I asked, "What are we going to do with ourselves, Shirley?"

"Ger, I need to take my teaching to the next level—I need a currency exchange. There is way too much craziness out there now, and it's dragging me down. Worse, it could drag us down. Ger, this Vietnam War is speeding up, and you might get drafted for it at a most inopportune time. I don't know what to do about that yet, but for everybody's sake, I'm working on it."

"Well, for me it all comes back to the bloody bomb."

"Ger, take it all to the next level. Humankind is launched on a big, steep climb to get beyond the bomb, and we are just starting to experience our climb's antithesis. As I told you last night, there are no guarantees that we will make it through to synthesis. Frankly, from what I'm seeing in the world, we as a species are not doing very well."

Still rocking, I replied, "*Om* my goodness Shirley! Saying the mystic mantra helps, but it's not enough. We have to do a lot more then just sit around and chant, right?"

"Putting Prince's *Om* in the air certainly won't hurt, and I feel that it will definitely help. Ger, humankind's climb may be a very close call. Consider that our collective *Om* in the air may be the straw that tips the scales in favor of sanity and survival. Never give up on the mantra. However, you're right; we have to do more than chant. For myself, I know that to do any good, I have to get rid of my monkey mind, and to do that I need to separate myself from the madness and become a broker for harmony. Love, I've applied for the Peace Corps."

"Yes, I know."

"Ger, how could you possibly know that?"

"Shirley, like you, I have no intention of sitting on a cushion in the valley meditating in a vain attempt to get rid of my body. How do I know that you applied for the Peace Corps? That's easy. For the same reasons, I've applied too, and I saw your name on a list."

"*Om*! Ger, for once you're ahead of me! I didn't know that you had applied as well." After a minute, Shirley gave me a penetrating look, and asked, "Ger, what country did you apply for?"

"Shirley, I picked the toughest country that I could imagine. You must realize by now that it's the same country that you picked."

After pausing to ponder and gaze toward Orizaba, Shirley said, "Well, Ger, that's it then. We go to India as a team."

Tingling anew, I whispered, "Yes!" Then, after reflecting for a minute, I added in a low voice, "Shirley, in order to actually live together on a Peace Corps assignment, we would have to be married."

Giving me her effusive smile, Shirley said the most important single word that I had ever heard.

"So?"

Letting her round word roll back and forth between Popo and Izta, I finally squirmed around on the pumice to face Shirley squarely. I had no trouble finding her intense gaze. "Shirley, did you just ask me to marry you?"

Now it was Shirley's turn to study all three volcanoes. When her smile came back to me, she said in her lowest love voice, "Ger, we are not just playing footsie here—this is the big one. Take your time, and answer when you are ready."

After nuzzling in her lap for several minutes, I said, "Shirley, I have always known that we would get married. Love, for me the Peace Corps is just a beginning. My currency exchange also needs to include the mountains—I need to figure out how to climb for peace."

Two days after lifting
our veil, we left to
save the world, but
that's another tale.

Stroking the top of my head, Shirley replied, "You have a partner who can help you with that now. Ger, your climbs are a perfect model for humankind's climb for peace. Every time you reach a summit, you have demonstrated how to move from thesis through antithesis to reach synthesis. Each climb gives the world an example to emulate. Better yet, when you achieve a Transcendent Summit, you give the world an example of the opportunity for its collective spirit to transcend. Oh my love, there *is* a way out from under the bomb. If humankind's spirit can transcend and shed its current shackles, then it can exist in a brave new land where the bomb is locked out behind a wall of peace. Oh! Gotta breathe!"

"I'm with you, Shirley. When do we start?"

"We're on our way right now. Are you still tingling?"

"Nonstop!"

"Ger, think about where we're going to be. From India, we can visit the Himalayas!"

Letting her strength caress me, I mused, "I'll bet that's a good place for a married couple to go shadow bagging!"

"We can do better than that, husband. Never mind volcanoes; right now, I feel strong enough to climb Everest! Om belay?"

"Om belay, wife!"

Then, entwining our fingers and twinkling at each other anew, we chanted in chorus, "*Om Mani Padme Aum!*"

Gerry Roach

Guides to climbing Colorado's famous peaks

Colorado's Thirteeners—
13,800 to 13,999 feet
From Hikes to Climbs

ISBN 1-55591-419-5
6 x 9, 352 pages
PB $19.95

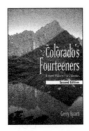

Colorado's Fourteeners
From Hikes to Climbs

ISBN 1-55591-412-8
6 x 9, 336 pages
PB $19.95

Colorado's Lost Creek Wilderness
Classic Summit Hikes

ISBN 1-55591-238-9
6 x 9, 160 pages
PB $14.95

Longs Peak DVD

ISBN 1-55591-513-2
$24.95

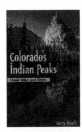

Colorado's Indian Peaks
Classic Hikes and Climbs

ISBN 1-55591-404-7
6 x 9, 208 pages
PB $16.95

Fulcrum Publishing
16100 Table Mountain Parkway, Suite 300
Golden, Colorado 80403
(800) 992-2908 • (303) 277-1623
www.fulcrum-books.com